Music and Child Development

Music and Child Development

Edited by
J. Craig Peery   Irene Weiss Peery
Thomas W. Draper

With 51 Illustrations

Springer-Verlag
New York Berlin Heidelberg
London Paris Tokyo

J. Craig Peery
Department of Family Sciences
College of Family, Home, and Social Sciences
Brigham Young University
Provo, Utah 84602, USA

Irene Weiss Peery
Department of Music
Brigham Young University
Provo, Utah 84602, USA

Thomas W. Draper
Department of Family Sciences
College of Family, Home, and Social Sciences
Brigham Young University
Provo, Utah 84602, USA

Library of Congress Cataloging in Publication Data
Music and child development.
   Bibliography: p.
   Includes index.
   1. Children as musicians   I. Peery, J. Craig.
II. Peery, Irene W. (Irene Weiss)   III. Draper, Thomas.
ML83.M97 1987   372.8′7   86–22045

Typeset by Publishers Service, Bozeman, Montana.
Printed and bound by R.R. Donnelley & Sons, Harrisonburg, Virginia.
Printed in the United States of America.

9 8 7 6 5 4 3 2 1

ISBN 0-387-96422-3 Springer-Verlag New York Berlin Heidelberg
ISBN 3-540-96422-3 Springer-Verlag Berlin Heidelberg New York

To Joseph, Christie, Samuel, Tom,
Janine, Robert, and Michael

Preface

I acknowledge a deep debt of gratitude to my coeditors: my wife Irene, and my friend and colleague Tom Draper. They have worked with diligence and insight to bring this work to completion. They have delegated the task of writing the Preface to me.

As the scientific study of human development matures it is not only natural, but it is necessary to reach beyond understanding the ways humans develop capacities, to study the ways emerging capacities fit into the larger sphere of human undertakings. Music is one of the most significant of those endeavors. As I attend the several piano competitions that are on my agenda each year, and see children seated at the keyboard drawing forth the magnificent sounds of Bach, Chopin, and Ravel, I am always a little awed. Surely, it seems to me, the piano* is among the best of man's creations; the creative energies of great composers are among mankind's greatest expressions; and encouraging children to associate themselves seriously with both instrument and composer can be one of the great blessings to their young lives and, by association, to the larger society.

Music touches the entire range of our lifespan on a daily basis. Involving children with music and music training has high market, and common sense, validity. Parents understand intuitively that children will benefit, and their lives will be enriched, if they are influenced by music and music training. Yet among both human development specialists and educators, the systematic study of how music weaves into the fabric of our progress through life is only beginning.

This book is intended both as a resource and a catalyst. There are attempts here to make some preliminary approaches to conceptualizing the ways music may be considered in children's lives. Examples of several of the kinds of music-child development research, and reviews of research findings relating to music and child development are also included. In the case of the actual research reports we have tried to identify some areas (in cognition, language, reading, socialization, and creativity) where the study of music may fruitfully merge with more tradi-

---

*To be fair, the other instruments need to be included, even if the piano is my personal favorite.

tional topics in child development. At times the boundary between what we know and what we ought to be discovering is fuzzy. Some chapters contained here push into those blurry borders. We trust that time will disclose if we were following correct intuitions in identifying new paths.

As a catalyst, by its existence we hope this volume will help to focus attention on the importance, in the lives of children, of studying music. We trust this work may be of some use in the search for topics for research projects, masters' theses, and doctoral dissertations. Clearly there remain far more intriguing questions than answers, both in the more abstract, and particularly in the applied realms of research on music and development. Further integrating research on music and children into the larger context of developmental knowledge will continue to be an important and potentially exciting task. Beyond the academic research, we also hope that an occasional teacher, or even possibly a parent, will be encouraged to consider broader implications, and perhaps broader involvements of music in children's lives.

There is one aspect of the study of music and development that I wish might have been more fully explored here. Just as I find a certain goodness and wholesomeness in music itself, I frequently find these qualities in those who involve themselves with music. It has been my observation over a number of years that those who involve themselves with, and love, music seem to have humor, common sense, a wholesome decency, emotional openness, a hearty love of life, and a sort of cosmic wisdom in larger doses than many others. Of course these perceptions may just be my own personal proclivity (after all I did marry a Juilliard student). But the impressions continue with me as I compare the many young pianists I have been privileged to get to know at regional and national competitions with other children in my acquaintance. I am not sure whether music inoculates people against some of the more common intellectual, social, and personality ills, whether people with these positive qualities are drawn to music, or whether studying music draws these latent qualities out. However, this "righteous" factor in the lives of young people involved with music is a significant impression for me; I trust it awaits further study.

The broader context for the study of music and children, which we have been cultivating in other work, also needs to be mentioned. We have been working on developing a Program for Optimal Human Development at Brigham Young University, which has supplied both resources and a framework for this effort. We agree with many who have observed that the needs for remediation of problems inevitably outstrip resources. We are also sympathetic with those who have been pointing toward prevention as a wiser and more cost effective course. However, the orientation of a prevention perspective is implicitly facing towards problems. In addition to prevention, particularly in the health arena, wellness promotion has become a more frequent theme. We have conceptualized the term *Optimal Human Development* to refer to the confluence of personal characteristics and socially desirable outcomes which characterizes the most desirable aims toward which development should be guided. For me the development of musical talent, abilities, and appreciation are definitely a part of what Optimal Human Development should come to mean.

A word of appreciation is in order to James Mason, Dean of the College of Fine Arts and Humanities at BYU, who was among the first to organize conferences where professionals in music education and in child development could be brought together. In this continuing effort, Jim was a key person in organizing the conference on Music and Early Childhood, at BYU in 1984. That conference provided some important impetus for this project. Another debt of gratitude is owed to Martin Hickman, the former dean, and to Stan Albrecht, the current Dean of the College of Family Home and Social Sciences at BYU, for their administrative assistance in bringing this project to completion.

Finally, I know I speak for my coeditors and for all the chapter authors and coauthors when I say we recognize that both music and children have given much to our lives and this book is a modest way to give a little something back.

Provo, Utah   J. Craig Peery
December 1986

Contents

Contributors

Amy Brown
  School of Music, Florida State University, Tallahassee, Florida 32306, USA

Bernadette Colley
  Project Zero, Harvard University, Cambridge, Massachusetts 02138, USA

Lyle Davidson
  Project Zero, Harvard University, Cambridge, Massachusetts 02138, USA

Thomas W. Draper
  Department of Family Sciences, College of Family, Home, and Social Sciences, Brigham Young University, Provo, Utah 84602, USA

Claire Gayle
  Department of Family Sciences, College of Family, Home, and Social Sciences, Brigham Young University, Provo, Utah 84602, USA

C. Ray Graham
  Department of Linguistics, Brigham Young University, Provo, Utah 84602, USA

Carolyn Hildebrandt
  Institute of Human Development, University of California at Berkeley, Berkeley, California 94720, USA

John M. Holahan
  College of Music, Temple University, Philadelphia, Pennsylvania 19122, USA

Linda Kelley
  3 Milkwood Drive, RD1, Chadds Ford, Pennsylvania 19317, USA

Jean M. Larsen
  Department of Family Sciences, College of Family, Home, and Social Sciences, Brigham Young University, Provo, Utah 84602, USA

Albert LeBlanc
Department of Music, Michigan State University, East Lansing, Michigan 48824, USA

Linda Bryant Miller
Department of Curriculum and Instruction, University of Wyoming, Laramie, Wyoming 82071, USA

Dale Nyboer
Young Keyboard Artists Association, Grand Rapids, Michigan 49509, USA

Irene Weiss Peery
Department of Music, Brigham Young University, Provo, Utah 84602, USA

J. Craig Peery
Department of Family Sciences, College of Family, Home, and Social Sciences, Brigham Young University, Provo, Utah 84602, USA

Brian Sutton-Smith
Graduate School of Education, University of Pennsylvania, Philadelphia, Pennsylvania 19104, USA

Rena Upitis
Faculty of Education, Queen's University, Kingston, Ontario, Canada U7L 3N6

Peter R. Webster
Department of Music, Case Western Reserve University, Cleveland, Ohio 44106, USA

Part I
Introduction

1
The Role of Music in Child Development

J. CRAIG PEERY and IRENE WEISS PEERY

Music is a part of development from the strains of the first lullaby. Music enters a child's life from experiences in the family, from the media, as a part of religious worship, in the school curriculum, in play and organized recreation. Although this chapter does deal directly with the reason for music in society per se, we personally believe that the elements of music are a reflection of the organization of the human central nervous system. We also believe that in music and musical experience we reproduce, in an emphasized and stereotypical way, many of the behaviors and experiences necessary to human social communication. By including music so naturally as an integral part of a child's world we may unconsciously be recognizing such fundamental parallels between music, normal neurological functioning, and normal social communication. So basic is music to human society that Margaret Mead has said it is a fundamental human *need* that bridges cultural diversity (Mead, 1972).

Considerable research related to children and music has been done, but surprisingly little attention has been paid to developing a systematic view of the role and significance of music in childhood. This chapter is an attempt to begin to formulate a model for considering the ways music can have significance for children, and to examine the research findings currently available, which are encompassed by the proposed model.

We suggest two major divisions for conceptualizing the influence of music on children. First, music is important because it has *inherent merit* in itself. As a part of life and one of the beauties of human culture, many see value in exposing, training, and enculturating children with regard to music because music is good and desirable. Second, developing music skills may have *attendant benefits* that generalize to other categories of personal and social competence. By developing performance, listening, and appreciation abilities in music, music educators, child development experts, and parents have believed that children may also be developing or enhancing cognitive, physical, and social development. These two divisions are illustrated in Figure 1.1. Some work has commenced on both these approaches to music and children, but the exploration has only begun. The following material gives an overview of the state of the art in each, and suggests that the interrelationships between these two approaches (represented by the broken

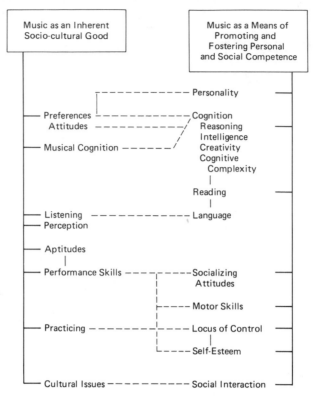

FIGURE 1.1. A model for considering the role of music in child development.

lines in Figure 1.1) could be a fruitful area for furthering our understanding of music in children's lives.

Music as Music: Developing Understanding, Appreciation, Aptitudes, Skills, and Abilities

There is a theory in the psychology of the arts that accumulating information and ideas about the performing and fine arts is a way of "banking" cultural capital that can later be "spent" in attaining and maintaining social status and influence. Beyond such a role for social manipulation, many parents feel musical exposure and training is enriching and positive as a part of human experience. We have divided the available research on music-for-its-own-sake in the lives of children into eight topics for this section: preferences, musical cognition, listening, perception, musical aptitude, performance skills, practicing, and cultural issues.

Musical Preferences

LeBlanc (Chapter 7, this volume) has discussed the history of research in musical preferences, presented a comprehensive theory of the development of musical preferences, and discussed its implications in detail. There are three frequently occurring hypotheses regarding the formation of musical preference. First, music training (Geringer, 1979, 1982; Gordon, 1971) or repeated exposure to particular music (either a specific piece or a particular style) increases liking for that music, or "What you hear is what you like." Second, musical preference is influenced by salient variables identified in social learning theory, that is, children tend to model their musical preferences using important people in their lives as the pattern. Such models include authority figures (Radocy, 1976), adults and teachers (Steele, 1967), and adolescent peers (Inglefield, 1971). This approach to understanding the development of musical preferences might be called, "You like what significant others like." Third, certain qualities inherent in the music itself influence preference (Kalanidhi, 1970; Kulka, 1981; McMullen, 1974)—particularly style (LeBlanc, 1979) ("popular is preferred to classical"); tempo (LeBlanc & McCrary, 1983) ("faster is better"); and performing medium (LeBlanc, 1981; LeBlanc & Cote, 1983) ("instruments are [slightly] preferred to voice").

REPETITION

Getz (1966) identified the importance of repetition in increasing liking for classical music in seventh-grade students. Heingartner and Hall (1974) found both college students and fourth graders increased their liking of Pakistani music after repeated hearing. Similarly, Bradley (1971, 1972) and Mull (1957) found repeated exposure and classroom training had a positive influence on the musical preferences of young adolescents and college students even when discordant modern music was scheduled for their repeated listening. Repeated exposure seems to increase liking for a variety of music.

SOCIAL INFLUENCES

Peers have a significant influence on music preference for adolescents (Inglefield, 1977), but Marks (1972) was unable to support his hypothesis that adolescents were looking to rock musicians for role models in life or for developing strategies to help resolve adolescent developmental problems. Approval and support by adults and teachers can also have a positive influence on music selection for grade-school children (Dorow, 1977; Greer, Dorow, & Hanser, 1973; Greer, Dorow, Wachhaus, & White, 1973).

STYLE

Preschool children seem to like most musical styles. Greer, Dorow, and Randall (1974) found no differences between preschoolers and first graders in their preference for popular versus classical music, but even at preschool and first-grade ages Greer et al. reported a trend to prefer rock music to nonrock. Schuckert and McDonald (1968) were not able to influence preschoolers' musical preference significantly by exposure to less preferred music alone. Peery and Peery (1986) found that at age 4 children have eclectic musical tastes and like classical and popular music equally well. They found evidence that sometime during the fifth or sixth year there is a shift away from liking classical music. However, they also found this shift away from preferring classical music can be avoided by exposing children to classical music and to music appreciation training in a preschool classroom setting. Geringer (1977) found preschool children play most frequently with timpani, piano, step bells, ukulele, metallophone, and slide whistle, in that order, in nondirected free-play activities; other orchestral instruments were not available to the children in his study, however.

In the studies with grade school children, there is a consistent finding that musical style is the most salient variable influencing musical preference. Popular music is increasingly preferred to classical music as children get older (Greer et al., 1974; LeBlanc, 1979; Rogers, 1957). LeBlanc has conducted systematic studies of music preference in grade school (fifth- and sixth-grade) children. He has found musical style has a significant preference effect independent of tempo and medium, with popular (but not necessarily rock) music being preferred to classical.

Heyduk (1975) stated that both personal characteristics and aspects of the music itself influence preference. Wapnick (1976) suggested dividing the variables related to the development of musical preference into three categories: (a) personal characteristics of the listener, (b) music characteristics, and (c) situation characteristics. Similarly LeBlanc (1982, and Chapter 7, this volume) has developed an elaborate theory of musical preference identifying personal characteristics of the listener, characteristics of the music, and cultural environment as the key variables. In his theory of the development of musical preference, LeBlanc is one of the few who has attempted to relate musical issues to other characteristics of personal and social competence, as the model we present in this chapter suggests should be done.

Musical Cognition

Dowling (1982) discussed a developmental sequence for melodic information processing. He noted that infants can detect changes in temporal presentation, rhythm, and pitch intervals of melody (Chang & Trehub, 1977a, 1977b; Kinney & Kagan, 1976; Melson & McCall, 1970). In older children the ability to remember melodies is dependent on at least three subskills: (a) remembering melodic contour, (b) remembering pitch intervals, and (c) identifying tonality (and distinguishing between tonal and atonal music). Training enhances these skills for adults (reviewed in Bartlett & Dowling, 1980); with children these abilities develop with age (and therefore presumably experience with music).

Ability to recognize pitch direction in 3-, 4-, and 5-year-olds was studied by Webster and Schlentrich (1982). They found some children of each age could make pitch direction discriminations accurately, although the skill improved with age. However, about one third of the children they tested could not perform this discrimination well, even when performance-based modes of responding were used instead of verbal responses.

Bartlett and Dowling (1980) discovered it is easier to distinguish between melodies from harmonically distant keys than from harmonically similar keys. They also found that adults were generally better at remembering melodies than children, and that older children (grades 1 and 2) were better than kindergartners in these memory tasks. Their results suggest that harmonic "key" becomes a part of the cognitive-cultural structure that we use to understand music at an early age.

Billingsley and Rotenberg (1982) tested the ability to remember sequences of random musical intervals in first-, fourth-, and seventh-grade children. The seventh graders did significantly better than the first graders, and there was evidence of consistent improvement as children got older. Interval memory was also correlated with musical aptitude in the older grades. However, children at each age could remember intervals at a better than chance level.

For tonal aspects of melody, an understanding of diatonic scale characteristics seems to develop first, followed by understanding pitch relationships in the tonic triad as children reach third to fifth grade (Krumhansl & Keil, 1982). Children in the 4- to 9-year-old age range do not identify the octave as "sounding like" test pitches (Sergeant, 1983). Sergeant concluded that the octave is a learned concept, not an innate perceptual characteristic of human hearing. Similarly, Krumhansl and Keil's (1982) data indicated that octave relations are preferred to other notes in the tonic triad more by adults than by first graders, and this preference seems to develop over time, indicating cognitive rather than strictly perceptual influences at work.

Five to seven-year-olds can remember musical phrases well enough to be able to recognize actual repetitions from variations (Abel-Struth, 1982). Abel-Struth (1982) also found recognition for musical phrases was better for complex than for simple musical phrases, and that girls were slightly better at recognition tasks than boys.

Ability to perform cognitive operations (in the Piagetian sense) on musical tasks is related to other cognitive skills. Preschool children incapable of performing concrete operational tasks involving number were also incapable of combining musical sounds in memory. Children who exhibited concrete operations were more successful at the tasks requiring musical cognition (Serafine, 1981). Children's understanding of the concept of meter in music becomes increasingly sophisticated as their cognitive development proceeds through the stages outlined by Piaget (Jones, 1976). Starting at about 9½ years, it is easier for children to understand and to talk about concepts of meter (Jones, 1976). Although Upitis (Chapter 3, this volume) found that 7-year-olds could frequently respond meaningfully to meter in music, the ability to conceptualize about meter and to verbalize those concepts clearly increases with age and cognitive development (Davidson & Colley, Chapter 6, this volume). Once again, training can improve a child's ability to use Piagetian conservation skills on tonal and rhythmic patterns (Foley, 1975). There is also evidence that training in conservation of musical concepts facilitates development of conservation with nonmusical concepts (Botvin, 1975).

Macdonald (1974) found a relationship between intelligence and musical concept formation for middle-class subjects, but not for lower class subjects. Bartlett (1973) found that training in understanding elements of classical musical style positively influenced college students' affective response to classical music, but not their preference for it.

There is evidence some children as young as first grade have abilities in all these areas, although most children do not develop facility with musical cognition until approaching adoelscence. Just why there are some early bloomers and others take longer in developing skill at musical cognition is not clear. Neither prodigious musical talent nor general intelligence seems to account for the early appearance of these abilities. One finding does emerge. The results consistently point to the importance of experience with and exposure to music in order to enhance pitch, melodic, and metrical abilities of musical cognition. Few of the skills in musical cognition are innate. The more exposure to music children have, both through direct training and by indirect experience, the more readily their ability to grasp musical ideas seems to progress.

Listening

Hedden (1973) believes listening to music involves multifaceted abilities that differ among individuals. Among the aspects important in listening that Hedden identifies are: making mental associations such as pictures; cognitive skills (e.g., focusing on note relationships or formal organization); physical items (e.g., beating time); involvement (e.g., passive listening versus engrossment); and enjoyment. Hedden followed Cattell's lead in attempting to discover relationships between personality variables and approaches to listening, but found complex factors and discriminant functions that were difficult to interpret. The link between personality styles and reaction to music deserves further exploration.

Very young infants can listen attentively to music (Kelley & Sutton-Smith, Chapter 2, this volume). Music listening skills are positively influenced by age and experience in the first three school grades; there is a greater improvement between first and second grade than between second and third grade in listening and performing ability (Simons, 1976). Age, experience, and intelligence all combine to increase ability to discriminate rhythmic patterns, pitch, and tonal sequences. Older children (adolescents) are better able to listen to and duplicate complex rhythmic patterns, although even 6-year-olds can be quite skilled in rhythm duplication (Gardner, 1971). Macdonald (1974) found that middle-class fourth-grade children were significantly better at perceiving changes in duration, loudness, and pitch in standard orchestral literature than lower class children, pointing again to possible exposure to and experience with music as key variables. Hickman (1970) found that children perceive the octave, minor seventh, and perfect fifth as intervals that are more "unitary" that other intervals. Hickman also found that perception of rhythm was influenced by pitch, intelligence, and practice, and that the perception of timbre was influenced by experience. Both Macdonald's and Hickman's work supports the utility of our model of proposing relationships between musical skills and other areas of social and personal competence.

Krumhans and Keil (1982) described what they identified as an acquisition of the hierarchy of tonal functions in music. Students from first to sixth grade and college students expressed their preference for tonal sequences; ratings showed a pattern of increasing differentiation of scale tones, tonic triad tones, and other scale components with age. The ability to discriminate similar interpretations of melodic passages from dissimilar interpretations also improves significantly from first to third grade, but only modestly from third grade to fifth grade (Heller, Campbell, & Gibson, 1982).

Morgan and Lindsley (1966) found that listening to music was a sufficiently powerful reinforcer to maintain sustained rates of operant response. They also found that subjects verbally reported preferring stereo to monophonic music, but that only two of their four subjects actually showed a preference for the stereo music in terms of their operant behavior.

MacGregor (1968) found an increase in preference for listening as a musical activity for fourth-grade girls during the school year. MacGregor introduced a balanced music curriculum during the year, including singing, listening, instrumental, and rhythmic activities. His finding of increased preference for listening in girls (but not in boys) may have been influenced by his music curriculum, or "maturation and motivation may be operating concurrently" to influence his results.

Both age and experience (probably correlated with social class in Macdonald's [1974] study) have an important impact on listening and discrimination skills. MacGregor's (1968) observation that either training or maturation could be influencing changes in musical abilities or preferences is fundamental to the future study of the influence of music in the lives of children. Developmental psychologists believe both maturation and experience can influence individual changes, and maturation and experience can interact to produce changes that are different than either factor might produce separately. A major difficulty with most research in music and child development has been a failure to consider both of these variables in planning and evaluating research studies.

Perception

H. T. Moore (1914) believed both personally and historically that the difference between consonance and dissonance is more a function of experience with hearing certain sounds than of absolute physiological or mathematical properties of sound. The importance of experience and training emerge in a wide range of studies of musical understanding, perception included.

Buckton (1977) stated that pitch discrimination and tonal memory, but not melodic abilities, could be improved by training programs for 6- to 8-year-olds. Children as young as first grade can perceive and identify ascending and descending sequences of tone presentation (Hair, 1982); understanding the relationship between cross-modal aural and visual representations of the concepts of "ascending" and "descending" is more difficult, with fourth graders performing better than first graders on cross-modal tasks (Hair, 1982). The relationship between pitch discrimination and pitch matching are not strong, and indeed these may be separate abilities. Fourth-grade children are better at pitch matching than preschool children, but this could be due to vocal and muscle maturation (Geringer, 1983).

Musical Aptitude

Considerable attention over many years has been given to developing ways to measure musical aptitude. The distinction between musical aptitude and musical achievement should be noted (Shuter-Dyson, 1982). Musical aptitudes are thought to remain relatively stable over time (Gordon, 1971) and are not improved by drills or exercises (Colwell, 1972). Musical achievement concerns the actual abilities that an individual can demonstrate, and these should improve with practice, experience, and training. Children with musical aptitude will demonstrate achievement in response to training and experience. Identifying aptitude is important so decisions about musical training can be guided intelligently.

To identify superior performers, panels (or juries) of teacher-performers are used (Peery, Nyboer, & Peery, Chapter 13, this volume). While teacher-performer's opinions are necessary in judging musical competitions, the purpose of these activities is focused more on recognizing achievement among individuals who have musical aptitude than identifying aptitude per se.

If parents are seeking an answer to the question, "Is my child musically talented enough that he or she should be given music lessons?", an audition with a competent teacher may provide sufficient information. However, it is possible for an individual child to have understanding and insight into sound, but lack the psychomotor ability necessary for performance. Such a child might benefit greatly from exposure to music and training in music appreciation. Some believe that teachers' opinions may not be completely accurate in assessing aptitude (Rubenger, 1979); this may be particularly true when considering musical aptitudes that are not linked with psychomotor skills necessary for success in performance training.

Freeman (1976) reported that the difference between musically and artistically talented children lies not in differences between innate abilities (which were approximately equal between the two groups in his study), but in differences of opportunity and encouragement provided by parents in the home environment.

Specifically, families of musically talented children provided many musical instruments, support for orchestra playing, support for extra lessons, incentive to practice music, an important status for music education, others in the family who played music, and good-quality music in the home. These findings are consonant with the theory that exceptional talent can be developed by "the earliness, intensity, persistence, regularity, family concentration, tutorial approach, and the presence of dominant family intellectual cultural value orientations" in the child's life (Fowler, 1969). In fact, Fowler (1962) has shown music to be one of the specialized abilities that can be fostered by this kind of family environment that focuses on music attitudes and abilities.

Musical aptitude probably includes a number of perceptual and motor skills in constellation. Lewandowska (1976–77) has begun to conceptualize the structure and development of musical aptitude. Barrett and Barker (1973) found a significant relationship between musical aptitude and three of five separate perceptual tasks supporting a multifaceted approach to musical aptitude. Jones (1976) found that the child's ability to understand the concept of meter in music was related to age and a development of the concept of time as Piaget outlines it. Buckton (1977) found that pitch discrimination and tonal memory, but not melodic abilities, could be improved by training programs for 6- to 8-year-olds. Wilcox (1969, 1971) has found that scores on the Seashore Measures of Musical Talent decline from ages 11 to 13 for children from disadvantaged environments. Wilcox believes this result parallels the general findings of decline in mental test scores from children in disadvantaged environments. So although training can enhance musical ability, deprived environments may retard development of musical aptitude.

Dorhout (1982) and Shuter-Dyson (1982) reviewed the many methods currently available for assessing musical aptitude, and reminded us that information from multiple sources (tests, teachers' opinions, parental feedback, etc.) may be helpful. "A coordinated effort should be undertaken to pool the information derived from all available sources" Dorhout suggested. There are a number of tests of musical aptitude. Most of these would be relevant to teachers in a school setting trying to devise and organize a musical curriculum.

The oldest, and perhaps best known test of musical aptitude is the *Seashore Measures of Musical Talent*, currently published by the Psychological Corporation. For children from fourth grade up this test assesses abilities in pitch, loudness, rhythm, time, timbre, and tonal memory. Gordon (1965) has developed the *Musical Aptitude Profile* for children from fourth grade up. This test measures tonal imagery, rhythmic imagery, and musical sensitivity. Attempts to measure musical aptitude by examining music audiation have been made by Gordon (1979) in order to illuminate musical aptitudes of children 5 to 8 years old. It is important to continue work on identifying aptitudes of younger children. Children seem to respond to music in potent ways (e.g., Zimny & Weidenfeller, 1962) and clearly enjoy music before they can conceptualize about it verbally. Other tests of musical aptitude are reviewed by Dorhout (1982), and discussed extensively by Shuter-Dyson (1982).

Absolute pitch (AP), or perfect pitch, is one of the most highly regarded musical abilities. An individual who possesses AP is able to state the name of a pitch upon hearing it and frequently can sing a given pitch on command. The etiology of AP has received attention (e.g., Crozier, Robinson, & Ewing, 1976–77). Some believe AP is hereditary, whereas most have argued that AP is learned either as a result of rigorous training, or as a combination of experience and maturation. In their excellent and comprehensive discussion of AP, Ward and Burns (1982) concluded that neither the hereditary nor the training-imprinted models for explaining AP have demonstrated conclusive proof of their validity. Some young children demonstrate the ability with matter-of-fact ease, whereas others struggle to develop AP with limited or no success. Stories like the one about the 4-year-old girl who was told the names of the notes on the piano keyboard one day and was able to match the names of the notes with the pitches the next day, "Because you said so yesterday, Mommy," seem incredible to someone who does not have AP, but are quite common among those who have this ability. The earlier the ability is manifest, the more accurate it is likely to be (Sergeant, 1969; Wellek, 1938). Apparently early exposure and experience is important, but the child must have the innate "gift" for the experience or training to be effective.

Performance Skills

In comparison to research on the mental aspects of music and child development, work on performance skills in children is much harder to find. This is unexpected since much of the intensity of the experience of studying a musical instrument is involved with practicing, which is a motor performance concern. The relative paucity of research on performance skills suggests that parents, and teachers, believe studying and practicing a musical instrument falls into the category of activities that are desirable for their own sake, and do not need ancillary improvement in other areas to justify them.

Gilbert (1979) has developed a Motoric Music Skills Test (MMST) to provide information on the development of motoric music skills. The test measures motor pattern coordination, eye-hand coordination, speed of movement, range of movement, and compound factors. Her preliminary findings with the test indicated these motor skills improve with age, and that girls perform better than boys on three of the subtests: motor pattern coordination, eye-hand coordination, and compound factors. Longitudinal research with the MMST (Gilbert, 1981), with two data points taken a year apart from the same children, revealed that individuals did improve consistently from year 1 to year 2. Gilbert also found significant predictive relationships between scores taken a year apart on the speed of movement, motor pattern coordination, and range of movement subtests. There was an overall positive correlation from year 1 to year 2 on all subtests except eye-hand coordination. These findings indicate that skills at one time are good predictors of skills in later development.

Gilbert (1979, 1981) did not find any difference between boys and girls in the improvement of motor skills, but she did find that 4-year-olds improved significantly more than 6- or 7-year-olds in the year that elapsed between testing. Gilbert believes the finding that young children seem more plastic and susceptible to improvement has several implications. First, it is parallel with research findings in other domains (e.g., Rarick, 1961) that "most fundamental motor patterns emerge before the age of 5, and that skills are merely stabilized beyond that point" (Gilbert, 1981). For example, training 4-year-olds in motor skills related to gymnastics has demonstrated levels of improvement subsantially greater than would be predicted by observations of motor development in children without such training (Leithwood & Fowler, 1971). Second, since the 4-year-olds showed the greatest gain scores in every subtest of the MMST, greater attention should be given to helping preschoolers develop the motor skills required in musical performance, and practice with motor skills might well be integrated into the preschool curriculum. Additionally, these observations about improvement in motor skills between age 4 and age 5 reinforce the practical experience of the second author of this chapter as a piano teacher, that the best time to start a young child on piano lessons is late in the fourth or early in the fifth year.

Heller et al.'s (1982) research point to the time between first and third grade as one when children become able to discriminate different styles of musical interpretation. Such sensitivity is critical in developing musical technique beyond the basics of notes and meter. Kuhn and Gates (1975) found a tendency to increase tempo in clapped examples of different note values across ages.

The link between performance skills and the concept of using music as a means of promoting intellectual, social, and personal competence is perhaps the strongest of any in the model we are presenting. Children in the 4- to 7-year age range seem particularly susceptible to improvement in motor performance skills with training. Many of these skills are likely to have carryover to other large and small motor tasks from game playing to penmanship.

Practicing

The business of learning to play a musical instrument consists of regular lessons sandwiched in between hours of lonely and demanding practice. Practicing is seldom the motivation for musical study and it is frequently the reason lessons are terminated. The rigor of practice yields amazing results in the lives of millions of children every year; they actually learn to play instruments and make music. Yet millions of children doing tens of millions of hours of practicing notwithstanding, research concerning practicing a musical instrument is surprisingly lacking. What children do most when learning to play a musical instrument is not well studied at all; to date we have been unable to find a single study related to practicing. Yet research on the motivations and methods for encouraging practice and on the results of practice, both musically and nonmusically, seem logically to be among the most important for enhancing our understanding of the role of music in children's lives.

Cultural Issues

In addition to the cultural capital concept, Gordon (1967) made an attempt to identify musically talented students in culturally disadvantaged environments; he found that disadvantaged environments generally depress musical sensitivity, but that some children from disadvantaged environments showed considerable musical talent. Freeman (1976) and Shuter-Dyson (1979) showed that music in the home environment was a significant factor in children displaying musical aptitudes.

Giving further understanding to the importance of cultural differences, Igaga and Versey (1977) found that cultural differences favored an English over a Ugandan sample in tests of rhythmic perception. They noted, however, that there are major cultural differences in experience with the meaning of rhythm between Uganda and England. Using a test of rhythmic performance Igaga and Versey (1978) studied Ugandan and English children from ages 10 to 15. They found a steady and accelerated increase in rhythm performance skills for Ugandan children in comparison to English children, with the biggest improvements in scores coming in the 10 to 13 age range. They suggested that rhythm has an all-pervading role in Ugandan society, and that children learn the subtleties of rhythmic performance better as a result of this cultural exposure.

Zern (1983) found a relationship between childrearing practices and the structure of folk music in many cultures. Zern had postulated that childrearing pressures toward obedience would yield music that was more complex. This hypothesis was not confirmed, and the results of his statistical analysis were difficult to interpret.

Further inquiries about the relationship between cultural influences in childrearing and music certainly seem appropriate and needed. One phenomenon that has intrigued the authors of this chapter is the relatively high proportion of children with an oriental racial heritage who perform successfully in music competitions (Peery, Nyboer, & Peery, Chapter 13, this volume). We have guessed that cultural differences in childrearing practices may be influential, but the nature of the salient variables is not obvious.

In the broader view substantial cultural and social enrichment results from exposing children to and involving them with music. Parents seem to understand such enrichment from both a practical and an aesthetic perspective. Once again, however, we are confronted with a domain of child development that is being driven in the real world by parents' intuitive understanding but for which virtually no research has been accomplished. Perhaps substantial face validity is a contraindication for research scrutiny.

Music as a Means of Promoting and Fostering Personal and Social Competence

In this section we turn attention to the second reason for exposing children to music proposed in our model: that developing music skills may have attendant benefits that generalize to other categories of personal and social competence.

Our purpose here is not so much to provide evidence that confirms music as a means of fostering other aspects of personal and social competence as it is to explore the possibilities of what is known. Relationships and proposed relationships between music and personal and social competence have long been part of the music education scene. As Draper and Gayle (Chapter 11, this volume) have pointed out, we have a long-standing cultural tradition that, by developing music performance, listening, and appreciation abilities, children may also be developing or enhancing cognitive, physical, and social development. It is not clear from much of the research cited in this section whether involvement with music is the salient influence, or if other confounding variables associated with music study may be the critical force. It is possible that music might be seen as a contextual catalyst for many developmental outcomes, doing little by itself by enlarging the effect of certain kinds of activities. It is also possible that music and musical tasks do indeed promote specific developmental outcomes. In most cases the precise relationship between what causes which effects is not clearly explicated in the studies below. And, as is often the case in science, one is left with more intriguing questions than clear answers.

We have divided this section on music as a means of promoting and fostering personal and social competence into nine areas: personality, cognition (including reasoning, intelligence, creativity, and cognitive complexity), reading, language skills, socializing attitudes, motor skills, locus of control, self-esteem, and social interaction.

Personality

One long-standing hypothesis is that musical preferences are an indication of personality style. Cattell and Anderson (1953) first developed a musical preference test as part of the Institute for Personality Ability and Testing battery (IPAT). Cattell and Saunders (1954) sought to discover factors for musical preferences on the IPAT battery, and related these to personality diagnosis. They were only moderately successful in identifying music preference factor structures that correlated with personality factor structures. Cattell and Eber (1954) further refined a musical test of personality as a part of the IPAT battery. In a check of the reliability and validity of the Musical Preference Test (MPT), Healey (1973) found a high degree of agreement with the factor loadings identified by Cattell and Eber, but a lower level of agreement on the correlation with personality disorder. Healey reported that some of the factors did not discriminate between normal and clinic populations; some factors did, but in the opposite direction proposed by Cattell and Eber; and some factors did indeed discriminate between normal and clinic populations in the direction Cattell and Eber suggested. Sample and Hotchkiss (1971) found that junior high school children who performed in the school band scored higher on musical interest and tendermindedness scales of the IPAT battery. Clearly the IPAT MPT raises some intriguing issues, but it falls short of being definitive. It is interesting that Healey confirmed the factor structure of the MPT 20 years after it was first presented. Perhaps some aspects of musical preference are relatively resistant to sociocultural variation over time.

Healey also reported a clinical observation confirmed by others (Simon, Holzberg, Alessi, & Garrity, 1951; Weidenfeller & Zimny, 1962)—that the ability to appreciate music can remain relatively intact during times of severe psychological disorder.

Listening to music can reduce anxiety (Peretti, 1975); women in particular experience anxiety reduction when listening to music (Peretti & Swenson, 1974). Stimulating music increases student anxiety during a test situation, whereas sedative music has no effect on test anxiety (Smith & Morris, 1976). Music can be as effective as muscle relaxation training in reducing state anxiety (Stoudenmire, 1975). State anxiety can be increased by hearing "happy" music, whereas "sad" music tends to decrease state anxiety (Biller, Olsen, & Breen, 1974). In an interesting twist on the music-affect relationship, Cantor and Zillmann (1973) found that exposure to emotional-affective arousal influenced subsequent reaction to music; in particular, highly arousing stimuli increased positive responses to music.

A high degree of personal insecurity is associated with either overfavorable or underfavorable response to unfamiliar music, suggesting that social as well as personality factors may influence response to music (Fisher & Fisher, 1951). Individual mood influences emotional response to music, with cheerful individuals responding to a broad range of music positively and gloomy individuals responding more pessimistically to the same music (Sopchak, 1955). Emotionally disturbed children with moderate to severe need for structure did significantly worse on tasks requiring duplication of rhythmic patterns (Gibbons, 1983). Giacobbe and Graham (1978) were unable to find differences in musical preference between groups of normal and aggressive emotionally disturbed boys, although they did not use as complex a range of responses as did Fisher and Fisher (1951) or Sopchak (1955).

Krugman (1943) found that repeated exposure to music increased an affective response of increased "pleasantness" in the music. It is likely that pleasantness and preference are confounded in this and in the preference research. Verveer, Barry, and Bousfield (1933) also found that positive affect was associated with repeated listening up to a given level of repetition, but then additional repetition produced a decline in positive affect for some pieces, unless an interval of time intervened between the subsequent repetitions. The Krugman (1943) and Verveer et al. (1933) work does point to a possible relationship between affective development and exposure, or at least the development of affective states associated with music. Beyond these findings no one has speculated about the correlation of the development of musical preferences and personality characteristics. Since several researchers have reported relationships between these two variables, their development over time is an intriguing area of potential inquiry.

Cognition

McDonald and Ramsey (1978) argued that music helps develop cognitive skills in many curricular areas. Gardner (1973) found that children conceptualized the arts in increasingly sophisticated ways as they grew older. This work points to an interface between cognitive development and art appreciation. Castell (1982) found that children between ages 8 and 11 are remarkably sensitive to musical style, using instrument cues to identify classical music and tempo cues to identify popular music. Castell also found that older children were more fluent in their ability to express verbal descriptions of musical style, but both 8- and 11-year-olds had some difficulty verbally describing perceived differences in musical style, leading to the conclusion that education in describing music would be helpful for children at this age.

Several attempts have been made to bridge the gap between involving children in music as a good in itself and involving them in music to stimulate positive mental abilities. Some tantalizing indications of an important link between musical performance skills training and other cognitive abilities have emerged.

FIELD DEPENDENCE, SPATIAL ABILITY, SOCIAL ADJUSTMENT, ANALYTIC ABILITY

Parente and O'Malley (1975), for example, found that training in the performance of musical rhythms significantly improved the performance on the rod and frame task in 6- to 9-year-old children; their evidence parallels research indicating that field independence improves with perceptual-motor training. Even though the motor-music training in their study was much less sophisticated, and much less structured than the gymnastics training, Leithwood and Fowler (1971) did find that 4-year-olds who received either gymnastic performance training or motor-music training also improved in analytic ability, and in social adjustment with peers and relationships with adults. Karma (1982) has found that verbal-analytic skills are correlated with musical ability in younger subjects and spatial abilities correlate with musical ability in adolescents and adults. Wagley (1978) discovered that children enjoyed learning cognitive skills more when training was accompanied with musical experiences.

Cognitive skills of classification, seriation, spatial understanding, and temporal relations can also be improved through guided music listening (Parker, 1973). Hurwitz, Wolff, Bortnick, and Kokas (1975) found that boys improved on tests of spatial cognition after they had training in a Kodaly Music Curriculum. Botvin (1974) found that training sixth graders to be able to perform Piagetian-type conservation tasks with melody also improved their performance on non-musical concepts of mass, weight, and number. Nelson (1980) found third graders able to conserve meter both verbally and behaviorally, and that kindergartners had some, but much less, ability with meter conservation tasks. Musical ability is related to auditory conservation, but visual conservation skills and auditory conservation skills may not be related (Norton, 1978).

INTELLIGENCE

After reviewing the research of Getz (1966), Keston and Pinto (1955), and Rubin-Rabson (1940), Wapnick (1976) concluded that there is probably no relation between intelligence and music preference. Music aptitude and intelligence are more likely to be related. Young (1971) found intelligence to be related both to music reading ability and to developing music performance skills.

Gordon (1968) noted that several studies have shown low but consistently positive correlations between musical aptitude scores and scores on intelligence tests, and Gordon's (1968) study replicates such a finding. Research in the early part of this century suggested that high ratings of musical performance were correlated with intelligence. Both Gordon (1968) and R. Moore (1966) noted the traditional conclusion that intelligent people are not necessarily musical, but musical people are necessarily intelligent.

Phillips (1976) studied relationships between the Wing battery of musical aptitude tests and several measures of intelligence. He concluded that there is considerable relationship between musical aptitude and intelligence. However, Phillips believes family and social influence play major roles in influencing ability to score well on all his tests. Most psychologists believe the kind of ability measured on standard IQ tests is largely genetic in character; consequently Phillips' (1976) work may be confounding intelligence and other kinds of information variables. Wingert (1972) found an increase in intelligence manifested by retarded children after exposure to a music enrichment program.

Gardner (1983) has proposed a theory of multiple intelligences with music as one of the specific intelligence types. Gardner believes music abilities, aptitudes, and talents result from physiological and personal differences in individuals that may not be detectable using a standard intelligence test. He cited evidence, for example, that verbal skills seem to be produced in the left hemisphere of the brain, whereas musical perception and skills seem to function in the right hemisphere. Neal's (1983) research comparing children with high musical aptitude to children of normal musical aptitude relates to Gardner's suggestion. Neal found that right ear (therefore left cerebral hemisphere)-dependent scores distinguished high-aptitude from normal-aptitude children. Neal suggested that children with high musical aptitude learn to analyze musical concepts with their left brain (verbal/analytic) functions, in addition to right brain abilities found in children with normal musical aptitude.

CREATIVITY

Cleall (1981) believes that cognition is promoted by creative activity. Musical play fosters positive creative experiences as children try different instruments, modes, melodies, and so on. Plummeridge (1980) acknowledged the frequent call for curriculum activities that will foster creativity, and noted that music training or activities are often proposed as vehicles for stimulating creativity. However, Plummeridge (1980) believes one must distinguish between creative *productivity* and creative (or imaginative) *thinking* styles; he also indicated that substantial differences in perspective may lead discussions of music and creativity to focus on very different matters. Cleall (1981) believes children should be allowed to "play" with musical elements to foster creativity.

Lowery (1982) tested three curricula designed to increase creativity in children. Two of these curricula were nonmusical, and one (Music and Imagery) was musical in orientation. Lowery reported significantly higher creativity scores in verbal fluency, verbal originality, figural originality, total verbal, and grand total creativity for the children who had the Music and Imagery curriculum.

COGNITIVE COMPLEXITY

McMullen (1974) found that melodic complexity influenced preferences of junior high and high school students, with melodies of moderate complexity being preferred to less complex and more complex melodies. Heyduk (1975) theorized that personal preference for psychological complexity and the complexity of the music combine to predict preference in many individuals. Heyduk proposed a theory that corresponds to McMullen's (1974) findings that moderate musical complexity will be preferred to simple or very complex music structure. Heyduk (1975) argued that the preference perception of a musical excerpt is also a function of the individual's usual level of psychological complexity. Several researchers have postulated that complexity, and therefore psychological arousal, is positively correlated with preference (Berlyne, 1971; Fiske & Maddi, 1961; Zajonc, 1968). According to this line of reasoning, expanded in Heyduk's (1975) research, individuals who are accustomed to higher levels of psychological complexity will prefer more complex music than individuals who are accustomed to lower levels of psychological complexity. It is not clear how preference for particular levels of psychological complexity may be developed. Temperament could play a significant role. In terms of musical preference, exposure and instruction in the characteristics of classical music seem likely to render the relative cognitive complexities of classical music more familiar, and therefore less psychologically complex and more preferred. If this is the case, one might argue that training in classical music decreases the likelihood that an individual will be "satisfied" with stimulation by relatively less complex musical forms, and increases the probability of preferring classical music.

An analysis of the correlation between musical style and psychological complexity has not been undertaken. It seems likely that both classical and popular music might be conceptualized accurately on a continuum of psychological complexity. However, it is tempting to speculate that, overall, classical music has a greater range of variation on a complexity continuum. If Heyduk is correct, it would be logical that a naive listener would prefer the simpler pieces regardless of style. Given the relatively greater amount of study usually required to compose classical music successfully, study leading to a cognitive grasp of the music may be required in order to reduce the psychological complexity of classical music to an acceptable level for enjoyment and appreciation. Therefore, one might expect both that individuals who spend a good deal of their time in psychologically complex tasks (mathematicians, for example) prefer classical music, and that individuals who come to appreciate classical music in its more complex forms prefer to be engaged in psychologically complex tasks. If the development of preferences for complex thinking and for classical music are mutually interactive, a parent who encourages his or her child to appreciate classical music (and/or relatively more complex popular music) may be fostering a preference for cognitive complexity in other areas. At least this kind of theorizing suggests numerous avenues of research both in musical preference and in developmental domains.

Reading

Music has been found to be a potential distraction when used as a background for other tasks. Fogelson (1973) found that music interfered with reading test scores for eighth graders. However, Wolf and Weiner (1972) found that listening to rock music did not impair college students' performance on arithmetic problems. Apparently if the music is familiar the distracting effect on reading ability is decreased (Etaugh & Michals, 1975).

On the other hand, the opportunity to listen to popular music can be a reinforcer for such tasks as math performance or paying attention in school (Madsen, Moore, Wagner, & Yarbrough, 1975). The notion that access to music is reinforcing, or more generally that music can be a pleasant accompaniment to and can strengthen learning in other domains, has been discussed but not widely researched or practiced. Integrating music with other academic pursuits is an intriguing idea deserving further attention.

Cohen (1974) suggested music and song as a vehicle for facilitating children's developing an interest in reading, but (as Draper & Gale, Chapter 11, this volume, suggest is frequently the case) he presented no data demonstrating the efficacy of this approach. Hurwitz et al. (1975) reported an improvement in reading skills for grade school children who have been involved in Kodaly Music Curriculum training (see Brown, Chapter 10, this volume, for a description of the Kodaly approach). This improvement in reading ability was measured on standard reading tests that were a part of the school's student evaluation and had nothing to do with music. Children with two years of Kodaly training (through second grade) continued to have higher reading scores than a matched control group, indicating a potential long-range improvement over increasingly complex reading skills (Hurwitz et al., 1975). Weeden (1971) found no improvement on reading or math skills in black children who had been involved in one semester of Suzuki violin training. However, Weeden himself suggested that one semester may be too short a time to generate appreciable differences in other skills.

Montessori developed a program for early childhood education that has had a major impact on early childhood education curricula (see Chattin-McNichols, 1981). Montessori planned and discussed an approach to music education requiring student experience for learning (Montessori, 1965). Although aspects of children's perceptual, motor, and intellectual functioning in relation to the Montessori classroom approach have been examined, little is known about the effect of the Montessori music curriculum (McDonald, 1983). Montessori clearly saw parallels between music learning and other kinds of learning, but research integrating the Montessori methods of music education with other education issues has yet to appear.

Language Skills

Papousek and Papousek (1981) pointed out the paucity of information relating to infant vocalization, music, and language, and they suggested that important relationships may indeed exist. Kokas (1969) has conducted preliminary studies indicating that participation in a Kodaly Music Curriculum can improve a child's ability with language development.

Jalongo and Bromley (1984) suggested that picture song books help children develop linguistic competence. They believe bilingual children and children with learning difficulties benefit from the added exposure to vocabulary, syntax, semantics, and rhythm. Gifted children also benefit linguistically from exposure to picture books, according to Jalongo and Bromley (1984), because the songs add extra dimensions of comprehension and encourage teaching/learning activities that encourage divergent thinking. Information about the song's history, social context, or cultural context can also lead to expanded abilities to deal with the song from a more meaningful linguistic base. Similarly, Kuhmerker (1969) advocated learning songs to facilitate adoption of beginning reading vocabulary; she believes the rhythm and phrasing of the words and the actions and kinesthetic experiences associated with the song help the child associate words with a wider variety of linguistic experience.

Socializing Attitudes

In a study of the effects of musical aptitude, instruction, and social status on attitudes toward music, Williams (1972) found none of these variables particularly effective with college students. Williams did find socioeconomic status to be a better predictor of liking for classical music than the other variables; and he found music instruction to be relatively ineffective in changing attitudes. Williams' (1972) findings suggest that early experience may be a key factor in socializing musical attitudes.

We have noted that several researchers (e.g., Greer et al., 1974; Peery & Peery, 1986) who have studied the development of musical preferences agree that exposure to a particular kind of music (especially at young ages) influences musical taste. There is substantial reason to believe cognitive and listening skills required to understand a particular musical style are enhanced by exposure, and furthermore that social attitudes that result from *being able* to understand and appreciate a particular musical style are also influenced as preferences develop.

Research in aesthetic education is relatively new. However a consensus is emerging that music may be one medium that can help children understand how art "works" (Saffle, 1983). Saffle (1983) also believes music can be a vehicle that can communicate information about culture and aesthetics from different cultures. In fact, Stone (1983) suggested that including elements from the pop music culture into a music education curriculum may help children develop a variety of skills necessary to general music appreciation. If such a generalization hypothesis is true, music's ability to spread an appreciation for aesthetics and additional aspects of other cultures may be one of the most potent reasons for teaching a variety of music to children.

The development of attitudes about music parallels the "cultural capital" concept. If one wants to associate on a "highbrow" level, one needs to have an understanding of "highbrow" attitudes and tastes. We suspect that many children have been taken involuntarily to orchestral concerts by parents who want them to be able to appreciate the "finer" things.

In Japan a mandatory, progressive system of music education is incorporated into elementary and secondary school curricula. Every child in Japan must take 6 years of music in elementary school, plus additional exposure in junior high school. Such a broad national commitment means, "almost every person who graduates from junior high school [in Japan] can read music and has the basic historical and theoretical tools to appreciate and enjoy it" (Abdoo, 1984). The United States lacks commitment and will at present to devote such energy to music training. Yet the data presented in this chapter at least point to the possibility of enhancing cognitive and motor skills, as well as music appreciation, by the blanket approach adopted by the Japanese.

Motor Skills

Although practicing an instrument is a specific case of motor skill training, little is known about the interrelationships of these issues in normal human development. Groves (1966) found no relationship between training or home musical background and children's ability to synchronize body movements to rhythmic stimuli. Groves did find that overall motor ability and age were correlated with rhythmic movement ability, as did Christianson (1953). Hurwitz et al. (1975) found significantly better scores on tests of sensorimotor rhythmic behavior for first-grade children who had been involved with Kodaly training.

Locus of Control

Locus of control is a psychological construct for describing whether individuals basically see themselves in charge of their lives (internal locus of control) or see their lives as primarily controlled by people and events outside themselves (external locus of control). Internality is positively correlated with many socially desirable skills and social characteristics (e.g., school performance, low incidence of delinquency), but the relation between locus of control and music skill development has also not been examined. Lawrence and Dachinger (1978) found that self-taught child pianists continued to be involved with music as adults, whereas children who had formal piano training frequently were not involved with music as adults. This suggests that an internal locus of control may be helpful in maintaining interest in music across the life span. Lawrence and Dachinger (1978) also reported that studying the piano *and* another instrument as a child increased the individual's involvement with music as an adult.

Self-Esteem

Eleven percent of the teacher education and early childhood education textbooks studied by Draper and Gayle (Chapter 11, this volume) state that music can be used to enhance self-esteem. Although self-esteem enhancement is a frequently stated goal of early childhood education programs, we have been unable to find any research actually relating music to self-esteem.

Social Interaction

Music is frequently used in the classroom as a mechanism of social interaction. Musical performance is inherently social from several aspects, but little is known about the interplay of these issues in child development. Chertock (1974) reported a non-statistically-significant but intriguing finding that social cooperation was higher under conditions of background art and mood music than with background noise of adult reading, or silence. Facilitating social interaction is one of the major functions of music, from pep bands at football games to dance bands at dances. The relationship between social encounters and music deserves much more scrutiny.

Summary and Conclusions

This chapter has reviewed much of the past research relating music and child development. We proposed a model for considering the role of music in child development that divides motivations and research problems into two major sub-headings: music as an inherent good in itself, and music as a means of promoting and fostering personal and social competence. The model is helpful in conceptualizing music research related to children. There are some research findings in almost every topic outlined in our model (Figure 1.1). It should be said, however, that little attempt has been made to demonstrate that musical experiences themselves cause changes in children. The fact that music is associated with certain child characteristics does not mean music causes the development of those characteristics; in statistical jargon, correlation is not causality. Studies that carefully control for potentially confounding variables will be necessary before it is possible to detail exactly which kind of musical experience influences which developmental characteristic; or if music is a catalyst or conjunct medium for other causes of change.

A wide perspective reveals little more than peripheral study on any given topic with the possible exceptions of the development of musical preferences. These gaps in research findings are an invitation to scholars from many disciplines to expand and refine our knowledge of the influence of music on childhood. The dotted lines between the two conceptual columns in our model (Figure 1.1) represent areas where there might be a logical relationship between issues in studying music as music and in studying music to facilitate other development. We did not find any research specifically focusing on trying to make such a bridge. Relationships between these domains seem logical—is there a relationship between listening-perception skills in music and abilities in language development, for example—but questions of this order await future research.

Three general themes run through the music and child development research. First, there is considerable evidence supporting the importance of the role music can play in a child's life, both as he or she comes to enjoy and appreciate music for itself, and because music involvement can enhance other aspects of cognitive, physical, and social development. Second, the processes of maturation in normal child development are an important part of a child's developing music-related abilities. Parents, teachers, researchers, and curriculum developers need to take into consideration a child's age-appropriate skills and developing capacities when planning how to integrate music into the child's life. Finally, even more important than being innately musically gifted, the data point again and again to the importance of experience in encouraging and refining musical aptitudes and abilities. Musical experiences need to be planned and monitored. Developing a taste for classical music, for example, is not a likely outcome for a child left strictly to the public school system and the network television and radio producers. Having carefully designed musical experiences in the classroom, however, can make an important difference in the way children appreciate music. Parents are particularly important and influential in encouraging music involvement. Starting children's musical life very early and promoting music consistently in terms of time and resources pays dividends as children become musically enculturated. Neither the schools nor private lessons alone are likely to be as effective as parental influence and a consistent family environment that synthesizes these outside educational experiences with a musically supportive home atmosphere.

References

Abdoo, F. H. (1984). Music Education in Japan. *Music Educators Journal*, *70*(6), 52–56.

Abel-Struth, S. (1982). Experiment on music recognition. [Special Issue]. *Psychology of Music*, 7–10.

Barrett, H. C., & Barker, H. R. (1973). Cognitive pattern perception and musical performance. *Perceptual and Motor Skills*, *36*, 1187–1193.

Bartlett, D. L. (1973). Effect of repeated listenings on structural discrimination and affective response. *Journal of Research in Music Education*, *21*(4), 302–317.

Bartlett, J. C., & Dowling, W. J. (1980). Recognition of transposed melodies: A key-distance effect in developmental perspective. *Journal of Experimental Psychology*, *6*, 501–515.

Berlyne, D. E. (1971). *Aesthetics and psychobiology*. New York: Appleton.

Biller, J. D., Olson, P. J., & Breen, T. (1974). The effect of "happy" versus "sad" music and participation on anxiety. *Journal of Music Therapy*, *11*, 68–73.

Billingsley, R., & Rotenberg, K. J. (1982). Children's interval processing in music. *Psychomusicology*, *2*(1), 38–43.

Botvin, G. J. (1974). Acquiring conservation of melody and cross-modal transfer through successive approximation. *Journal of Research in Music Education*, 22(3), 226-233.

Bradley, I. L. (1971). Repetition as a factor in the development of musical preference. *Journal of Research in Music Education*, 19, 295-298.

Bradley, I. (1972). Effect on student musical preference of a listening program in contemporary art music. *Journal of Research in Music Education*, 20(3), 344-353.

Buckton, R. (1977). A comparison of the effects of vocal and instrumental instruction on the development of melodic and vocal abilities in young children. *Psychology of Music*, 5, 36-47.

Cantor, J. R., & Zillmann, D. (1973). The effect of affective state and emotional arousal on music appreciation. *Journal of General Psychology*, 89, 97-108.

Castell, K. C. (1982). Children's sensitivity to stylistic differences in "classical" and "popular" music. [Special issue]. *Psychology of Music*, 22-25.

Cattell, R. B., & Anderson, J. C. (1953). The measurement of personality and behavior disorders by the IPAT MPT. *Journal of Applied Psychology*, 37, 446.

Cattell, R. B., & Eber, H. W. (1954). *Handbook for the IPAT music preference test of personality*. Champaign, IL: Institute for Personality Ability and Testing.

Cattell, R. B., & Saunders, D. R. (1954). Musical preferences and personality diagnosis: I. A factorization of one hundred and twenty themes. *Journal of Social Psychology*, 39, 3-24.

Chang, H-W., & Trehub, S. (1977a). Auditory processing of relational information by young infants. *Journal of Experimental Child Psychology*, 24, 324-331.

Chang, H-W., & Trehub, S. (1977b). Infants' perception of temporal grouping in auditory patterns. *Child Development*, 48, 1666-1670.

Chattin-McNichols, J. P. (1981). The effects of Montessori school experience. *Young Children*, 11, 49-66.

Chertock, S. L. (1974). Effect of music on cooperative problem solving by children. *Perceptual and Motor Skills*, 39(2), 986.

Christianson, H. (1953). *Bodily rhythmic movements of young children in relation to rhythm in music*. New York: Bureau of Publications, Teachers College, Columbia University.

Cleall, C. (1981). Notes toward the clarification of creativity in music education. *Psychology of Music*, 9(1), 44-47.

Cohen, M. (1974, February). Move him into reading with music. *Instructor*, 60-62.

Colwell, R. (1972). Review of *Measures of Musical Abilities*. In O. K. Buros (Ed.), *The seventh mental measurements yearbook* (Vol. I). Highland Park, NJ: Gryphon Press.

Crozier, J., Robinson, E., & Ewing, V. (1976-77). Etiology of absolute pitch. *Bulletin de Psychologie*, 30, 792-803.

Dorhout, A. (1982). Identifying musically gifted children. *Journal for the Education of the Gifted*, 5(1), 56-66.

Dorow, L. G. (1977). The effect of teacher approval/disapproval ratios on student music selection and concert attentiveness. *Journal of Research in Music Education*, 25, 32-40.

Dowling, J. W. (1982). Melodic information processing and its development. In D. Deutsch (Ed.), *The psychology of music*. New York: Academic Press.

Etaugh, C., & Michals, D. (1975). Effects on reading comprehension of preferred music and frequency of studying to music. *Perceptual and Motor Skills*, 41, 553-554.

Fisher, S., & Fisher, R. L. (1951). The effects of personal insecurity on reactions to unfamiliar music. *Journal of Social Psychology, 34,* 265–273.

Fiske, D. W., & Maddi, S. R. (1961). A conceptual framework. In D. W. Fiske and S. R. Maddi (Eds.), *The functions of varied experience.* Homewood, IL: Dorsey.

Fogelson, S. (1973). Music as a distractor on reading test performance of eighth grade students. *Perceptual and Motor Skills, 36,* 1265–1266.

Foley, E. A. (1975). Effects of training in conservation of tonal and rhythmic patterns on second-grade children. *Journal of Research in Music Education, 23*(4), 240–248.

Fowler, W. (1962). Cognitive learning in infancy and early childhood. *Psychological Bulletin, 59,* 116–152.

Fowler, W. (1969). The effect of early stimulation: The problem of focus in developmental stimulation. *Merrill-Palmer Quarterly, 15*(2), 157–170.

Freeman, J. (1976). Developmental influences on children's perception. *Educational Research, 19*(1), 69–75.

Gardner, H. (1971). Children's duplication of rhythmic patterns. *Journal of Research in Music Education, 19,* 295–298.

Gardner, H. (1973). Children's sensitivity to musical styles. *Merrill Palmer Quarterly, 19,* 67–77.

Gardner, H. (1983). *Frames of mind.* New York: Basic Books.

Gardner, H., Winner, E., & Kircher, M. (1975). Children's conceptions of the arts. *Journal of Aesthetic Education, 9*(3), 60–77.

Geringer, J. M. (1977). An assessment of children's musical instrument preferences. *Journal of Music Therapy, 14,* 172–179.

Geringer, J. M. (1982). Verbal and operant music listening preferences in relationship to age and musical training [Special issue]. *Psychology of music,* 47–50.

Geringer, J. M. (1983). The relationship of pitch-matching and pitch-discrimination abilities of preschool and fourth-grade students. *Journal of Research in Music Education, 31*(2), 93–99.

Getz, R. P. (1966). The influence of familiarity through repetition in determining music preference. *Research in Music Education, 14,* 179.

Giacobbe, G. A., & Graham, R. M. (1978). The responses of aggressive emotionally disturbed and normal boys to selected musical stimuli. *Journal of Music Therapy, 15*(30), 118–135.

Gibbons, A. C. (1983). Rhythm responses in emotionally disturbed children with differing needs for external structure. *Music Therapy, 3*(1), 94–102.

Gilbert, J. P. (1979). Assessment of motoric music skill development in young children: Test construction and evaluation procedures. *Psychology of Music, 7*(2), 3–12.

Gilbert, J. P. (1981). Motoric music skill development in young children: A longitudinal investigation. *Psychology of Music, 9*(1), 21–25.

Gordon, E. (1965). *Musical aptitude profile.* Boston: Houghton Mifflin.

Gordon, E. (1967). A comparison of the performance of culturally disadvantaged students with that of culturally heterogeneous students on musical aptitude profile. *Psychology in the Schools, 4*(3), 260–262.

Gordon, E. (1968). A study of the efficacy of general intelligence and musical aptitude tests in predicting achievement in music. *Council for Research in Music Education, 13,* 40–45.

Gordon, E. (1971). *The psychology of music teaching.* Englewood Cliffs, NJ: Prentice-Hall.

Gordon, E. (1979). Developmental music aptitude as measured by the Primary Measures of Music Audiation. *Psychology of Music*, *7*(1), 42–49.

Greer, R. D., Dorow, L. G., & Hanser, S. (1973). Music discrimination training and the music selection behavior of nursery and primary level children. *Council for Research in Music Education*, *35*(4), 30–43.

Greer, R. D., Dorow, L. G., & Randall, A. (1974). Music listening preferences of elementary school children. *Journal of Research in Music Education*, *22*, 284–291.

Greer, R. D., Dorow, L. G., Wachhaus, G., & White, E. R. (1973). Adult approval and students' music selection behavior. *Journal of Research in Music Education*, *21*, 345–354.

Groves, W. C. (1966). Rhythmic training and its relationship to the synchronization of motor-rhythmic responses. *Dissertation Abstracts*, *27*(3-A), 702–703.

Hair, H. I. (1982). Microcomputer tests of aural and visual directional patterns. *Psychology of Music*, *10*(2), 26–31.

Healey, B. J. (1973). Pilot study on the applicability of the music preference test of personality. *Journal of Music Therapy*, *10*, 36–45.

Hedden, S. K. (1973). Listeners' responses to music in relation to autochthonous and experiential factors. *Journal of Research in Music Education*, *21*, 225–238.

Heingartner, A., & Hall, J. V. (1974). Affective consequences in adults and children of repeated exposure to auditory stimuli. *Journal of Personality and Social Psychology*, *29*, 719–723.

Heller, J., Campbell, W., & Gibson, B. (1982). The development of music listening skills in children [Special issue]. *Psychology of Music*, 55–58.

Heyduk, R. G. (1975). Rated preference for musical compositions as it relates to complexity and exposure frequency. *Perception and Psychophysics*, *17*(1), 84–91.

Hickman, A. (1970). Experiments with children involving pitch, rhythm and timbre. *Research in Education*, *3*, 73–86.

Hurwitz, I., Wolff, P. H., Bortnick, B. D., & Kokas, K. (1975). Nonmusical effects of the Kodaly music curriculum in primary grade children. *Journal of Learning Disabilities*, *8*(3), 167–174.

Igaga, J. M., and Versey, J. (1977). Cultural differences in rhythmic perception. *Psychology of Music*, *5*, 1.

Igaga, J. M., & Versey, J. (1978). Cultural differences in rhythmic performance. *Psychology of Music*, *6*(1), 61–64.

Inglefield, H. G. (1972). Conformity behavior reflected in the musical preferences of adolescents. *Contributions to Music Education*, *1*, 56–65.

Jalongo, M. R., & Bromley, K. D. (1984). Developing linguistic competence through song picture books. *Reading Teacher*, *37*(9), 840–845.

Jones, R. L. (1976). The development of the child's conception of meter in music. *Journal of Research in Music Education*, *24*, 142–154.

Kalanidhi, M. S. (1970). Preference for concordant and discordant intervals: A study among school children. *Manas*, *17*, 111–118.

Karma, K. (1982). Musical, spatial and verbal abilities: A progress report [Special issue]. *Psychology of Music*, 69–71.

Keston, M. J., & Pinto, I. M. (1955). Possible factors influencing musical preference. *Journal of Genetic Psychology*, *87*, 101–113.

Kinney, K. D., & Kagan, J. (1976). Infant attention to auditory discrepancy. *Child Development*, *47*, 155–164.

Kokas, K. (1969). Psychological tests in connection with music education in Hungary. *Journal of Research in Music Education*, *8*(3), 102–114.

Krugman, H. E. (1943). Affective response to music as a function of familiarity. *Journal of Abnormal and Social Psychology*, *38*, 388–392.

Krumhansl, C., & Keil, F. C. (1982). Acquisition of the hierarchy of tonal functions in music. *Memory and Cognition*, *10*, 243–251.

Kuhmerker, L. (1969, January). Music in the beginning reading program. *Young Children*, 157–163.

Kuhn, T. L., & Gates, E. E. (1975). Effect of notational values, age, and example length on tempo performance accuracy. *Journal of Research in Music Education*, *23*(3), 203–210.

Kulka, J. (1981). Preference choice and identification of simple musical structures by children. *Studia Psychologica*, *23*(1), 85–92.

Lawrence, S. J., & Dachinger, N. (1967). Factors relating to carryover of music training into adult life. *Journal of Research in Music Education*, *15*(1), 23–31.

LeBlanc, A. (1979). Generic style music preferences of fifth-grade students. *Journal of Research in Music Education*, *27*, 255–270.

LeBlanc, A. (1981). Effects of style, tempo, and performing medium on children's music preference. *Journal of Research in Music Education*, *29*, 143–156.

LeBlanc, A. (1982). An interactive theory of music preference. *Journal of Music Therapy*, *19*, 28–45.

LeBlanc, A., & Cote, R. (1983). Effects of tempo and performing medium on children's music preference. *Journal of Research in Music Education*, *31*, 57–66.

LeBlanc, A., & McCrary, J. (1983). Effect of tempo on children's music preference. *Journal of Research in Music Education*, *31*, 283–294.

Leithwood, K. A., & Fowler, W. (1971). Complex motor learning in four-year-olds. *Child Development*, *42*(3), 781–792.

Lewandowska, K. (1976–77). Structure and development of musical aptitude in childhood. *Bulletin de Psychologie*, *30*(14–16), 804–809.

Lowery, J. (1982). Developing creativity in gifted children. *Gifted Child Quarterly*, *26*(3), 133–139.

Macdonald, D. (1974). Environment: A factor in conceptual listening skills of elementary school children. *Journal of Research in Music Education*, *22*, 205–214.

MacGregor, B. (1968). Music activity preferences of a selected group of fourth-grade children. *Journal of Research in Music Education*, *16*, 302–307.

Madsen, C. K., Moore, R. S., Wagner, M. J., & Yarbrough, C. (1975). A comparison of music as reinforcement for correct mathematical responses versus music as reinforcement for attentiveness. *Journal of Music Therapy*, *12*(2), 84–95.

Marks, J. E. (1972). "On the road to find out": Adolescent development and rock music preferences. *Psychology, General*, (Abstract).

McDonald, D. T. (1983). Montessori's music for young children. *Young Children*, *39*(1), 58–63.

McDonald, D. T., & Ramsey, J. H. (1978). Awakening the artist: Music for young children. *Young Children*, *33*(2), 26–32.

McMullen, P. T. (1974). Influence of number of different pitches and melodic redundancy on preference responses. *Journal of Research in Music Education*, *22*(3), 198–204.

Mead, M. (1972, October). Music is a human need. *Music Educators Journal*, 24–29.

Melson, W. H., & McCall, R. B. (1970). Attentional responses of five-month girls to discrepant auditory stimuli. *Child Development*, *41*, 1159–1171.

Montessori, M. A. (1965). *A Montessori handbook: Dr. Montessori's own handbook* (R. C. Orem, Ed.). New York: Putnam.

Moore, H. T. (1914). The genetic aspects of consonance and dissonance. *Psychological Monographs, 17*(2, Whole No. 73).

Moore, R., (1966). The relationship of intelligence to creativity. *Journal of Research in Music Education, 14*, 243-253.

Morgan, B. J., & Lindsley, O. R. (1966). Operant preference for stereophonic over monophonic music. *Journal of Music Therapy, 3*, 135-143.

Mull, H. K. (1957). The effect of repetition upon the enjoyment of modern music. *Journal of Psychology, 43*, 155-162.

Neal, C. (1983). Dichotically stimulated cerebral hemisphere asymmetries in children with high music aptitude and normal music aptitude. Ann Arbor Michigan: *University Microfilms International.*

Nelson, D. J. (1980). The conservation of metre in beginning violin students. *Psychology of Music, 8*(1), 25-33.

Norton, D. (1978). Relationship of music ability and intelligence to auditory and visual conservation of the kindergarten child. *Journal of Research in Music Education, 27*(1), 3-13.

Papousek, M., & Papousek, H. (1981). Musical elements in the infant's vocalization: Their significance for communication, cognition, and creativity. *Advances in Infancy Research, 1*, 163-224.

Parente, J., & O'Malley, J. (1975). Training in musical rhythm and field dependence of children. *Perceptual and Motor Skills, 40*, 392-394.

Parker, J. J. (1973). Discriminative listening as a basis for problem solving among four year olds. *Dissertation Abstracts International, 33*(8-A), 4460-4461.

Peery, J. C., & Peery, I. W. (1986). Effects of exposure to classical music on the musical preferences of preschool children. *Journal of Research in Music Education, 34*(1), 24-33.

Peretti, P. O. (1975). Changes in galvanic skin response as affected by musical selection, sex, and academic discipline. *Journal of Psychology, 89*, 183-187.

Peretti, P. O., & Swenson, K. (1974). Effects of music on anxiety as determined by physiological skin responses. *Journal of Research in Music Education, 22*(4), 278-283.

Phillips, D. (1976). An investigation of the relationship between musicality and intelligence. *Psychology of Music, 4*(2), 16-31.

Plummeridge, C. (1980). Creativity and music education—the need for further clarification. *Psychology of Music, 8*(1), 34-40.

Radocy, R. D. (1976). Effects of authority figure biases on changing judgments of musical events. *Journal of Research in Music Education, 24*, 119-128.

Rarick, G. L. (1961). *Motor development during infancy and childhood.* Madison, WI: College Printing and Typing Co.

Rogers, V. R. (1957). Children's musical preferences as related to grade level and other factors. *Elementary School Journal, 57*, 433-435.

Rubenger, R. (1979, Summer). Identification and evaluation procedures for gifted and talented programs. *The Gifted Child Quarterly.*

Rubin-Rabson, G. (1940). The influence of age, intelligence, and training on reactions to classic and modern music. *Journal of General Psychology, 22*, 413-429.

Saffle, M. (1983, Spring). Aesthetic education in theory and practice: A review of recent research. *Bulletin of the Council for Research in Music Education, 74*, 22-38.

Sample, D., & Hotchkiss, S. M. (1971). An investigation of relationship between personality characteristics and success in instrumental study. *Journal of Research in Music Education*, *19*, 307–313.

Schuckert, R. F., & McDonald, R. L. (1968). An attempt to modify the music preferences of preschool children. *Journal of Research in Music Education*, *16*(1), 39–44.

Serafine, M. L. (1981). Musical timbre imagery in young children. *Journal of Genetic Psychology*, *139*(1), 97–108.

Sergeant, D. (1969). Experimental investigation of absolute pitch. *Journal of Research in Music Education*, *17*, 135–143.

Sergeant, D. (1983). The octave: Percept or concept. *Psychology of Music*, *11*(1), 3–18.

Shuter-Dyson, R. (1979). Music in the environment: Effects on the musical development of the child. *International Review of Applied Psychology*, *28*(2), 127–133.

Shuter-Dyson, R. (1982). Musical ability. In D. Deutsch (Ed.), *The psychology of music*. New York: Academic Press.

Simon, B., Holzberg, J. D., Alessi, S. L., & Garrity, D. (1951). The recognition and acceptance of mood in music by psychotic patients. *Journal of Abnormal Social Psychology*, *64*(4), 307.

Simons, G. M. (1976). A criterion-referenced test of fundamental music listening skills. *Child Study Journal*, *6*(4), 233–234.

Smith, C. A., & Morris, L. W. (1976). Effects of stimulative and sedative music on cognitive and emotional components of anxiety. *Psychological Reports*, *38*, 1187–1193.

Sopchak, A. L. (1955). Individual differences in responses to different types of music in relation to sex, mood, and other variables. *Psychological Monographs*, *69*(No. 11).

Steele, A. L. (1967). Effects of social reinforcement on the musical preferences of mentally retarded children. *Journal of Music Therapy*, *4*(2), 57–61.

Stone, M. (1983). Some antecedents of music appreciation. *Psychology of Music*, *11*(1), 26–31.

Stoudenmire, J. (1975). A comparison of muscle relaxation training and music in the reduction of state and trait anxiety. *Journal of Clinical Psychology*, *31*(3), 48–50.

Verveer, E. M., Barry, H., & Bousfield, W. A. (1933). Change in affectivity with repetition. *American Journal of Psychology*, *45*, 130–134.

Wagley, M. W. (1978). The effects of music on affective and cognitive development of sound-symbol recognition among preschool children. *Dissertation Abstracts International*, *29*(3-A), 1316.

Wapnick, J. (1976). A review of research on attitude and preference. *Bulletin of the Council for Research in Music Education*, *48*, 1–20.

Ward, W. D., & Burns, E. M. (1982). Absolute pitch. In D. Deutsch (Ed.), *The psychology of music*. New York: Academic Press.

Webster, P-R., & Schlentrich, K. (1982). Discrimination of pitch direction by preschool children with verbal and non-verbal tasks. *Journal of Research in Music Education*, *30*, 151–161.

Weeden, R. E. (1971). A comparison of the academic achievement in reading and mathematics of negro children whose parents are interested, not interested, or involved in a program of Suzuki violin. *Dissertation Abstracts International*, *32*(3582-A).

Weidenfeller, E. W., & Zimny, C. H. (1962). The effects of music upon the GSR of depressives and schizophrenics. *Journal of Abnormal Social Psychology*, *64*(4), 307.

Wellek, A. (1938). Das absolute Gehor. *Seitschrift fur Angewandte Psychologie & Charakterkunde-Beihefte*, *83*, 1–368.

Wilcox, R. (1969). Music ability among Negro grade school pupils: Or, I got rhythm? *Perceptual and Motor Skills*, *29*(1), 167–168.

Wilcox, R. (1971). Further ado about Negro music ability. *Journal of Negro Education*, *40*(4), 361–364.

Williams, R. O. (1972). Effects of musical aptitude, instruction, and social status on attitudes toward music. *Journal of Research in Music Education*, *20*, 362–369.

Wingert, M. L. (1972). Effects of a music enrichment program in the education of the mentally retarded. *Journal of Music Therapy*, *9*, 13–22.

Wolf, R. H., & Weiner, F. (1972). Effects of four noise conditions on arithmetic performance. *Perceptual and Motor Skills*, *35*, 928–930.

Young, W. T. (1971). The role of musical aptitude, intelligence, and academic achievement in predicting the musical attainment of elementary instrumental music students. *Journal of Research in Music Education*, *19*(4), 385–398.

Zajonc, R. B. (1968). Attitudinal effects of mere exposure. *Journal of Personality and Social Psychology*, *9*, (Monograph Supplement 2, Part 2).

Zern, D. S. (1983). The relationship of pressure toward obedience to production in art and music: A cross-cultural study on the effects of certain child-rearing practices. *Journal of Social Psychology*, *120*(2), 213–221.

Zimny, G., & Weidenfeller, E. (1962). Effects of music upon GSR of children. *Child Development*, *33*, 891–896.

Part II
Development of Musical Abilities

2
A Study of Infant Musical Productivity

LINDA KELLEY and BRIAN SUTTON-SMITH

Detailed information on the early musical responses and productivity of normal children prior to 2 years of age is notably absent, except for such prodigies as Mozart. In contrast, other areas of child development such as language acquisition have been widely studied. This void led to the present exploratory study of three children of three contrasting musical backgrounds. One family included parents who were professional musicians, one family had parents who were musically oriented but not musicians by profession, and a third family had parents who were not musically oriented. The study involved the observation of each child in relevant family settings over a period from birth to 2 years of age and provided an earlier period of observation (0–12 months), more family context data, and more child performance data than the other studies presently in the literature (McKernon, 1979; Holahan, Chapter 5, this volume) of children from 1 to 2½ years.

The study was directed by three questions: (a) How is musicality differently expressed in these families? (b) What are the distinctive features of the children's early musical response and performance? and (c) What is the immediate context that signals the beginning and end of musical behavior? By and large this paper is confined to noting the contrasting features of parental and child expression across these three families in order to provide a background for the later study of more specific causal assessments.

Observing the Children

The three children selected were all firstborn females of similar socioeconomic status. Each was observed weekly during their first 24 months in a variety of contexts. Length of observation varied from 15 minutes to half-day sessions. On each visit, an attempt was made to sample a variety of settings and times of day such as eating, playtime, nap time, birthday parties, and, for Case I, the parents' music practice (keyboard, voice), music lessons, and music performances. During the observation, the observer recorded any spontaneous music productions such as pitch modulations, vocalizations, or body rhythmic movements, noting at the same time the contingencies of situation, persons, objects, and sounds involved as agencies for these responses. Musical instruments or other music present in the setting was noted along with the child's responses to them. Each family was interviewed concerning their musical history, modes of transferring musicality from one generation to the next, and such aspects of the child's performance as: favorite songs, records, instruments, and occasions for musical behavior. Mothers were observed in their use of lullabies with the babies. All parents sang adequately and all claimed grandparents who were professional or actively proficient musicians.

In the following description of cases we will deal in sequence with each family's level and kind of musicality, the child's responses to this context, and the child's own musicality in these settings. Particular attention will be given to the child's own songs, which will be analyzed in terms of their song-form (phrasing of words and melody, endings), substructures (rhythm, melodic contours, intervals), and performance (renderings, interpretation).

Case I: Professionally Musically Oriented Context

Family Musicality

These parents were both professional musicians, were actively involved in study, practice, teaching, and performance, and attended productions in the arts. Music was present in the home in a multitude of forms, from parents' and grandparents' performances and practice to records and instruments. All adults were aware of this child's musical response, reporting changes and activity to the investigator and one another in technical terms such as singing in "thirds." They arranged musical experiences via instruments (piano, guitar, autoharp), singing, or recordings. At family gatherings music played an important role, with frequent singing around the piano, performing, and listening to recordings and television performances. This was truly a musically "literate environment" comparable to the linguistically "literate environments" reported for early readers.

Mother and grandmother engaged in singing conversations with Child I (Figure 2.1). Here the adults modified melodies sung to the child, perhaps somewhat similar to "motherese" in early language development ("singerese"). These melodies and "conversations" had well-defined characteristics: repetition of a

Bye-oh   bye,   Bye-oh   baby   bye.

FIGURE 2.1. Case I: Example of mother's song.

ah ------,   This   is   a   forth.

FIGURE 2.2. Case I: Example of mother's singing.

short motive, frequently of narrow (up to a fourth interval) range and usually holding the baby and rocking in rhythm with the song. Later, as we shall see, the child initiated these simple songs together with the mother and grandmother, starting with the basic element and then extending the song. These songs took place during caretaking periods, while rocking, and interacting throughout the day.

Regarding lullabies, the mother and grandmother sang two lullabys originally sung by the great grandmother and "handed down" to the daughters: one an original tune by the great grandmother and the other the carol "Away in a Manger." The mother also created high-pitched lyrical, soft melodies without words to accompany rocking for lullabys at other times.

Child's Responses

During the first 5 months, music production consisted of a continuous blend of sound, oscillating over a rather narrow range and punctuated by higher, loud screeches. These songs occurred most frequently as a response to and in conjunction with the mother's songs. It is possible that other musical behavior may have been present and developing during the first 5-month period but remained unobserved by the investigator. Whatever the case, the present intensive account shows there is more to the first stage of "musical babble" than other evidence in this volume might imply (cf. Holahan, Chapter 5). For example, distinctive features for melodic performances were apparent with a descending glissando (gliding effect by sounding adjacent tones in rapid succession) on "ah" at 6 months in the mother-infant and grandmother-infant context at nap times. At the 6- to 7-month period, the glissando was repeated and expanded with repetition of the final pitches; this was later reversed to an ascending pattern. At 8 months, alternating third and fourth intervals were added to the repertoire, induced by the cuckoo clock. Additionally, early songs sung by the grandmother and mother were made up of fourth and third intervals. The mother would sing and describe third and fourth intervals to the baby and tell her to sing the interval (Figure 2.2).

Along with these alternating intervals, a three-note pattern emerged at 8 months. This pattern was first heard during nap times, prior to sleep or upon waking (Figure 2.3). This 3-note pattern was expanded with the vocabulary of earlier pitch productions described above. The final note of the pattern was sung with the

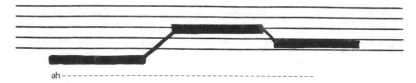

FIGURE 2.3. Case I: 3-note pattern at 8 months.

glissando inverted to rise in pitch at the end. This pattern was further altered by speed changes—fast and slow. These elements were combined and recombined during the next 3 months. It is important to note that none of the features mentioned here for the ages 6 to 12 months are reported in the McKernon (1979) article. Judging by her remarks, these phenomena may have occurred in her sample from 12 to 18 months.

During the ninth month, the father played the piano and the child sang and played with one finger on one note at a time. While her father played "Old MacDonald" on the piano, she sang a sustained "ah" following the general contour of the melody, but gliding over the notes between. These performances were accompanied by leg movements or "dancing" while held by the mother. When placed on the floor with the autoharp or guitar, she would pluck a single string, cock her ear to the side to listen to the string with a more serious expression, and respond with shrieks of laughter as the resonance died away.

At 13 months the child sat at the piano and played with two hands, one finger each, sounding two notes together, while she sang. This led to performances where the whole family listened, clapped, and praised. This was a new social event to which the family gradually increased responsiveness on occasions when they noticed her sitting alone. With this constant musical interaction, Child I developed an extensive song repertoire by 24 months.

Primary singing time was during car rides, nap times, early morning waking, and interactions with mother, grandmother, and father at the piano. Agencies for music production were: voice, piano, guitar, autoharp, cuckoo clock, records, and radio music. Music entering her awareness led to cessation of any activity, attentive listening, then clapping and dancing or singing with the music. Interruptions of the music occurred more often as the result of voices or nonmusical sounds, although the appearance of favorite books could also end music behavior. She usually returned to the music after the interruption.

Songs

Songs appeared at about 12 months, with an extensive repertoire by 24 months. Singing was characterized by accurate pitch and rhythm, distinct diction, basically correct lyrics, vocal technique, and musical expression. These songs primarily developed from the mother reading and singing nursery rhymes and stories at bedtime using a "scaffolding" procedure mentioned by Ninio and

Bruner (1976), where the child filled in words. On morning waking and at play, the child would sing or pretend-read songs to herself. The mother corrected songs and sang along on difficult passages. At times the father accompanied the songs at the piano. Of interest here is the development of vocal technique. On one occasion the child was having difficulty with an octave interval jump. Noticing this problem while riding in the car, the grandmother told her she could sing that note if she "breathed in a great big breath with lots of air, opened her throat as if she yawned a great big yawn, and then sang the note." The child followed these instructions and the note was easily sung. The results of these kinds of teachings was a great reduction in the kinds of pitch, rhythm, and melody errors more characteristic in previous research accounts and in Cases II and III below.

Song-Form

The melodic contour appeared first, followed by the rhythm, and then the words. Child I began with the standard tune contour at 9 months, perceiving first the basic melodic structure of the song, its first phrase, and its most salient features. This was expanded through practice to the overall expression of the melodic contour of the song. She participated in extensive manipulations of songs, making up and adding new words to old tunes. The rhythm was increasingly incorporated, with the words following later and performed with very clear, precise diction at 24 months.

Substructure

Rhythm developed from random groupings to groups with an underlying beat, with a regular beat maintained, by 2 years. Vocal range was G# to C#'. One of the most salient observations at this age was Child I's demonstration of self-correction, which implied her assimilation of harmonic and rhythmic structure. For example, in the song "Happy Birthday" (Figure 2.4), tonal correction was demonstrated in the third to fourth phrase. Here she lost the tonality in the third phrase but still managed to end correctly, no small task with such wide jumps in a rather difficult tune. The singer also demonstrated her knowledge of vocal

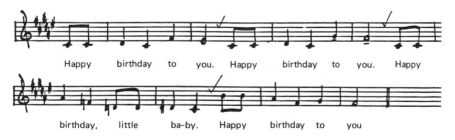

FIGURE 2.4. Case I: "Happy Birthday," illustrating tonal self-correction.

one   for the   little   boy who   lives   down   the   lane.

FIGURE 2.5. Case I: "Baa, Baa Black Sheep," illustrating self-correction.

technique in this song by opening her mouth wide, taking large breaths, and "throwing the air" to sing these leaps.

In her rendering of "Baa, Baa Black Sheep," she became confused with the variation performed in "Twinkle, Twinkle, Little Star" (Figures 2.5 and 2.6) and began to lose the melody line. Realizing that she had lost the melody, she self-corrected and got back on the original pitch, ending with strong emphasis on "yes sir, yes sir" and then retarded the ending almost as if to distract our attention from the difficulty. Perhaps even more striking is that she was almost successful in transposing the variation from "Twinkle, Twinkle" into "Baa, Baa Black Sheep," which is essentially the same tune.

Rhythmic adjustments are seen in "Old MacDonald," in which she alternated 4-count measures with 5-count measures, so employed as to fit the words. Remarkable rhythmic development is demonstrated in her piano and voice rendition of "Mary Had a Little Lamb." The preciseness of the dotted eighth with the sixteenth notes followed by the even eighths on "little lamb" was striking. Even more remarkable was the piano accompaniment, which she played evenly on the beat and in which she utilized the motive "little lamb" (♫ ♩). Her emphasis at the beginning of the phrase musically reinforced the rhythmic beat together with slurring "Mary had," extending the initial consonant as "MMMary." Two verses were accurately sung. A representative portion of the song illustrating these points is reproduced in Figure 2.7.

Performance

Performance was an important feature of Child I's musical development. Her songs, performed for an audience and in private, demonstrated developing musicality. Examples of this developing musicality were found in her use of ritards, accented words, lyrical phrasing, and melodic variations.

little   tiny   'tar

Twinkle,   twinkle   little   star,   how I   wonder   what you   are

FIGURE 2.6. Case I: "Twinkle, Twinkle Little Star" variation.

FIGURE 2.7. Case I: "Mary had a Little Lamb," illustrating rhythmic development with voice and piano accompaniment.

Summary

Child I's progress is summarized in Tables 2.1 and 2.2, which list the major "features" of her development as described above. Table 2.1 includes a listing of the agents and agencies of musical influence observed in the homes of this and the other two children over the 2-year period of study. Table 2.2 includes the same contrast across the three children for the developmental sequence of their vocalizations.

Case II: Musically Oriented Context

Family Musicality

These parents were not professionally trained musicians but were musically oriented insofar as music played a major role in the home at family gatherings, singing together, and sharing musical experiences with recordings and concert attendance. Both parents sang and the mother played the piano at an elementary level. Both parents sang songs with the child and provided musical experiences via recordings, piano, and music at church. They were aware of and interested in the child's musical responses, although they did not report the productions and responses in technical language, as in Case I, but rather sang examples to the investigator. The mother did not create songs for the child as in Case I, but she did sing nursery rhymes and parts of nursery rhymes to her. The mother sang two lullabies, "Muffinman" and "Silent Night."

Child's Responses

Development was similar to Child I but at a later age. Music response was first observed at 4 months, involving arousal modulation with a music box within the mother-infant relationship. When the mother played the music box at nap time, the baby expressed excitement by waving her arms rapidly and screeching repeatedly at the sound of the music box. At this time the mother began to sing simple

TABLE 2.1. Agents and agencies in musical influences in each of the 3 cases

Child I Professionally musically oriented context	Child II Musically oriented context	Child III Non-musically oriented context
Mother-infant context		
Mother sings—baby listen attentively, smiles, vocalizes (1–3 weeks)	Mother sings—baby "sings" and listens (1 month)	
Mother rocks—baby rocks or moves body rhythmically, later claps and dances (8 months)	Mother plays music box— baby waves arms and screeches (1–2 months)	
Lullabies	Lullabies	
Mother says "Sing" — baby "sings"		
Instruments		
Child placed near piano, begins to play one note at a time, changes expression (9 months)	Mother plays piano—child listens and sings along	Tambourine—infrequent Guitar (introduced by observer)—regular beat maintained (24 months)
Father plays piano—child listens attentively, plays piano with one finger at a time	Toy xylophone—infrequent use, no perceived pattern	
Guitar or autoharp placed on floor—child plucks string, smiles, and becomes excited (9 months)		
Media		
Records, radio—child stops activity, listens attentively, gets excited	Records, radio—child listens and sings	Records—child dances and "sings" (18 months) TV (Mickey Mouse, Sesame Street)—child sings with TV, not readily audible
Outside contexts		
Parents' rehearsals and performances—child stops activity, listens attentively	Church—child listens and sings along Parades—child claps and dances to music	
Independent productions		
Car rides	Singing into curtain pull cord	
Nap times	Nap times	
Early morning waking	Play	
Play	Private performance	
Private performance		
Singing with the piano alone		

TABLE 2.1. *Continued*

Child I Professionally musically oriented context	Child II Musically oriented context	Child III Non-musically oriented context
Instruction		
Mother/child singing conver- sations ("singerese")	Mothers plays songs at piano	
Song/Nursery rhyme scaffolding—child practices on waking		
Vocal technique		
Interval and song corrections		
Father plays songs at piano with child beside and on lap		

childhood songs and nursery rhymes while the baby watched her face intently, listening and vocalizing on a sustained pitch or oscillation, carrying the phrase with each breath. At 8 months Child II responded consistently by clapping and "dancing" with recorded music. The descending glissando was observed at 10 months, and at 15 months, alternating third intervals and the three-note contour were repeated during play. These did not receive the degree of manipulation as in Case I. Beginning attempts at songs appeared at 16 months, and were clearly distinguished at 20 months in the context of the mother singing and playing nursery rhyme songs at the piano. The mother reported that the child frequently accompanied her play with singing either standard songs or original tunes. By 24 months the child created story songs to accompany play and performed either for her family or a pretend audience, singing into the curtain pull cord as a microphone.

Agencies for music were the mother's voice, records, radio music, piano, music box, the toy xylophone, and singing into the curtain pull cord. Productions were observed during mother-child and father-child interactions, initially prior to nap time and then as an accompaniment to play or caretaking activities. The parents reinforced productions with attention and repetition, but did not expand them with the singing conversations as in Case I. Interruptions occurred as a result of loud noises or of people, although typically Child II returned to musical activity directly afterward.

Songs

Songs developed while interacting with the mother. The earliest observed attempts were at 16 months, and they increased at 20 months in accuracy and frequency. The mother played songs at the piano while Child II sang along. Child II extended these songs during play times as an accompaniment to any activity and

TABLE 2.2. Developmental sequence of children's vocalizations

Child I Professionally musically oriented context	Child II Musically oriented context	Child III Non-musically oriented context
Body movement		
Rocks (self, duck, book)	Rocks	Dance (18 months)
Claps	Claps	
Dances	Excited movements	
Waves arms	Some facial expressions	
Varies facial expressions		
Excited movement, hysteria		
Melodic features		
Glissando (6 months)	Glissando (10 months)	Beginning songs (20–21 months)
Glissando with repetition of final sound	3-note contour (15 months)	
Glissando reversal	Alternating third interval	
3-note contour (8 months)	Beginning songs (18 months)	
3-note contour with alteration of final pitch— raising and shortened duration		

Alternating third
interval (9 months)

Alternating fourth
interval

Combining 3-note contour with alternating thirds
Attempted reproduction of mother's songs (11 months)

Rhythmic features
Claps in time (8 months)
Dances (9 months)
Elongation and shortening
Meter (8 months)

Plays tambourine

Claps in time (8–9 months)

Standard songs
Melodic contour followed by rhythm (11–12 months)
Accurate pitch and rhythm by 24 months
Precise diction (24 months)
Self-corrections
Musicality via accents, retards, phrasing
Audience performance with piano

Melodic contour followed by rhythm (18 months)
Beginnings and endings (21 months)
Characterized by idiosyncratic kernals, final cadences,
    complex rhythms
Less accurate lyrics, rhythm, pitch than Case I
Audience performance—curtain pull cord microphone

Words followed by
    rhythm and
    melodic kernal
    (20–21 months)
Few spontaneous
    songs
No performance
Inaccurate pitch—
    tone more spoken
    than sung

then in her performances for family and pretend audiences. She also requested that her songs be tape recorded.

Song-Form

Child II, as did Child I, began with the tune contour holding together the event, and adapting idiosyncratic kernals that functioned to end songs and maintain structure. Words followed rhythmic melodic development but lacked the precise diction and tonal-rhythmic accuracy of Child I. The performance of the song, however, maintained the overall flavor of the song. The characteristics of Child II's songs were definite beginnings and cadences, and complex rhythms with typically a basic rhythmic motive suggested or maintained. Lyrics did not appear to be as important to her, as they were to Child I, since when unsure of words she willingly substituted a syllable or words from other songs, or just skipped and continued. The overall production was the main event, as is also contended to be the case in children's story production (Scollon & Scollon, 1981). Nevertheless, her diction was unclear and difficult to understand at times; she did, however, sing in phrases, and her original songs contained a story content.

Substructure

Although the basic character of the song was maintained, Child II was not as accurate in pitch as Child I. There was not a definite key or tonality maintained throughout but rather a shifting of these. Songs did, however, finish with a definite ending. She did not seem to be as aware of these changes as Child I, who self-corrected her errors. At 24 months Child II sang a vocal range of "B" to "B'" ("Do-Re-Mi"). Most interesting was her use of cadence to end a song, even though the tonality of the ending cadence was not related to the rest of the song. This formula was demonstrated in most of her songs. Figures 2.8 through 2.10 show examples of her use of final cadences.

The most tonally consistent song was her original composition, "Kitty Song" (Figure 2.11), sung to a pretend audience into the curtain pull cord. This song was the most rich in musical features compared with her own standard songs. Although there were frequent pauses, we find examples of melodic sequence, a final cadence, and complex rhythm patterns along with a story content. This song suggests that this child may feel a greater degree of freedom to experiment in her own creations than in the standard songs she sings.

FIGURE 2.8. Case II: Final cadence example in "Jack and Jill."

Eb'-ry where 'at Mary went, the lamb was sure to go-woh.

FIGURE 2.9. Case II: Final cadence example in "Mary Had a Little Lamb."

My comb, my *------ in it *------

FIGURE 2.10. Case II: Final cadence example in child's original song. Asterisks mark inaudible words.

um----------------my kitty him plays out in the sun

Him comes out in the sun. Him feels like some birds.

and the sun (smiles?) at baby bird the sun

uh- jah and the birds and the

and sadly him went home

FIGURE 2.11. Case II: "Kitty Song," illustrating melodic sequence, final cadence, complex rhythm patterns and story content.

FIGURE 2.12. Case II: "Dog Song," original song showing contrasting rhythms. Asterisk marks inaudible words.

The "Dog Song" (Figure 2.12), another original tune, was sung into the tape recorder at the child's request. This song was made up of two distinct phrases. The dotted rhythm in the first phrase contrasted with the even eighth notes in the definite ending of the last phrase.

At 24 months Child II was not as rhythmically accurate as Child I. She did, however, group regular, consistent rhythmic patterns within phrases. "Mickey Mouse" and "Do-Re-Mi" particularly showed incorporation of the basic rhythmic element of the standard tune (Figures 2.13 and 2.14).

Performance

Performance was a key ingredient of Child II's songs. The overall musical character of the tune was communicated through musical techniques such as phrasing, word emphasis, and final cadences with ritards. These demonstrated a growing musicality.

Tables 2.1 and 2.2 again sum up the contrasts we have made here between Case I and Case II. Note the great difference across all the categories, although, as is noticeable, Cases I and II are more like each other than either is like Case III.

Case III: Non-Musically-Oriented Context

Family Musicality

In contrast with the above cases, the parents in Case III were not music oriented in the home, although both parents sang adequately and participated in church

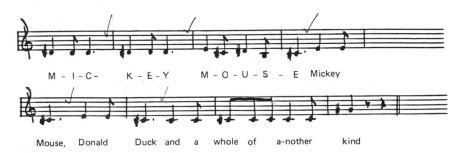

FIGURE 2.13. Case II: "Mickey Mouse," demonstrating incorporation of basic rhythm elements.

A song I will sing to you Doe   a deer   a female deer H   a drop of

FIGURE 2.14. Case II: "Do-Re-Mi," illustrating basic rhythm incorporated in song production.

choirs. The parents were not aware of their child's musical responses and productions and did not report any details of the child's music activity to the investigator. They did not provide musical experiences in the environment, with the exception of infrequent records and television. The mother did not report any particular lullaby and was not observed singing any lullaby to the child. Music did not play a role at family gatherings as in Cases I and II. In fact, Child III's mother almost forgot to sing "Happy Birthday" at the child's birthday party. She then sang one verse, whereas in the other two cases three verses were sung, and a "sing along" time occurred during the celebration with both children singing performances for the respective gatherings.

Child's Responses

Music behavior was first observed at 18 months in the context of "Sesame Street" with dancing and "singing" on a single sustained tone that was unrelated to the tonality of the music presented. At this same time the mother began to sing Christmas carols and the child responded with dancing to the music. Noticing this enthusiastic response, the mother then began to play records more frequently for the child, who responded with dancing rhythmically to the music. The mother also read nursery rhymes regularly and at times sang them for her. Response was increasingly evident at 20 months, with the child attempting to sing along. The features of this singing were basically the words, which were more spoken than sung; only later was there the inclusion of part of the tune.

Transitions for this child occur particularly when toys or people entered the boundary. She did not typically return to the singing or music after an interruption. She did not readily sing when asked and did not sing in accompaniment to activities, such as play, naps, car riding, and general interactions, as with Cases I and II. Singing and music were a separate and distinct activity initiated by singing on the television or specific listening to records started by the mother.

Songs

Standard song development emerged just prior to 2 years of age. However, few spontaneous opportunities to observe songs presented themselves. Singing was initiated by the mother or requested by the observer. At times the child responded to "Sesame Street" with "singing" as described above, although she did not often sing at an audible level. It may be important to note that she did speak with an audible, clear voice in verbal interactions.

Song-Form

Child III demonstrated a different approach than Child I or Child II, beginning with the words, as reported by McKernon (1979), then including rhythm, as structured by the words, and finally melodic development, preceding from the kernal or first phrase to the general overall melody contour. For Child III, then, the words and rhythm held the event together.

Substructure

Songs progressed from lyrics to rhythm to increasing levels of melodic incorporation. As mentioned above, Child III did not always produce discrete tones, but rather spoke the tune, at times on a unitary pitch degenerating progressively into speaking the songs. Figure 2.15 shows an example where she incorporated the general rhythm of the words. By 24 months she sang parts of the songs along with the spoken sections. Figure 2.16 shows an expansion of "Old MacDonald" illustrating this melodic development.

Attempting to stimulate response, the investigator brought a guitar at 24 months and allowed the child to strum the strings while the chords were changed. The child requested songs to be played and heartily strummed (not to say violently strummed) the guitar. She sang very little and almost inaudibly. The following weeks the guitar playing continued at the child's request. At this time she made up the spontaneous song notated in Figure 2.17. The chords were fingered by the investigator, while the child strummed the guitar and sang. It is interesting to see that she strummed the guitar with a steady, regular beat while she sang, demonstrating an internalization of the beat.

Performance

Songs were not observed to be performed for any audience, real or imaginary, but were primarily private events, usually in conjunction with television music, records, or nursery rhymes with the mother, and later at the investigator's prompting with the guitar. Few, if any, musical interpretative devices were apparent by 24 months, except for some variations in dynamics—loud and soft as emphasis of words.

Old Mac-Donald had a farm,   E - I, E - I, oh.

FIGURE 2.15. Case III: "Old MacDonald," incorporating rhythm from the lyrics.

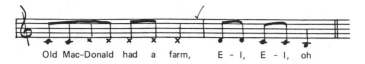

FIGURE 2.16. Case III: "Old MacDonald," illustrating melodic development.

Discussion and Conclusions

The differences between the above three children, particularly I and II versus III, which are summarized in Tables 2.1 and 2.2, suggest a strong relationship between home stimulation and the speed of development. This is hardly an unexpected finding in the light of developmental literature on early stimulation, which usually associates such stimulation with precocious development. Naturally we can only speculate about the genetic factor. What is perhaps more important is the discovery that the character of developmental stages varies for Cases I and II, the "musical" children, versus Case III, the relatively "nonmusical" child. Just as there are different ways in which children first learn language, so there appear to be different ways in which children learn to be musical. The musical children (Cases I and II) proceeded to music from a musical base; the relatively nonmusical child (Case III) proceeded from words and the incorporated rhythm. The stage of musical development between 1 and 2 years, when language usually develops, might be critical in determining which of these kinds of progress is adopted. Perhaps the acquisition of musical skill prior to the acquisition of language makes the owner an inherently musical thinker, whereas the acquisition of musical skill after the acquisition of language may interpose that latter competence between the learner and his or her music.

Furthermore, Child I and Child II followed a similar developmental path and produced clearly distinguished pitches prior to age 2. Discrete pitch developed out of a diffuse glissando to specific intervals with increasing levels of manipulation. With Child III no pitch was clearly distinguished from any other pitch prior to 18 months, and a meager amount of vocal singing was observed in the early period.

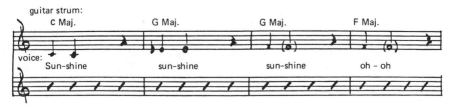

FIGURE 2.17. Case III: Original "Sunshine Song," illustrating internalization of beat.

Concerning the role of environmental influences, it is possible that the rich musical environment provided a large amount of material for abstraction and manipulation by the children. As Tables 2.1 and 2.2 show clearly, parental influences are much more striking in Cases I and II than in Case III. The greater number of musical agencies found in the environment appears to have provided input for increased music productivity and accuracy. In addition, reinforcement and valuing of music by the significant others most probably indicated to those children the importance of music and its role in their lives. Specific parental input of musical conventions led to greater, earlier, and more accurate musical behavior, particularly in Case I, where the mother and grandmother corrected and shaped the child's response. Needless to say, attention and repetition added further support to this music development.

When these results are compared with those of McKernon (1979), it becomes clear that her subjects are of the musical status of Case III in the present study. She described the development of musical progress in terms of words followed by the elaboration of song structures by rhythmic and melodic expansion. The present musical children, on the contrary, began with the melodic contour as the main event, which then held together rhythm and words as they were added. Furthermore, there was extensive pitch development prior to 18 months for Child I and Child II, but a complete absence of pitch development in McKernon's subjects and our Child III. It is also possible that the organization for a given child may not necessarily be tonal, but may be around the words, the rhythm per se, body movements, or even a particular contextual setting of a song. It would be surprising if there are not such individual variations in music development, because they are usually found in other forms of development where they have been similarly longitudinally examined (e.g., language development). Finally, with respect to performance, again McKernon is confined to comments on children like Child III, who are essentially nonperformers in the present terms. Both Child I and Child II performed before parents and other audiences in their second year of life. In fact, as mentioned earlier, performance is a key to child development in music as it is in narrative.

Finally, with respect to our initial questions, the present study makes the home context appear to be of vital importance. In Cases I and II overdetermination seems to be the rule, although this study cannot assess which or how many of these multiple influences were critical for the children's development. Our own guess is that the parents' own singing was probably the most important variable. What Tables 2.1 and 2.2 show is that there are individual variations even across these three cases in the developmental sequences of musical vocalizations, although the parallels between Cases I and II are also quite striking. This study, therefore raises as an important issue: the extent to which musical development must follow a set path or can allow variations. Again, as the data in the text show, there are multiple agencies for instigating and terminating musical responses, but, more importantly, such interpolations have less durable impact on Cases I and II than on Case III.

In summary, there are implications suggested by these findings for the importance of the musical environment and context in early childhood musical literacy, much as in creating the literate environment for language and reading development. In addition, there are clues to individual differences in musical production. The major value of the paper, however, must consist in laying before the reader these descriptions of just how intensive and in how many ways musical parents socialize their musical children. The developmental literature to date is largely lacking in such evidence.

References

McKernon, P. E. (1979). The development of first songs in young children. In D. Wolf (Ed.), *Early symbolization: New directions for child development* (Vol. 3, pp. 43–58). San Francisco: Jossey-Bass.

Ninio, A., & Bruner, J. (1976). The achievement and antecedents of labelling. *Journal of Child Language, 5,* 1–15.

Scollon, R., & Scollon, S. B. K. (1981). *Narrative, literacy and face in interethnic communication.* New Jersey: Ablex.

3
Toward a Model for Rhythm Development

RENA UPITIS

Definitions of Musical Rhythm

It is indisputable that rhythm plays a fundamental role in the organization, under-standing, and enjoyment of music. However, despite the primacy of rhythm in music, little is known about how children develop a "sense" of rhythm. Indeed, so many definitions of rhythm have been explored (cf. Cooper & Meyer, 1960; Fraisse, 1982; Lerdahl & Jackendoff, 1983; Ruchmich, 1913) that it is difficult to articulate just what a "sense" of rhythm entails.

In the present chapter, rhythm in music in the most general sense is taken to mean the temporal structure of music. This temporal structure is created by the progression of notes, including relations among the various musical dimensions such as melody, harmony, duration, and timbre. On another level, rhythmic organization in music is defined in terms of two qualitatively different, but inter-related organizational forms: figural and metric. The presence of these two forms of rhythmic structure is central to the view of rhythm development described in the present chapter.

Figural Organization

Figural rhythmic organization refers to the listener's ability to naturally organ-ize the sounds he or she hears into meaningful groups or figures. This chunking ability is found in many areas of human cognition besides rhythm, where the person "spontaneously segments or chunks the elements or events into groups of some kind" (Lerdahl & Jackendoff, 1983, p. 13). A rhythmic figure is a small cluster of notes (usually five or fewer) that the listener perceives as belonging together, where the meaning attached to any single event in the figure is depen-dent on its function in relation to the other events. Figural boundaries are often defined by a change in duration, so that a new duration marks either the end of one figure or the beginning of the next. In the figural form of rhythm organiza-tion, all events are perceived as belonging to one figure or another. In addition, small figures of the type described may be grouped hierarchically, that is, the listener may infer different levels of figural groups. In standard music notation rhythmic figures are often encoded by slurs, which are added to the notation to denote pitch and duration.

Metric Organization

The listener also infers a kind of rhythmic organization that underlies the surface events of the melody. Even though the surface notes of a melody most often vary in duration, the listener can respond to an underlying system of regular or invariant patterns of beats. This is the essence of metric organization of rhythm. The ability to infer such invariant patterns is manifested by people's ability to keep time to music; tapping along at a steady rate while the surface durations vary in rhythmic texture. Furthermore, since people can keep time at different rates in response to the same piece of music, metric organization, like its figural counterpart, is hierarchical. That is, various beats are generated by a single piece of music, some fast, some slow. The beats are related to one another proportionally and this system of beats defines the meter of a piece. Thus, if some of the beats generated by a given melody occur in a 4:2:1 ratio, the meter is called duple.

Because of the invariant nature of the metric mode of rhythmic organization, the metric hierarchy provides a standardized system for classifying duration. In standard music notation, durations are depicted according to a measured or metric system, so that all events of the same duration are encoded with the same symbol, *regardless* of their figural function. A musical example illustrating the relationships between the figural and metric modes is given in Figure 3.1.

It is argued here that in order to explain children's rhythm development, including the commonly encountered difficulties in teaching music notation, one needs to take a close look at children's responses in terms of the figural-metric distinction. Little is known about how the figural and metric knowledge structures develop, and the research described in this chapter is a beginning attempt to outline trends in rhythm development. The following review of the literature shows how previous attempts have neglected to provide a firm basis for a theory of rhythm development, largely because of a lack of attention either to psychological processes across different response domains, or to the figural and metric structures in the context of a musically derived model.

Review of the Literature and Rationale for the Experimental Tasks

Many strikingly different viewpoints have been taken to explain rhythm development. Some researchers have described rhythm in terms of perception—what patterns the listener is able to perceive from discrete stimuli presented in different conditions—for example, at faster versus slower tempi (e.g., Fraisse, 1964, 1981, 1982; Handel, 1974; Handel & Buffardi, 1969; Povel, 1981). Others have chosen to describe rhythm understanding in terms of a model from another discipline.

Standard music notation

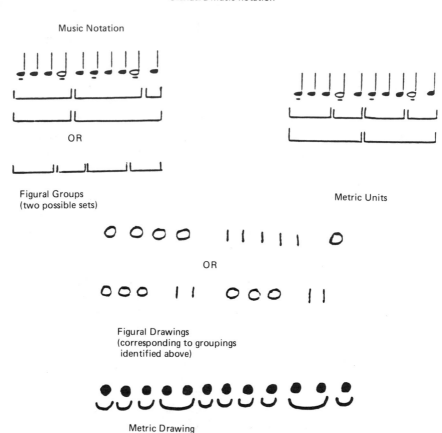

FIGURE 3.1. Figural and metric descriptions of a simple rhythm.

For example, the linguistic model has been used to formalize the relationship between the physical events of the music and the psychological processes of the listener (e.g., Kassler, 1963; Lerdahl & Jackendoff, 1981, 1983). This approach is more satisfactory than the perceptual approach for two important reasons. First, researchers attempting to apply a linguistic model to rhythm processing are concerned primarily with the *psychological* processes used by the listener in making sense of music. Second, researchers applying the linguistic model, such as Lerdahl and Jackendoff (1983), usually evaluate people's understanding of rhythm in more "ecologically valid" contexts than the perceptual researchers, that is, in "real" rather than laboratory musical settings. Indeed, research findings reported in other chapters in this volume are also derived from ecologically valid musical settings (e.g., Holahan, Chapter 5, on music babble; Kelley and Sutton-Smith, Chapter 2, on musical productivity).

However, as Holahan (Chapter 5, this volume) indicates, even though the linguistic model adds an important dimension to the perceptual research, the linguistic model cannot fully account for rhythm processing. The analogy between language and music, both with their respective deep and surface structures, is, at best, only an analogy. Kelley and Sutton-Smith (Chapter 2, this volume) also report that music development has similarities to language development, and may even have an interactive effect with language development, but do *not* claim that the same mechanisms can be used to explain both music and language development. There are other reasons for the failure of the linguistic model to explain music development. For example, Deutsch (1975) has demonstrated that the psychological mechanisms for pitch perception and memory are fundamentally different from those used to process language sounds. Also, Gardner (1983) has cited evidence for different physiological bases for language and music processing (for example, loss of language-processing ability does not usually result in loss of music-processing ability).

Where, then, does one turn to find a model for rhythm development? Just as the linguistic model was developed from a careful look at how language is acquired, so too can a model for rhythm be developed by studying how children's understanding of rhythm, in its varied forms, is acquired.

Unfortunately, studies on the development of rhythm cognition are few. Most of the studies on children's musical development have been concerned with pitch, where rhythm is only examined insofar as it affects pitch perception (e.g., Petzold, 1963). Three notable exceptions are the work of Pflederer (1964), Bamberger (1980, 1982), and Smith (1983).

Pflederer (1964) concerned herself with children's ability to conserve meter. However, she used the term "meter conservation" to mean the ability to identify or discriminate duple and triple meters, which is not conservation in the Piagetian sense. The Piagetian conservation tasks involve changing one dimension of a situation while keeping or conserving another. The child is said to "conserve" if he or she realizes that, even though some parameters may change, another parameter is constant or "conserved." A meter conservation task would involve changing one dimension (for example, tempo) while keeping the meter (e.g., triple) constant. Prior to forming the ability to conserve meter, then, a child would regard the change in tempo as indicating a change in meter. This might be on the basis of some rule such as "faster is triple." However, a child who could conserve meter would realize that meter is unchanged so long as the metric hierarchy remained the same. Conservation in this sense has not been established by Pflederer's research. However, even though it can be argued that Pflederer's tasks were discrimination tasks ("tell if the pattern is in two or three") and not conservation tasks, her work is important for several reasons. First, she used tasks that make sense in the child's musical world. Second, she introduced a Piagetian outlook to questions on rhythm cognition—a marked improvement over the perceptual view. Third, she concluded that children actively make sense of the music they hear, as expectations are generated by the music and modified by the child as the music is played. The view of the child as one who actively constructs musical coherence is taken in the present chapter, and is clearly reflected in the nature of the experimental tasks.

Bamberger's (1980, 1982) research on children's descriptions of simple rhythmic patterns also bears consideration. Bamberger studied children's spontaneous descriptions of rhythmic patterns, and developed a typology for classifying children's descriptions according to the figural-metric distinction described earlier. However, although Bamberger's research indicates that children are capable of spontaneously producing figural and metric descriptions of various levels of sophistication, her research does not describe how such abilities are affected by factors such as prior musical training and general cognitive development. Furthermore, her research is focused on children's pen-and-paper descriptions, and does not include an examination of children's responses in related domains. Is there a relationship among the child's aural and motor skills and his or her ability to make and read written descriptions of rhythm?

Smith's (1983) recent work addresses the effect of musical training on skill at reproducing and remembering rhythm patterns in terms of the figural-metric framework. Her findings indicate that children and adults with musical training are far more likely to focus on metric organization when reproducing and remembering rhythmic sequences, whereas untrained subjects tend toward figural groupings for rhythmic coherence. This preference for metric organization by trained musicians is also illustrated by Bamberger's (1982) observation that adult musicians often prefer metric descriptions of rhythm, and may even be unable to understand figural descriptions or may consider them incorrect.

Comparisons between musically trained and untrained children across domains and ages are regarded as central to the development of a model of rhythm development. Accordingly, the experimental tasks in the research described here give children the opportunity to respond aurally, motorically, and symbolically in the figural and metric modes. The variety of tasks and media also reflects the view that learning involves the development of multiple descriptions, rather than improving or changing on a single unidirectional measure, and furthermore, that the building of new knowledge is based on a broad existing knowledge base (Boden, 1980; Brown, 1975, 1979; Goodman, 1978; Piaget, 1981).

Method

Sample

Seventy-two children, 7 to 12 years of age, participated in the study. Half of the children had musical training in addition to the school music program, and were classified as musically trained. Children were considered musically trained if they had received music lessons out of school for at least 1 year, including note reading instruction.

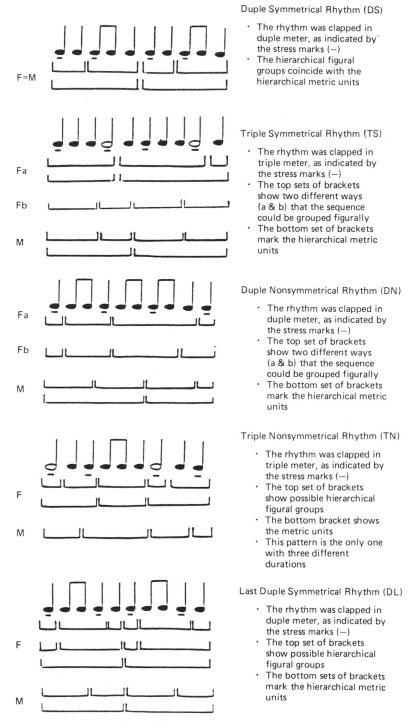

Duple Symmetrical Rhythm (DS)

· The rhythm was clapped in
  duple meter, as indicated by
  the stress marks (−)
· The hierarchical figural
  groups coincide with the
  hierarchical metric units

Triple Symmetrical Rhythm (TS)

· The rhythm was clapped in
  triple meter, as indicated by
  the stress marks (−)
· The top sets of brackets
  show two different ways
  (a & b) that the sequence
  could be grouped figurally
· The bottom set of brackets
  mark the hierarchical metric
  units

Duple Nonsymmetrical Rhythm (DN)

· The rhythm was clapped in
  duple meter, as indicated by
  the stress marks (−)
· The top set of brackets
  show two different ways
  (a & b) that the sequence
  could be grouped figurally
· The bottom set of brackets
  mark the hierarchical metric
  units

Triple Nonsymmetrical Rhythm (TN)

· The rhythm was clapped in
  triple meter, as indicated by
  the stress marks (−)
· The top set of brackets
  show possible hierarchical
  figural groups
· The bottom bracket shows
  the metric units
· This pattern is the only one
  with three different
  durations

Last Duple Symmetrical Rhythm (DL)

· The rhythm was clapped in
  duple meter, as indicated by
  the stress marks (−)
· The top set of brackets
  show possible hierarchical
  figural groups
· The bottom sets of brackets
  mark the hierarchical metric
  units

FIGURE 3.2. Nonpitch rhythms.

FIGURE 3.3. Melodies.

Five experimental tasks were presented individually through a standardized clinical interview. The children's descriptions and responses were coded by independent observers.

The nonpitch rhythms and melodies that were used for tasks appear in Figures 3.2 and 3.3, respectively. The stimuli are described in terms of figures and meter. The nonpitch rhythms were clapped by the experimenter, with stressed notes where indicated. Melodies were computer generated and audiotaped; thus all notes were generated with equal intensity.

Describing Simple Rhythms (Task 1)

This task is a replication of the task described by Bamberger (1982). The child listened to the experimenter clap the first pattern in Figure 3.2, and was asked to clap back what he or she heard. Once the child had clapped the sequence correctly, he or she was invited to describe the rhythm by "put[ting] down on paper whatever you think will help you remember the . . . piece tomorrow or help someone else to play it who isn't here today" (Bamberger, 1982, p. 194). After the child had made the drawing, he or she was asked to "put in some numbers under the drawing that seem to fit with the marks you have made." The same procedure was used for the first four sequences described in Figure 3.2.

Interpreting Descriptions of Simple Rhythms (Task 2)

The experimenter showed the child a "different kind of drawing," figural if the child made a metric drawing, and vice versa (see Figure 3.4). The figural drawings were described by the experimenter as showing "groups of claps that sound like they belong together." The metric drawings were described as depicting how "long and short claps compare with each other." The child was then asked to clap from his or her drawing, then from the different kind of drawing. Finally, the child was asked to identify which drawings were the most helpful for "figuring out the rhythm."

Next, the child was shown several drawings of the duple nonsymmetrical sequence, some figural, some metric (see Figure 3.5). The child was told that all of the drawings were of the same rhythm, and was asked to "guess the mystery

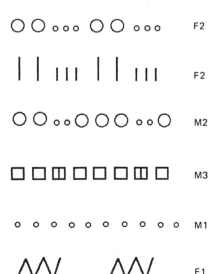

FIGURE 3.4. Descriptions of the duple symmetrical rhythm used in Task 2.

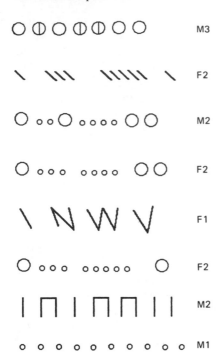

FIGURE 3.5. Descriptions of the duple non-symmetrical rhythm used in Task 2 (mystery rhythm).

rhythm by clapping it, using the drawing that you find easiest to read." The child was also asked to clap the other drawings as well, and to identify the "most helpful" drawing.

Finally, the child was asked to describe the last rhythm in Figure 3.2, following the procedure from the first task.

Keeping Time (Task 3)

The child was first asked to "drum a steady beat on the drum," without music. Then the child was asked to drum a faster beat and a slower beat. Next, the child was asked to drum along with a melody played on a tape recorder. The instructions to the child were: "See if you can use this drum to keep time with the tune that you will hear. I'd like you to try to find more than one beat for each tune, like you did just now without a tune." This procedure was carried out for all five melodies that appear in Figure 3.3.

Identifying Congruent Beats (Task 4)

The melodies for this task were the first two unfamiliar tunes in Figure 3.3. An electric metronome was used to generate eight different beats. The beats were identified by whole numbers, 2 through 9, rather than using the more cumbersome metronome settings (e.g., M.M. quarter = 130 corresponded to "2"; similarly for the others). Three of the beats corresponded with the surface durations of the duple melody (beats 2, 4, and 8); two corresponded with the triple melody (beats 3 and 9). The child was asked to pick a number between 2 and 9. After hearing the beat with the tune, the child was asked if the beat "fit" with the melody. After the child tried all of the beats with each melody, he or she was asked to identify his or her favorite beat for each melody.

Describing Beats (Task 5)

The child was asked to "imagine that you have gone back to your classroom and you find that an orchestra has appeared. Most of the members of the orchestra have parts, and they're playing the first tune (duple unfamiliar melody). But there are three drummers without parts, and when you come into the classroom, your teacher asks you to write something down for the drummers. One of the drummers is going to drum a fast beat, one will drum a medium beat, and one will drum a slow beat." The above scenario was repeated for the second tune (triple unfamiliar melody) for "only two drummers."

After the child completed the drawings, he or she was shown "how some kids draw the drummers' parts," and was asked if he or she could "explain how the drawings work" (see Figure 3.6).

Finally, the child was asked to add drum beats to a spatial analog version of the varied durations of one of the melodies (duple unfamiliar melody): "This is one way of drawing of the notes of the first tune [experimenter sings tune, pointing to surface events while singing]. Can you draw in the drummers' parts with the

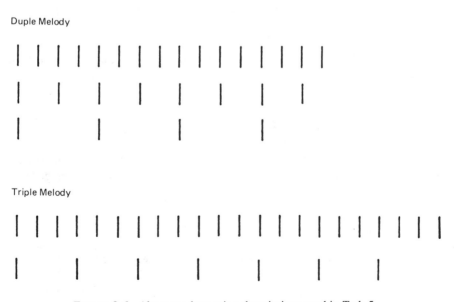

FIGURE 3.6. Alternate drumming descriptions used in Task 5.

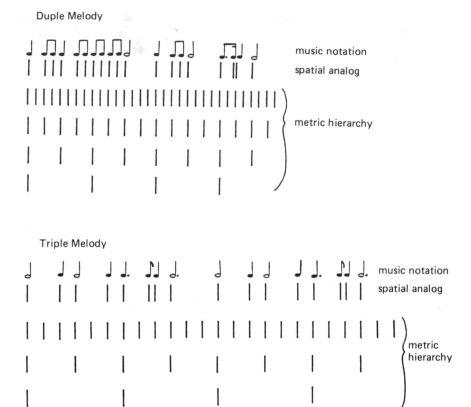

FIGURE 3.7. Spatial analogs of melodies with metric hierarchies used in Task 5.

melody part?" The instructions wre repeated for the second tune. The melodies, along with coordinated drawings of the metric hierarchy, are shown in Figure 3.7.

Classification of Responses

The various symbolic, motor, and aural responses were classified according to the set of criteria outlined below. Interrater reliability for all responses averaged $r = .97$, with a standard deviation of .026.

Motor Scores

The motor scores were based on the child's ability to keep time to the five melodies in Figure 3.3. The child was given a score of 1, 2, or 3 for each melody indicating good, fair, or poor beat keeping, respectively. The five scores were averaged and combined into a composite motor score on a 5-point scale, where a score of 1 represented excellent drumming ability, and a score of 5 represented poor drumming ability. (For a full explanation of the criteria for "excellent," "good," "fair," etc., see Upitis, 1985.)

Aural Scores

Two aural scores for the duple and triple unfamiliar melodies were used. First, the proportion of congruent beats identified for the melody were calculated (e.g., if the child said that 2, 4, 5, and 8 were congruent for the duple melody, then the proportion would be 3/4 or 75%). Second, it was noted whether the child's "favorite" beat was congruent with the melody.

Symbolic Scores

DESCRIPTION MAKING

The basis for classifying children's graphic and numeric descriptions of the non-pitch rhythm patterns was the typology developed by Bamberger (1982). Bamberger identified three basic types of drawings: Iconic (pictures describing the activity, such as a pair of clapping hands), Figural (depicting the rhythmic figures in the sequence), and Metric (consistently depicting the events in terms of duration). Different levels of figural and metric drawings were also identified, and are now described (see Figure 3.8 for examples of figural and metric descriptions).

Graphic Descriptions (Drawings) of Simple Rhythms

The Early Figural drawings (F1; example 1, Figure 3.8) depict the main figures in the pattern. The child "plays" the rhythm on the paper, lifting the pencil when one figure stops and putting the pencil back down when the next figure begins. Thus, the events within a figure are described by a single continuous mark, where changes in direction indicate discrete events.

True Figural drawings (F2; example 2, Figure 3.8) symbolize each of the events with a discrete mark, where the marks vary according to function. The marks also vary according to duration, but not consistently. For example, a small mark may be used to depict a long duration if the note occurs at the end of a figure, and the same mark may be used for a short duration in the middle of a figure. Thus, True Figural drawings can be used to reconstruct the actual rhythm if the "reader" knows the description is figural, and can read accurately from a True Figural description.

Counting Metric drawings (M1; example 3, Figure 3.8) do not differentiate events by duration, but merely record the number of discrete events with identical marks for each event.

Durational Metric drawings (M2; example 4, Figure 3.8) are characterized by the same type of mark for like durations, regardless of where the events occur within the sequence. However, one mark cannot be measured against a different kind of mark (e.g., a mark twice as long as another does not mean that the longer

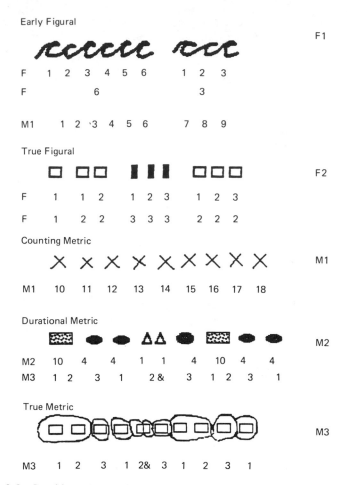

FIGURE 3.8. Graphic and numeric descriptions of the triple nonsymmetrical rhythm.

mark stands for an event that has twice the duration of the event depicted by the shorter mark).

Finally, not only do True Metric drawings (M3; example 5, Figure 3.8) use consistent symbols for each of the durations, but the symbols themselves can be mathematically related to one another to determine the relative durations for each of the surface events, based on a fixed reference unit. For example, a square may be used as a unit, and therefore two half-squares would denote two equal events that occur in the time of a square.

Numeric Descriptions of Simple Rhythms

One form of figural numeric description and three forms of metric numeric descriptions were identified. It is important to note that a child could give a figural numeric description with a metric drawing, and vice versa, as indicated by some of the examples in Figure 3.8.

Figural numeric descriptions (F; examples 1 and 2, Figure 3.8) depict the number of events in each of the figures. The child "counts up" the number of events in each figure. The child may use one number for each figure, adding up to the total number of events in the figure. Alternately, the child may use one number for each mark in the figure, beginning a new sequential count for each figure.

Counting Metric descriptions (M1; examples 1 and 3, Figure 3.8) are simply a series of sequential numbers, one for each element in the sequence (for example, the first symbol might be marked "1," the second "2," and so on). As for the Counting graphic description, each element is treated as the same except for its position in the sequence, regardless of its duration or of its function in a figural group.

For the Durational Metric description (M2; example 4, Figure 3.8), the same number is assigned to like durations. For example, a "4" might be used to describe all of the "short" events, a "10" might be used to describe all of the "long" events, and a "1" might indicate the "very shortest" event. However, the values of the numbers cannot be numerically compared to each other. In this example, a "10" is not to be interpreted as "two and a half times as long as '4'."

Finally, the True Metric numeric description (M3; examples 4 and 5, Figure 3.8) depicts the relative durational values of all of the events in the sequence. There is an interval relationship between the numbers, so that "4" means "twice as long as 2." Therefore, an invariant time unit is given by this kind of numeric description, by which the proportional relationships between the various durations can be measured.

Other Measures for Rhythm Descriptions

In addition to scoring the graphic and numeric descriptions according to the above criteria, the drawings were scored for accuracy (a yes/no score according to the type of description) symbol type (arbitrary or musical), and indications of figural groupings (use of devices to show groups, e.g., space, commas, barlines, etc., regardless of the form of description).

Descriptions of the Metric Hierarchy

As for the drawings of rhythm patterns, drawings of the drumming patterns or metric hierarchy were classified as Iconic, Figural (one type), or Metric (three types). Similar criteria were used here to follow Bamberger's (1982) typology for the classification of rhythm patterns of varied durations. (See Figure 3.9 for examples of drumming descriptions.)

Iconic descriptions are pictures of the activity rather than of the hierarchy of beats. For example, the child might draw a picture of a single drum. No information about the beats can be reconstructed from iconic descriptions.

In the Figural (F; Figure 3.9) drumming descriptions, the child attempts to show the periodic, invariant nature of each of the beats. However, the beats are

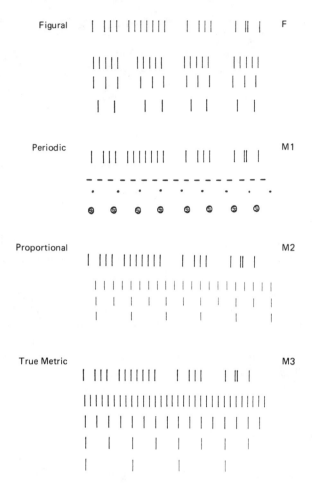

FIGURE 3.9. Drumming descriptions with the spatial analog of the duple unfamiliar melody.

not described consistently. Rather than drawing evenly spaced marks for the whole melody, the description is of groups of evenly spaced marks, where the groups correspond to the figures in the melody.

The Periodic drawing (M1; Figure 3.9) shows each beat level as a series of invariant events, by making equally spaced discrete marks to depict equal time intervals between events. A faster beat is therefore shown by marks that are relatively closer together spatially than the marks representing a slower beat. However, the different beat levels cannot be measured with one another in absolute terms.

The Proportional descriptions (M2; Figure 3.9) depict beat levels that can be measured in terms of each other. Thus, twice the spatial distance between the marks on one beat level as compared to another indicates twice the time interval between each event from one beat level to the next.

The True Metric (M3; Figure 3.9) description consists of a hierarchical system of proportionally spaced marks, corresponding to the metric hierarchy generated by the varied surface durations. This drawing is more sophisticated than the proportional drawing, since the marks for the hierarchy also line up with the marks of the spatial analog of the surface events.

INTERPRETATION OF DESCRIPTIONS

Verbal Interpretation of Proportional Metric Hierarchy Drawings

The explanation given by the child for the proportional drawings was scored as Intuitive, Periodic, or Proportional. Intuitive explanations were marked by the attention given to the number of symbols for a beat description, rather than to the spatial relationships among the symbols. Thus, the child would say that the drawing with closely spaced symbols was "faster because there are more." Periodic explanations recognized that the further apart the symbols appeared spatially, the slower the beat. However, periodic explanations did not relate the beat levels to each other in a measured way, except in terms such as "faster" and "slower." Proportional explanations were characterized by a measurement statement comparing the levels of the hierarchy, for example, "that one's twice as fast because there's two of those for every one of those."

Ability to Read Rhythm Descriptions

The children were rated on their ability to clap from their own drawings, and to clap the "mystery rhythm," using a 3-point scale similar to the one used for drumming ability. A score of 1 (good) indicated that the child clapped the rhythm without error. A score of 2 (fair) indicated that the child had made a minor error in clapping, for example, missing an event or making one or two durational inaccuracies. A score of 3 (poor) was given if the child made a major error in clapping, for example, missing more than three events or making five or more durational errors.

Other Measures for Reading Ability

The description(s) used to guess the mystery rhythm were noted, and those identified as "most helpful" and "least helpful" for depicting both the duple symmetrical and duple nonsymmetrical rhythms were identified according to type (F1, M1, M2, and M3).

Average figural and metric scores were calculated, with the Early Figural (F1) and Counting (M1) descriptions omitted from the average. Also if the child was able to understand both forms of description equally well, this was noted.

Findings

Responses were analyzed by both quantitative and qualitative methods. Some of the main findings are highlighted here, in terms of group differences and with regard to responses of individual children across tasks and domains. (For a full discussion of the findings and nonparametric statistics, see Upitis, 1985.)

Trends Related to Age

The ability to make and read descriptions of both the figural and metric forms was found to be a direct function of age. Not only did accuracy in description making increase with age ($p < .0001$), but so too did accuracy in description reading ($p < .0001$). Also, children were able to give a more sophisticated verbal explanation of the Proportional drawing of the metric hierarchy as they got older, moving from Intuitive to Periodic and finally to Proportional explanations ($p < .02$). Finally, the children's own descriptions of simple rhythms, whether figural or metric, became more sophisticated with age ($p < .0001$).

The ability to hear metrically congruent beats was also found to be a direct function of age, based on accuracy in identifying congruent beats ($p < .02$). Similarly, the ability to keep time to music improved with age ($p < .04$). Thus, in general, one can conclude that, with or without musical training, children's ability to generate and interpret descriptions of musical rhythm increases as a function of age.

Musical Training

Musically trained children were found to be the most fluent readers, showing an ability to read both figural and metric forms more accurately than children without musical training ($p < .0001$). Those children without musical training were more likely to be good readers of the figural form ($p < .01$).

Musically trained children performed significantly better on the keeping time task than did their untrained counterparts ($p < .03$). This somewhat surprising finding indicates that musical training may have an effect on metric gross motor abilities, even though music teaching is usually focused on note reading and the fine motor skills needed for performance.

Musically trained children were most likely to achieve the "highest" form of rhythm understanding, successfully integrating the figural and metric forms. Most children reaching the True Metric level of description of the metric hierarchy with spatial analogs were musically trained. Also, musically trained children were more likely than the untrained children to be able to describe rhythms both figurally and metrically, readily switching between the two different description forms.

The musically trained children were much more likely ($p < .002$) to change from a figural drawing to a metric drawing for the last representation task than were the untrained children. This indicates that the musically trained children may have preferred using a figural description at first, but nevertheless had the ability to process rhythm information metrically. This brings into focus the distinction between preference and ability: a child who makes figural descriptions is not necessarily unable to make metric descriptions, and vice versa. In fact, when encouraged to make two descriptions of a single rhythm, one graphic and one numeric, more than 40% of the children gave different description forms.

Age and Musical Training Interaction Effects

There were two important age and training interactions. First, children with musical training had better aural and motor scores up to about 10 years of age. After that time, almost all children exhibited good aural and motor abilities, as measured by the tasks for keeping time (Task 3) and identifying congruency (Task 4).

Second, the children reaching the "highest" level of rhythm understanding, characterized by the successful integration of the figural and metric forms, were almost all 10 years of age or older, and musically trained.

Clusters of Response Patterns

In order to describe patterns of responses across tasks and domains, responses were grouped by cluster analysis. Three distinct groups of children were identified by this method.[1] In order to perform the cluster analysis, the number of measures (47) was reduced to 7. The two factor variables, age and training, were retained. In addition, five response variables were chosen to represent each domain and type of task: the type of graphic description for the duple nonsymmetrical rhythm, the composite motor score, the proportion of congruent beats identified for the duple melody, and the reading abilities for the metric and the figural descriptions of the duple nonsymmetrical rhythm.[2]

One cluster (accounting for 20% of the subjects) was comprised of young children, 7 or 8 years of age, most of whom had musical training. The graphic descriptions generated by these children were varied, but tended to be of the more primitive forms: Iconic, the Counting Metric form, or in some cases, True Figural. The children also varied somewhat in their reading ability. On the whole,

---

[1]Since one of the assumptions of cluster analysis is the use of continuous data, and some of the measures in the present study were discrete, the cluster analysis should be regarded as a summary of the patterns in the data set, rather than as conclusive statistical evidence of clusters to be found in the population.

[2]The duple nonsymmetrical rhythm was chosen for a response variable in cluster analysis since this rhythm produced the most varied and representative responses in terms of children's abilities and preferences for describing rhythm patterns. In addition, the duple nonsymmetrical rhythm was used as the mystery rhythm, and therefore comparisons could be made between reading ability and description-making preferences for the same rhythm. The choice of the duple melody for the aural score was an arbitrary one (aural scores for the duple and triple melodies did not differ significantly).

these children were able to read figural descriptions well. Most were moderate to poor readers of metric descriptions. Only one child in this cluster was able to read both forms well. The children belonging to this cluster had good motor skills. One of the most distinguishing features of the children in this group is that they had poor aural ability. On average, only 60% of the beats that were thought to be congruent by these children were, in fact, congruent.

Another cluster, the largest of the three (including 44% of the subjects), represented the greatest variety of responses of all of the clusters. The children in this group ranged from 8 to 11 years of age, and were from both the musically trained and untrained groups. Classifying the children from this cluster further into two subgroups according to age and training helps to clarify the patterns.

One subgroup was formed by the 8- and 9-year-old children. Most of these children were fair-good readers of the metric forms, and good readers of the figural forms, regardless of training. However, they differed in motor and aural abilities according to training, with the trained subjects performing better in both the aural and motor domains. The graphic descriptions produced by these children were approximately evenly divided between the Counting Metric and True Figural forms.

Another subgroup was made up of the 10-year-old children and two 11-year-olds, most of whom were trained. Again, as with the 8- and 9-year-olds, those children with training tended to have excellent motor and aural skills, and were able to read both metric and figural descriptions well. These children were somewhat distinguishable from their younger counterparts in that their graphic descriptions were slightly more sophisticated: there were fewer Counting Metric drawings, and more of the higher level metric drawings.

The last cluster (36% of the total sample) included children mostly from the 11- or 12-year-old age groups, with the exception of three 10-year-olds. The 10-year-olds included in this cluster were unusual, however, in that, although they were all untrained, they nevertheless had excellent aural, motor, and reading skills, and thus were similar to the older children in this cluster. The 11- and 12-year-old children, regardless of training, tended to have good or excellent motor and aural skills, were able to read both forms of description well, and generated mixed high-level descriptions (True Figural and True Metric).

The clusters indicated that the strongest predicting variable was age. In some cases, the training variable also defined clusters, particularly where the motor and aural responses and metric reading abilities were involved.

Advanced Rhythm Understanding

Children who appeared to exhibit the most advanced understanding of rhythm were able to relate, describe, and interpret both the figural and metric aspects of rhythm organization across response domains. Of the 72 children sampled 6 children appeared to exhibit this high degree of understanding. They were identified on the basis of four criteria. First, all of these children produced True Metric drawings of the metric hierarchies generated by the duple and triple melodies.

That is, they indicated the proportional relationships among the various beats by their graphic symbols, and, furthermore, the placement of the symbols corresponded with the spatial analog of the melody that was provided for them. Second, these children had perfect aural and motor scores. That is, they were consistently able to identify and produce beats that corresponded or "fit" with the melodies provided. Third, these children were able to read all figural and metric descriptions provided by the experimenter of the duple symmetrical and nonsymmetrical rhythms. Finally, their explanations of the drumming drawings were Proportional. That is, they were able to relate how one drummer would play in relation to another in metric terms (e.g., "three times as fast"). The type of graphic and numeric descriptions produced by the children for the simple rhythm patterns was not a distinguishing factor. Some preferred metric descriptions, others figural.

All of these children were musically trained, and most (five of the six) were 10 years or older. One of the most intriguing features of the rhythm knowledge displayed by these children was the apparent ease by which they could move between the figural and metric forms, depending on the importance they attached to either the meter or the figural groups. For example, one child chose a metric drawing with standardized durational symbols as the best way of representing the more complex duple nonsymmetrical rhythm, but a figural drawing for the duple symmetrical rhythm, stating "It's sorta obvious to see the groups for that one." Another child, comparing a figural with a metric drawing of the duple symmetrical rhythm, commented "So it's the same thing, then. Just a different way. That little circle and a space is just like a big circle, right?" In other words, the child was able to compare the different use of the symbols to depict the same event.

Cross-Domain Relationships

There were four important cross-domain relationships that suggested underlying cognitive processes for making sense of musical rhythm. First, the figural aspect of rhythm was found to be salient at all levels of age and musical ability. Figural graphic and numeric descriptions were the most commonly produced form of description. Also, the figural form was usually the easiest form for children (musically trained and untrained) to read. Furthermore, musically trained children did not lose the ability to read and describe rhythms figurally; in fact, they often preferred figural descriptions to the metric ones. Indeed, if children made metric drawings, they often nevertheless indicated figural groupings by using extra marks such as commas and slurs, much like standard music notation for duration and phrasing. Finally, the scores for reading figural descriptions were generally higher than metric reading scores, regardless of age or musical training.

A second, extremely important trend was that a direct relationship was found between aural and motor abilities, and metric reading abilities. In other words, a child's ability to keep time to music and to identify congruency could be used to predict his or her ability to read metric forms of description. The one exception to this rule was a cluster of 7- and 8-year-old musically trained children with good motor ability, poor-moderate-good aural ability, and poor metric reading ability. Other results indicated that the poor reading may be due to these children having fewer reading skills in general than their older peers.

Third, there was evidence for a parallel development between the figural and metric forms. That is, it can be argued from the findings that the two forms of processing develop in tandem, rather than in serial order with the figural form preceding the metric form. Children making True Figural descriptions understood the Durational Metric descriptions better than the Early Figural descriptions. Also, children who had difficulty picking a favorite description for the interpretation task (Task 2) were often making a choice between figural and metric descriptions, not between two different levels (e.g., M2 and M3) of the same form. This finding has important implications for performance and teaching, discussed later in the chapter.

Finally, descriptions of a single rhythm were entirely figural or entirely metric. There was no mixing of description forms within a single description, even though children were capable of operating under more than one set of "rules" (i.e., figural vs. metric). Thus, children might use metric rules to depict a duple rhythm, and figural rules for a triple rhythm, but never a mixture of the two for a single rhythm. This finding is significant because it indicates that children's responses were consistent and rule driven, which can be taken as evidence for the existence of internal representations of rhythm made up of figural and metric rules.

Summary of Major Findings

The descriptions of the simple rhythms varied greatly. All forms of descriptions were represented in the children sampled, although there was only one Early Figural drawing. This result was somewhat surprising, since the more primitive Iconic form was produced in several cases. Since Bamberger (1982) found that Early Figural drawings were most commonly produced by 6- and 7-year-old children, it is odd that none of the 7-year-old subjects in the present study produced Early Figural drawings, since some of the children were clearly at an earlier (Iconic) stage. Although it could be argued that the Iconic drawings may not have been an accurate reflection of the children's abilities, but rather, a combination of misunderstanding the task instructions and/or evidence of the children's preferences rather than abilities, it is suggested that the discrepancy between the results of the present study and Bamberger's work may be due to the different methods for collecting data. In the present study, influences by peers were controlled for by interviewing children individually, while Bamberger's study was conducted in classroom settings where some sharing of ideas may have occurred, and hence skewed results. In any case, the lack of Early Figural drawings when all others were produced is reason for questioning the importance of the Early Figural drawings in the developmental sense. A study of descriptions made by children 4 to 8 years of age in individual clinical interviews is needed to shed further light on this issue.

There was a tendency for musically trained children to favor metric descriptions of simple rhythms, particularly in the change from figural to metric graphics from the first to the last rhythm. However, this finding was dependent on the musical sequence under investigation. Sometimes musically trained children who were readily able to use and read metric descriptions for the duple rhythms used figural forms for the triple rhythms, especially the triple nonsymmetrical rhythm. This finding may indicate that these children were able to encode the rhythms figurally, as a way of first making sense of the music or segmenting the input of events. In some cases, they proceeded to decode the information in a metric description, but in other cases, particularly where the metric structure was complicated, the information was decoded in a figural description.

It was also found that most children who were able to create metric descriptions were also often able to read the figural descriptions accurately, even though their preference for notating rhythms might be for the metric form. It is interesting to compare this finding with Bamberger's observations that adult musicians who make metric drawings may regard the figural drawings as "wrong" (Bamberger, 1980, 1982). It is not clear why musically trained children appear to respond differently to the figural drawings than their adult counterparts. It is possible that there are significant differences between adult and child judgments as a function of decreasing tolerance for alternate description forms with age. On the other hand, it may have been that the children were less likely to make "right" and "wrong" judgments in the present study because they were in a setting where many different forms of description were presented by the experimenter as valid and interesting. In any case, these apparent differences between musically trained adults and children bear further investigation.

Children were able to portray the figural groups in the rhythms, even if they used a metric graphic form of description. This portrayal was accomplished through the use of spaces, commas, barlines, and change of symbol. The indication of figural groupings in the metric drawings shows that these children were able to notate both the figural and metric aspects of the rhythms. Also, the use of more than one method or device to show grouping has potential for more complex forms of notation. If the child has two or more "devices" at his or her disposal, rather than using multiple devices to show a single characteristic of the rhythm (in this case, grouping), the child could be taught to use one of the devices to depict another feature of the rhythm (e.g., the metrical accents).

On the whole, most children were remarkably skilled at the two aural and motor tasks. There was also a strong correspondence between aural, motor, and metric reading abilities. Older children and children with musical training were usually the most skilled in the aural, motor, and metric reading tasks domains.

In short, the findings show the child as an active learner with many forms of rhythm knowledge at his or her disposal. The child's understanding of rhythm and its notational forms is complex, rule driven, and based on metric and figural organizational processes. Although there are similarities among children belonging to particular age/musical training groups, children are also in some ways highly individual in their responses. One needs always to consider that the figural-metric abilities should be assessed in terms of each of the relevant domains (i.e., symbolic, motor, aural). Thus, a child should not be considered as "metric" or "figural," but rather "metric in reading preference and motor response" and "figural in description-making preference." These considerations figure prominently in the following section, where implications for education and performance are discussed.

Discussion

Perhaps the singularly most striking finding was that all children, regardless of age and prior musical experience, were able to make sense of both metric and figural descriptions of rhythm. Equally important was the finding that children varied considerably across domains, often independent of any musical training they might have received. This finding stands in contrast to the research of Smith (1983), where much clearer divisions were found between musically trained and musically untrained children. However, these differences may be explained in part by experimental design differences. While Smith tested for memory of rhythm sequences in carefully controlled situations, here there was a broader range of tasks and possible responses. Even so, the results of the present work raise questions regarding the role of musical training in rhythm understanding. Clearly, the role of musical training is not a simple one: children with musical training may respond in metric terms, but the findings from the present study show that figural understanding prevails through all stages of development. Several educational implications that can be formulated on the basis of the results are now suggested.

Educational Implications

One of the most obvious educational implications for music teaching arising from the findings reported here applies directly to the teaching of rhythm notation and its effect on performance. Standard music notation is based on the metric structure of rhythm, but effective performance also requires the ability to respond to the figural grouping of surface events. Most traditional instruction emphasizes the metric aspects of rhythmic structure over the figural aspects. By emphasizing the metric or formal knowledge, teachers not only underplay the equally important figural aspect, but may also be speaking in terms that children cannot readily understand, since the metric notation may not match their internal figural representations. This internal figural representation may even be valuable to children with considerable musical training. Musically trained children may decode rhythms figurally if their internal metric structures will not prove strong enough to decode a given rhythm metrically. One of the advantages of the tasks described in this chapter is that they are simple enough for teachers to use with children in the course of their regular classroom activities. Teachers can therefore readily acquire "diagnostic" information about the abilities of their students to use the figural and metric modes in a variety of settings. With such diagnostic information at his or her disposal, the music teacher can then weave together the figural and metric faces of rhythm with the child. For example, if a child makes figural descriptions of simple rhythms but is also capable of responding to the metric hierarchy in the motor domain, then a music teacher might teach standard music notation by relating the child's figural descriptions to his or her ability to keep time to music, and in turn, relating these abilities to the metric description embodied in standard music notation. (See Upitis, 1985, for two examples where the motor and symbolic domains are related in this way.)

The importance of figural organization goes beyond its use as a tool for helping to teach metric relationships in standard rhythm notation. Another way of deepening musical knowledge is to demonstrate how figural grouping is closely linked with effective musical performance (Bamberger, 1982). By gaining an understanding of the sequence of development of children's figural and metric understanding of rhythmic structure, with and without formal musical training, music teachers will be able to both build and preserve the children's knowledge of metric and figural aspects of rhythm, in music cognition, description, and performance.

The results and implications of the present research can also be viewed on a more general level. Research that emphasizes the value of multiple descriptions in the context of ecologically valid tasks has powerful implications for views on teaching and learning. Teaching is more likely to be effective if the teacher realizes that children have different (from adult descriptions and from those of other children) but equally useful descriptions at their disposal (Nelson, 1978). Teachers can use existing modes of description available to the learners to move to other forms of understanding or different "language systems." For example, by building on a child's figural understanding the teacher can move to a metric (or formal) embodiment of the phenomenon—in much the same way as the formal notation evolved historically. Many forms of early music notation were figural in nature. For example, the cheironomic neumes used to notate rhythmic figures in plainsongs were in essence a series of marks to describe figural groups (Apel, 1961). This figural form of notation embodied only those aspects of the rhythms that were useful to the singers in that environment (Vollaerts, 1960). The need for metric rhythm notation only arose when the audience reading the notation was comprised of a more varied musical public. One of the more universal notations that was developed in the 15th century was "mensural notation," in which the temporal value of the notes was measured in terms of a fixed tactus. The modern system of music notation has evolved from the mensural notation (Houle, 1969). (For a full discussion of the development of music notation, see Apel [1961], Houle [1969], and Vollaerts [1960].) Teachers can use the historical development of rhythm notation as yet another way of fostering a deeper understanding of both the figural and metric forms.

Teachers can also relate historical development of rhythm notation to show how each of the figural and metric forms evolved to a sophisticated level. The early neumes, for example, underwent many forms of modification, and continue to be used even today in the form of the neume-like symbols used in the liturgical books of the Catholic church (Apel, 1961). Similarly, the early mensural notation began with one symbol that could stand for several durations, and over a period of many years that metric symbol evolved so that one symbol is now used consistently even for different meters. One can also find a striking parallel in written language. The emergence and development of several qualitatively different forms of notation for language have been identified—hieroglyphic or syllabic, ideographic, and alphabetic (Nathan, Temple, & Burris, 1982). All three are still in use today. However, as Nathan et al. pointed out, because the English system is alphabetic adults may be "blind" to the ideographic and syllabic forms that are often used by children in their early writing. This is much like a music teacher who may be "blind" to the figural forms used by students, having been so firmly indoctrinated with metric notation.

It is clear that the findings related in the present chapter are not limited to the understanding of rhythmic organization in music. Rather, there is a common thread running through the type of understanding and implications for teaching that have been described that encompass other areas of knowledge. Tolerance of different viewpoints from one's own, learning about how contrasting forms of descriptions are related and evolve, and being able to change one's view are fundamentally important for situations far beyond understanding the complexities of musical rhythm.

References

Apel, W. (1961). *The notation of polyphonic music, 900–1600*. Cambridge, MA: The Mediaeval Academy of America.

Bamberger, J. (1980). Cognitive structuring in the apprehension and description of simple rhythms. *Archives de Psychologie, 48*, 171.199.

Bamberger, J. (1982). Revisiting children's drawings of simple rhythms: A function for reflection-in-action. In S. Strauss (Ed.), *U-Shaped behavioral growth*. New York: Academic Press.

Boden, M. (1980). *Jean Piaget*. New York: Penguin Books.

Brown, A. L. (1975). The development of memory: Knowing, knowing about knowing, and knowing how to know. In H. W. Reese (Ed.), *Advances in child development and behavior* (Vol. 10). New York: Academic Press.

Brown, A. L. (1979). Theories of memory and the problems of development: Activity, growth, and knowledge. In L. S. Cermak & F. I. M. Craik (Eds.), *Levels of processing in human memory*. Hillsdale, NJ: Lawrence Erlbaum Associates.

Cooper, B., & Meyer, L. (1960). *The rhythmic structure of music*. Chicago: University of Chicago Press.

Deutsch, D. (1975). The organization of short-term memory for a single acoustical attribute. In D. Deutsch & J. A. Deutsch (Eds.), *Short-term memory*. New York: Academic Press.

Fraisse, P. (1964). *The psychology of time* (J. Leach, trans.). London: Eyre and Spottiswoode.

Fraisse, P. (1981). The multimodal aspects of rhythm perception. In R. Walk & H. Pick (Eds.), *Intersensory perception and sensory integration*. New York: Plenum Press.

Fraisse, P. (1982). Rhythm and tempo. In D. Deutsch (Ed.), *The psychology of music.* New York: Academic Press.

Gardner, H. (1983). *Frames of mind: The theory of multiple intelligences.* New York: Basic Books.

Goodman, N. (1978). *Ways of worldmaking.* Indianapolis: Hacket Publishing Co.

Handel, S. (1974). Perceiving melodic and rhythmic auditory patterns. *Journal of Experimental Psychology, 103,* 922–933.

Handel, S., & Buffardi, L. (1969). Using several modalities to perceive one temporal pattern. *Quarterly Journal of Experimental Psychology, 21,* 256–265.

Houle, G. L. (1969). *The musical measure as discussed by theorists from 1650–1800.* Wycomb, England: University Microfilms.

Kassler, M. (1963). A sketch for the use of formalized languages for the assertion of music. *Perspectives of New Music, 2,* 83–94.

Lerdahl, F., & Jackendoff, R. (1981). On the theory of grouping and metre. *Musical Quarterly, 67,* 479–506.

Lerdahl, F., & Jackendoff, R. (1983). *A generative theory of tonal music.* Cambridge, MA: M.I.T. Press.

Nathan, R. G., Temple, C. A., & Burris, N. A. (1982). *The beginnings of writing.* Boston: Allyn & Bacon.

Nelson, K. (1978). How children represent knowledge of their world in and out of language: A preliminary report. In R. S. Seigler (Ed.), *Children's thinking: What develops?* Hillsdale, NJ: Lawrence Erlbaum Associates.

Petzold, R. G. (1963). The development of auditory perception of musical sounds by children in the first six grades. *Journal of Research in Music Education, 11,* 21–43.

Pflederer, M. (1964). The responses of children to musical tasks embodying Piaget's principle of conservation. *Journal of Research in Music Education, 12,* 215–268.

Piaget, J. (1981). *The psychology of intelligence* (M. Piercy & D. Berlyne, trans.). Totowa, NJ: Littlefield, Adams & Co. (First published in 1947)

Povel, D-J. (1981). Internal representation of simple temporal patterns. *Journal of Experimental Psychology: Human Perception and Performance, 7,* 3–18.

Ruchmich, C. A. (1913). The role of kinaesthesis in the perception of rhythm. *American Journal of Psychology, 24,* 305–359.

Smith, J. E. (1983). *Memory for musical rhythm: The effect of skill.* Unpublished doctoral dissertation, Macquarie University, Sydney, Australia.

Upitis, R. (1985). *Children's understanding of rhythm: The relationship between development and musical training.* Unpublished doctoral dissertation, Harvard University.

Vollaerts, J. W. A. (1960). *Rhythmic proportions in early medieval ecclesiastical chants.* Leiden, The Netherlands: E. J. Brill, Inc.

4
Structural-Developmental Research in Music: Conservation and Representation

CAROLYN HILDEBRANDT

Research in the development of musical intelligence is concerned with questions of the following type. What is the nature of musical understanding? What is its source and how does it develop? Are there aspects of musical development that are universal? If so, to what extent are they learned and to what extent are they due to general or even domain-specific capacities of the human mind?

Some interesting attempts to answer these and other questions have been made by psychologists and musicologists who subscribe to a structural theory of development. In this chapter, a series of studies are reviewed that examine the growth of musical intelligence from a structural-developmental point of view. The chapter begins with a brief overview of structural-developmental theory. This is followed by a discussion of some experimental applications of the theory to the study of music. Among these are studies of musical conservation (the ability to understand theme and variation in music), and musical representation (the ability to read and write various forms of musical notation) in subjects ages 4 through adult.

Structural-Developmental Theory

Structural-developmental theory is concerned with the nature of mind and the acquisition of knowledge. One of the main assumptions of the theory is that knowledge is not innately predetermined, but is constructed through the interaction of the child with the environment:

... [K]nowledge does not result from a mere recording of observations without structuring activity on the part of the subject. Nor do any a priori or innate cognitive structures exist in man: the functioning of intelligence alone is hereditary and creates structures only through an organization of successive actions performed on objects. Consequently, an epistemology conforming to the data of psychogenesis could neither be empiricist nor preformationist, but could only consist of constructivism, with the continual elaboration of new operations and structures. (Piaget, 1980, p. 23)

The only innate structures in the system are physical ones that set broad limits on intellectual functioning. In addition to these physical structures, there are automatic behavioral reflexes (grasping, crying, and sucking), which are rapidly transformed into cognitive structures during the first few days of life.

According to structural-developmental theory, four factors influence development from one set of structures to the next: maturation, experience, social transmission, and equilibration. The most fundamental of these is equilibration, the process by which cognitive structures develop toward greater levels of differentiation, integration, and adaptation. Equilibration involves the invariant functions of assimilation and accommodation. Assimilation is the process by which external elements are integrated into evolving or completed cognitive structures. Accommodation is the process by which cognitive structures are modified by the elements that they assimilate.

The process of equilibration gives rise to qualitatively different and increasingly more powerful modes of understanding. Within certain domains of knowledge, qualitative differences in cognitive structures have been characterized as constituting stages in intellectual development. In the domain of physical and logical-mathematical thinking, four main stages have been identified: sensorimotor (age 0–18 months), preoperational (18 months to 7 years), concrete operational (7–12 years), and formal operational (12 years to adult). Although children may vary in their rate of development through these stages, it is hypothesized that the sequence of development is universal. The universality of these stages is due neither to genetic preprogramming nor to the influences of external environmental forces. One stage follows the next because it is itself a transformation of the previous stage.

In recent years, the precise nature of developmental stages has been a source of controversy and debate. Whereas some researchers subscribe to the notion of global structures, others have suggested that knowledge develops independently within separate domains (Turiel, 1983; Turiel & Davidson, 1985). Whether global structures exist across domains as diverse as time, space, logic, number, morality, and art is a question yet to be answered. This question is of particular interest to researchers in music and cognition, as can be seen in some studies that are reviewed here.

Structural-Developmental Research in Music

Structural-developmental research in music has been heavily influenced by the work of Jean Piaget. Although Piaget himself did not conduct research in musical cognition, many of his methods and ideas have had a powerful influence on studies of perception and learning in music. Initially, the main focus of this research was upon the development of musical analogs of tasks originally designed to reflect developmental differences in thought within the physical and logical-mathematical domains. Experiments in conservation of number, substance, length, continuous and discontinuous quantity, area, weight, and volume have led to experiments in the conservation of musical attributes such as melody, rhythm, and meter (Pflederer, 1964). Similarly, experiments in the seriation of length, weight, and other discontinuous quantities have led to experiments in the seriation of loudness and pitch (Sloan, 1973; Torrey, 1975).

Musical Conservation

One of the first well-known attempts to apply Piagetian theory to the study of musical development was made by Pflederer-Zimmerman in her work on musical conservation (Pflederer, 1964, 1966, 1967; Pflederer & Secrest, 1968a, 1968b; Zimmerman & Secrest, 1968, 1970). The aim of these studies was to demonstrate the existence of preoperational and concrete operational reasoning in the domain of music. The expectation in these experiments was that conservation in music would occur around the same age as conservation in other domains.

Piaget's original experiments in conservation involve physical quantities that undergo transformations in appearance, but not in physical amount (Piaget, 1941/1952, 1970, 1942/1974). For example, in the conservation of liquid task, the child is shown two identical glasses containing the same amount of water. Once the child agrees that each glass has the same amount, the contents of one glass are poured into another glass of a different size and shape. Typically, children below the age of 6 or 7 claim that the amount of water changes when it is poured into the other glass. They justify this assertion by pointing out that the water level in a tall, thin glass is higher than the water level in a short, stout glass. In contrast to younger children, older children maintain that the amount of water remains the same even when it is poured into the shorter glass. They justify this assertion by pointing out that (a) it is the same water—nothing was added or taken away (identity); (b) even though the glass is shorter, it is wider as well (reciprocity or compensation); and (c) if you poured it back, you would still have the same amount (negation). The response of the older child reflects an ability to decenter and to perform a reversible operation. In the case of conservation, the most important of these operations involves an understanding of reciprocity or compensation. The ability to perform reversible operations is a characteristic of the concrete operational stage of development.

Pflederer-Zimmerman's conservation tasks were devised as musical analogs of Piaget's tasks in the physical domain. According to Pflederer-Zimmerman, conservation is central to the development of musical intelligence. The ability to hold one aspect of a complex whole constant while other aspects change is intrinsic to the understanding and appreciation of such compositional techniques as theme and variation and thematic development in music.

In her initial study, Pflederer-Zimmerman (Pflederer, 1964) presented six tasks: (a) conservation of meter with change in durational values, (b) conservation of rhythm with change in tonal pattern, (c) conservation of melody with change in durational values, (d) conservation of tonal pattern with change in pitch level, (e) conservation of tonal pattern with change in rhythm, and (f) conservation of tonal pattern with changes in rhythm and harmonic accompaniment.

These tasks were administered to 5-year-olds and 8-year-olds. On all of these tasks, the 8-year-olds gave more correct responses than did the 5-year-olds.

Subsequent research extended and improved these measures (King, 1972; Larsen, 1973; Pflederer, 1966; Pflederer & Secrest, 1968a, 1968b; Webster & Zimmerman, 1984; Zimmerman & Secrest, 1968, 1970). In general, the relationship between age and successful performance on musical conservation tasks was positive. However, as with conservations in the physical domain, decalages between performance of different types of musical conservation were also found. For example, conservation of tonal sequence (i.e., pitch progression) preceded conservation of rhythm, and within conservation of tonal sequence, changes in instrument, tempo, and harmony yielded higher scores than changes in mode, contour, and rhythm.

Following Pflederer-Zimmerman's initial studies, a number of researchers became interested in the extent to which musical conservation could be improved with training. In some cases, focused training enhanced children's ability to perform musical conservation tasks. Botvin (1974) showed that the use of successive approximations and verbal rule instruction significantly improved the ability of first-grade children to conserve melody under tempo variations. Foley (1975) found significant increases in the ability of trained second-grade children to conserve melody under rhythmic variation and rhythm under melodic variation as a consequence of focused instruction and interaction with these stimuli. Other researchers, however, found no training effect. Zimmerman and Secrest (1968) conducted two training studies with children in grades K, 2, 4, 6, and 8. In both studies they found that, whereas age was a significant factor in performance, focused training was not. Serafine (1979) found children at both preoperational and concrete operational levels to be resistant to focused training in conservation of meter. Ashbaugh (1980) attempted to train second-grade children to conserve duple and triple meter with no significant result. Other researchers found that prior training in music had little effect on the ability to conserve rhythm (Nelson, 1984) and meter (Perney, 1976).

The relationship between conservation in music and conservation in other domains has also been examined. Serafine (1979) found a significant positive relationship between conservation of meter and conservation of space, number, continuous and discontinuous quantity, and weight in children ages 4, 5, 7, and 9. Nelson (1984) found a significant positive relationship between conservation of rhythm and conservation of area and length in children 4 to 8 years old. However, Bettison (1976) found no significant relationship between conservation of melody and conservation of number, substance, continuous quantity, and weight with a restricted range of 7-year-old children. More recently, Norton (1979, 1980) found that IQ and "musical aptitude" were better predictors of musical conservation than ability to perform conservations in other domains.

The results of these studies are not easy to interpret. This is in part because of the wide variety of methods used to assess musical conservation, as well as the nature of the statistical tests used to compare children's performance across different tasks. For the most part, studies of musical conservation have employed correlational procedures to assess the relationship between conservation in music and conservation in other domains. Here, as in all other studies that use correlational measures, it is important to recognize that significant positive relationships may or may not indicate the existence of a causal link. Hence, high correlations between performance in musical and nonmusical tasks do not provide conclusive evidence for the existence of a common, global structure. In order to provide evidence for the existence of global structures, logical analyses of the problems must be made that delineate the structural features that musical and nonmusical tasks have in common. Until this is done, the results of these tasks cannot be interpreted.

Although studies of musical conservation have made an important contribution to our understanding of children's recognition of theme and variation in music, the extent to which these studies involve conservation in the Piagetian sense of the term is unclear. Serafine (1980) has pointed out some major discrepancies between Pflederer-Zimmerman's and Piaget's use of the term, as has Wohlwill (1981). The difference between Piaget's and Pflederer-Zimmerman's formulations is most clearly seen with regard to her "laws of musical conservation."

In a theoretical article, Pflederer-Zimmerman (Pflederer, 1967) proposed five "laws of musical conservation":

1. *identity*—repetitions of a theme maintain the identity of that theme when played by different musical instruments or when treated sequentially (as in conservation of melody with change in timbre).
2. *metrical groupings*—when consistent accents bind together groupings of notes, the overall metric configuration remains invariant even though individual note values may change (as in conservation of meter with change in rhythm).
3. *augmentation and diminution*—the note values of a musical statement can be systematically increased or decreased while maintaining the identity of a musical phrase (as in conservation of melody with change in tempo).
4. *transposition*—a musical phrase maintains its identity when transposed to a key in which the intervalic relations between the pitches remain the same (as in conservation of melody with change of key).
5. *inversion*—harmonic and melodic identities can be maintained with the substitution of lower pitches for higher ones and vice versa (as in conservation of harmony with chord inversion).

According to Pflederer-Zimmerman, these laws of musical conservation are analogs of Piaget's "laws of conservation." However, the precise nature of the analogy is difficult to ascertain, since Piaget's "laws" were originally meant to define the properties of concrete operational structures. These properties include combinativity (the combination of two elements of the set yields an element that is itself a member of the set), associativity (elements of a set can be combined in any order and still yield another element of the set), identity (there is an element of the set that, when combined with any other element of the set, leaves that element unchanged), and reversibility (for each element of the set, there is an inverse element that, when combined with that element, yields the identity element).

In their present form, Pflederer-Zimmerman's laws do not define the properties of concrete operational structures in music. The first two laws describe musical attributes that remain the same under given transformations (e.g., a melody stays the same, even if played by a different instrument), and the last three laws describe transformations that can be made while leaving certain musical attributes unchanged (e.g., the tempo of a piece may be changed without changing the melody). Structurally, these laws are very different from the properties of concrete operations that Piaget proposed. The most significant difference concerns the property of reversibility (compensation or reciprocity). Pflederer-Zimmerman's tests of musical conservation cover variations involving changes in pitch (melody, harmony, and mode), timbre (instrument), accent/grouping (meter), and duration (rhythm and tempo). Of these variations, there are only two that involve compensation or reciprocity in the Piagetian sense of the term. These are conservation of meter under rhythmic variation and conservation of rhythm under tempo variation. The other variations that Pflederer-Zimmerman proposed do not involve compensation or reciprocity, since changes in one dimension are not necessarily accompanied by changes in another. For example, what Pflederer-Zimmerman called conservation of identity does not involve compensation or reciprocity, since an overall change in timbre (e.g., musical instrument) does not necessarily imply a change in any other dimension. The same is true for the other conservations. What Pflederer-Zimmerman has defined with her musical laws are not conservations, but simple classifications that do not involve reversibility in the quantitative sense of the term.

The only musical tasks that assess conservation in the Piagetian sense are those that involve changes of duration. Two of these are illustrated in Figure 4.1. Figure 4.1A is a spatial analog of conservation of meter under rhythmic variation. In this example, the long lines represent events that receive a strong metric accent and the short lines represent unaccented events. Here, the quantity of time between each accented event remains the same regardless of how many unaccented events occur in between. Reversibility is involved in that the rate at which the events occur is compensated by the amount of time between them.

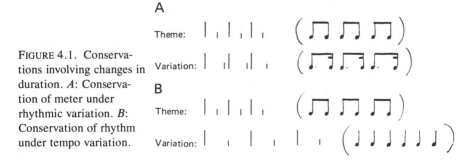

FIGURE 4.1. Conservations involving changes in duration. A: Conservation of meter under rhythmic variation. B: Conservation of rhythm under tempo variation.

Figure 4.1B is a spatial analog of conservation of rhythm under tempo variation. In this example, the overall rate at which a series of events occurs can increase or decrease while leaving the proportion of time between each event unchanged. Reversibility is involved since the rate at which the events occur is compensated by the overall amount of time it takes for them to occur.

Because time is the only musical dimension that can be conserved in a fully reversible fashion, many researchers have limited the focus of their studies to tasks involving temporal reasoning (Bickel, 1984; Jones, 1974; Perney, 1976; Serafine, 1979). One of the most interesting of these studies was conducted by Serafine (1979).

Serafine devised a task that measures the ability to recognize a steady, underlying pulse in the face of changes in a simultaneous surface rhythm. In an initial study, she found that most children between the ages of 4 and 9 can clap in time to a rhythm pattern like that in Figure 4.2. However, their perception of what constitutes a steady, underlying pulse differs with age. In this study, most of the 4-year-olds claimed that their clapping got "faster" or "slower" even though, from the teacher's point of view, they were making steady bodily movements. In contrast, most of the 9-year-olds said that their clapping "stayed the same." However, when children of both ages were asked to clap without the rhythm, most of them said that their clapping stayed the same. Serafine extended this task to other rhythms, with similar results.

In reviewing these results, at least three explanations seem possible for the judgments that the 4-year-olds made:

1. The child is able to clap steadily with a rhythm that changes, but is only able to focus on one aspect at a time: his or her clapping, or the rhythm. If the rhythm changes, the child might switch his or her focus to the rhythm and make his or her judgment solely on what the rhythm is doing.
2. The child does not focus on the rhythm alone, or the clapping alone, but the whole experience of his or her claps in conjunction with the rhythm. The child is, in a sense, responding to the relationship between the two sets of sounds. In this case, if the rhythm got faster, the claps might seem slower in relation to it, since they are coming in a ratio of 1:3 rather than 1:2.
3. The child is focusing on an underlying pulse, but one that is even slower than the one he or she is clapping. If we assume that the child is hearing the rhythm in a 4/4 meter, then it is difficult to imagine why he or she would say that his or her clapping "gets faster" or "gets slower." However, if the child changes meter, say from 4/4 to 2/4, then he or she may simply be describing the underlying accent structure.

Claps: x   x   x   x   x   x   x   x

FIGURE 4.2. Example of clapping in time to a rhythm pattern as used by Serafine (1979).

The ability to conserve an underlying pulse in the face of a changing surface rhythm is an important skill not only for musical performance, but for the reading and writing of music as well. Traditionally, one of the most difficult aspects of music for students to learn is rhythm representation. While most people can clap simple rhythm patterns with accuracy and ease, their ability to form written representations of these patterns differs significantly among individuals.

How do people experience rhythm in music? How do they form written representations of what they hear? Do systems of representation change with age and experience? These questions are the focus of a number of studies in the development of musical representation in children and adults.

Rhythm Representation

Formal analyses of the rhythmic structure of music suggest that certain elements and relations are necessary for a complete representation of rhythm (Cooper & Meyer, 1960). These are symbols for sounds, correspondences between sounds and symbols, serial order of events in time, accent, grouping, and duration. Given the hierarchical nature of musical rhythm and the problems that children of different ages normally encounter with tasks that require complex temporal reasoning (Fraisse, 1963; Friedman, 1982; Piaget, 1964, 1927/1969, 1970), one would expect interesting developmental trends to occur. Indeed, there is a growing body of evidence that suggests that children of different ages represent rhythm in qualitatively different ways (Bamberger, 1975, 1980, 1981; Brearly, 1970; Hildebrandt & Richards, 1978; Hildebrandt, 1984, 1985b; Smith, 1983; Upitis, 1985, and Chapter 3, this volume). One way of assessing children's representations of simple rhythms is through the analysis of their spontaneous drawings.

By the age of 4 or 5, most children can clap simple rhythms with accuracy and ease, but the problem of how to make *visible* marks represent *invisible* sounds is a difficult one. When children of this age are asked to imitate a rhythm and then to "put something on paper so that you could remember it next week or so that someone else could play it just like you did," many draw pictures of the instruments they have just used to perform the pattern (e.g., a drum mallet, or their own hands). The use of written symbols to represent sounds emerges somewhere around the age of 5 or 6. However, at this age the sounds and symbols are not always in full correspondence with each other. A one-to-one correspondence between sound and symbol can first be seen in rhythms that consist of a small number of events. Around the same time that sound/symbol correspondences are constructed, another problem of written representation is solved, that of the serial order of events in time. By the age of 7 or 8, other aspects of rhythm begin to be represented, including accent, grouping, and duration.

Figure 4.3 shows a developmental typology of children's representations of the rhythm that underlies the words "three, four, shut the door; five, six, pick up sticks." The last two drawings have been studied in detail by Bamberger (1975,

FIGURE 4.3. Examples of children's drawings of the rhythm for "three, four, shut the door; five, six, pick up sticks."

1980, 1981). Figural drawings are produced mainly by people who do not know how to read music, or by those who knew how to read it at one time but who no longer use it. Metric drawings are produced primarily by people who read music regularly from a score. When shown examples of figural and metric drawings of this pattern, most adults who do not read music agree that the figural drawings are better representations of the rhythm than the metric ones (Hildebrandt, 1985a; Hildebrandt & Bamberger, 1980). From the point of view of grouping, this is certainly the case. Figural drawings capture the change of pace between fast and slow claps, as well as the repetition of the main rhythmic motives. From a purely durational standpoint, however, the metric drawings are more accurate. To test this assertion, one needs only to construct a steady, underlying pulse, either at the rate of the shortest events (represented by the small symbols in Figure 4.3) or at the rate of the longest events (represented by the large symbols in Figure 4.3). If this is done correctly, the results should be similar to the metric drawing shown above. Here, the underlying pulse acts as a metric grid by which the duration of each event is measured. In the case of the metric drawing presented here, the large triangles represent two units of time and the small ones represent one unit of time.

There is another type of representation that does not appear in the typology presented above. This is called a spatial analog. Spatial analogs can be constructed by moving a pencil across a page and making a mark at the moment that each event occurs. A spatial analog of the rhythm "three, four, shut the door; five, six, pick up sticks" would look something like the drawing in Figure 4.4.

Several studies have examined children's use of space to represent simple rhythms (Birch & Belmont, 1965; Blank, Weider, & Bridger, 1968; Goodnow, 1970, 1972, 1977). However, these studies have not made use of rhythms that distinguish between figural and metric representations. Other studies have used spatial analogs as part of their experimental stimuli. Smith (1983) used spatial analogs in order to study rhythmic grouping in children and adults. Upitis (1985) used spatial analogs to study children's understanding of metric hierarchies. Spatial analogs have also been used as transitional representations in order to teach students to write rhythm patterns in standard music notation (Bamberger & Brofsky, 1979). Each of these studies assumes a certain level of competence on

FIGURE 4.4. Examples of spatial
analog of the rhythm shown in
Figure 4.3.

the part of subjects in the use of space to represent time. However, there is a prior question that needs to be addressed: To what extent do children of various ages actually understand the meaning of spatial analogs of temporal relations? This question was addressed in a study of children's use of spatial analogs to represent simple rhythms. This study is described in detail below.

Children's Use of Spatial Analogs to Represent Simple Rhythms

The purpose of the study was to trace the development of children's understanding of time through the examination of spontaneous representations of simple rhythm patterns. Forty-eight children participated in the study: 16 kindergarteners, 16 second graders, and 16 fifth graders. Half were girls and half were boys. None of the children had received any prior training in the reading and writing of standard music notation.

Each child was asked to clap and then represent four rhythm patterns. These rhythm patterns are presented in Figure 4.5. Children were asked to represent each of these rhythm patterns using four media of representation: drawings, numbers, circles of two sizes, and a mechanical toy. The mechanical toy is a dynamic spatial analog that children can use to construct and play simple rhythms by manipulating order, correspondence, distance, and velocity with visual and auditory feedback as a result. The toy consists of a Velcro conveyor belt mounted on a wooden frame. The conveyor belt is powered by a train motor that drives it forward and backward at different speeds. To play a rhythm pattern, the child puts wooden mallets on the conveyor belt and then turns the motor on. The mallets move past a photo cell. When this happens, a woodblock clicks or a bell rings. With this toy, children's understanding of spatial analogs of temporal relations can be explored. In addition, the toy makes it possible to observe two types of reversibility (negation and compensation or reciprocity) as well as various strategies for the augmentation (slowing down) and diminution (speeding up) of simple rhythms.

FIGURE 4.5. Rhythm patterns used in the study (one quarter note = M.M. 100).

The results showed that children's representations of these rhythms changed with age and experience. As grade increased, so did level of representation. The most marked age differences were observed with the mechanical toy. In this task, the main challenge for the kindergarteners was to establish a one-to-one correspondence between sound and symbol. Even with the simplest rhythm, only 68% of the kidnergarteners were able to establish a direct correspondence between the mallets and their claps. The second graders were primarily concerned with the use of space to represent rhythmic groupings, regardless of the pace at which the events within these groups occurred. In cases where the durations within rhythmic groups differed, changes in the speed of the belt were made in order to maintain the spatial integrity of the groups. In contrast to the second graders, the fifth graders attempted to use space to represent durations. However, unlike trained musicians, they did not make use of an underlying pulse to measure the amount of time between each event. This resulted in representations in which durations at the boundaries between rhythmic groups were shown to be longer than equivalent durations within rhythmic groups. Examples of children's representations of the most complex of these patterns (rhythm 4) are shown in Figure 4.6. The relation between age and level of representation for this pattern is shown in Figure 4.7.

After the children had played the rhythm patterns on the mechanical toy, they were asked if they could make the patterns sound "slower." There are two ways of achieving this. One way is to change the spacing of the mallets; the other way is to change the speed of the belt. In general, kindergarteners made exclusive use of speed to solve the problem. When asked to make the rhythm sound slower, they simply decreased the speed of the belt. In contrast to the kindergarteners, the second and fifth graders were able to use speed as well as space to solve the problem. However, they were unable to substitute one for the other in a fully reversible fashion.

Results of this and other studies suggest that children's understanding of time changes with age and experience. Previous research has focused primarily on children's ability to recognize musical excerpts as being "same" or "different" under tempo variations. In this experiment, the child is asked not only to

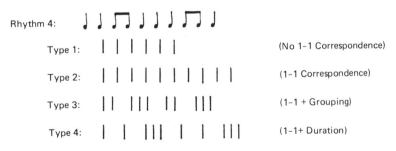

FIGURE 4.6. Examples of children's representations of rhythm 4.

Grade	Type of Representation			
	1	2	3	4
K	12	2	2	0
2	0	2	11	3
5	0	1	4	11

FIGURE 4.7. Relation between grade and type of representation on rhythm 4 with use of mechanical toy. The difference between age and level of representation was significant (for K vs. 2, $\chi^2 = 13.72, p < .001$; for 2 vs. 5, $\chi^2 = 3.18; p < .05$; Kruskall-Wallis pairwise comparisons).

represent the rhythm pattern in spatial terms, but to demonstrate the reciprocal relations that exist between distance traveled and velocity.

Teachers of young children should be aware of developmental differences in children's capacity to read and write standard music notation. Attempts to introduce notation too early in development could meet with disappointment and failure. Useful prereading activities include clapping simple rhythms and tapping in time to an underlying pulse. Gradual introduction of serial order and sound-symbol correspondence should precede attempts to represent rhythmic groups and durations.

Conclusions

In this chapter, a series of studies that examined the development of musical intelligence are reviewed. Common to all of these studies is a focus on the child's growing capacity to recognize variances and invariances in musical elements and relations across different musical contexts. With regard to musical conservation, it has been suggested that not all judgments involve reciprocity or compensation. Yet there is a marked improvement in performance of these tasks as a function of age and experience. How do we account for this phenomenon from a structural-developmental point of view?

There are two types of reasoning that can be identified in musical cognition. One is primarily "logical." The other is primarily "grammatical." Musical-logical reasoning is involved in tasks that require discrimination and classification of pitches, durations, timbres, tonal and rhythmic progressions, themes and variations, and larger musical forms. Classifications of these sorts involve the ability to recognize similarities and differences among musical elements and configurations. However, not all of these classifications involve reciprocity. A rose is a rose is a rose, regardless of its color, shape, or size. Similarly, a tune is a tune is a tune, regardless of the instrument, tempo, or key that is used to play it.

Also within the realm of musical-logical reasoning are seriation tasks, and representation tasks that involve the measurement of time. Rhythm representation is an example of a musical-logical task.

In contrast to musical-logical reasoning, musical-grammatical reasoning involves the understanding of the form and meaning of music within given styles and traditions. It belongs to a class of nonreversible structures described by Piaget:

[T]here is, of course, an immense class of structures which are not strictly logical or mathematical, that is, whose transformations unfold in time: linguistic structures, sociological structures, psychological structures, and so on. Such transformations are governed by laws ("regulations" in the cybernetic sense of the word) which are not in the strict sense "operations" because they are not entirely reversible (in the sense that multiplication is reversible by division and addition by subtraction). (1970, p. 15)

Whereas musical-logical knowledge makes it possible to classify musical excerpts as being "same" or "different," musical-grammatical knowledge makes it possible to recognize certain changes as constituting well-formed melodic variations within a given style of music. It also makes it possible to anticipate what sorts of musical events are likely to occur next. According to musical-logical reasoning, any change in pitch, time, or timbre would constitute a musical variation. However, according to musical-grammatical reasoning only certain changes are permissible within a given style of music. Although musical-grammatical knowledge is distinct from musical-logical knowledge, there are many cases in which they interact.

To date, most researchers within the structural-developmental tradition have concentrated primarily on the development of the logical aspects of musical development. Accordingly, the studies reviewed here have attempted to demonstrate commonalities between reasoning in music and reasoning in other domains. Judgments involved in conservation and representation are assumed to be global in that they can be observed in many different content areas. They are also assumed to be universal, in that they follow the laws of logical necessity. However, the existence of these global structures is still to be demonstrated in music and in other domains.

In order to further our understanding of musical development, more attention should be given to the musical-grammatical aspects of musical cognition. The ability to organize musical sounds and derive structure and meaning from them is an important aspect of musical development. Research in tonal organization, structural hierarchies, and generative grammars will help to expand our knowledge of musical development and make it possible to distinguish cognitive structures that are universal from those that are specific to the musical domain.

References

Ashbaugh, T. J. (1980). *The effects of training in conservation of duple and triple meter in music with second-grade children*. Doctoral dissertation, University of Iowa.

Bamberger, J. (1975). *The development of musical intelligence I: Children's representations of simple rhythms* (Artificial Intelligence Memo #342). Cambridge, MA: Massachusetts Institute of Technology.

Bamberger, J. (1980). Cognitive structuring in the apprehension and description of simple rhythms. *Archives de Psychologie, 48,* 171–199.

Bamberger, J. (1982). Revisiting children's descriptions of simple rhythms: A function for reflection in action. In S. Strauss (Ed.), *U-Shaped curves in behavioral growth.* New York: Academic Press.

Bamberger, J., & Brofsky, H. (1979). *The art of listening.* New York: Harper and Row.

Bettison, G. M. (1976). *The relationship between the conservation of certain melodic materials and standard Piagetian tasks.* Paper presented at the meeting of the Music Educator's National Council, Atlantic City, NJ.

Bickel, F. (1984). A time-velocity ratio investigation. *Journal of Research in Music Education, 32*(2), 105–111.

Birch, H., & Belmont, L. (1965). Auditory-visual integration, intelligence and reading ability in school children. *Perceptual and Motor Skills, 20,* 295–305.

Blank, M., Weider, S., & Bridger, W. (1968). Verbal deficiencies in abstract thinking in early reading retardation. *American Journal of Orthopsychiatry, 38,* 823–834.

Botvin, G. (1974). Acquiring conservation of melody and cross-modal transfer through successive approximation. *Journal of Research in Music Education, 22*(3), 226–233.

Brearly, M. (1970). *The teaching of young children.* New York: Schocken Books.

Cooper, G., & Meyer, L. B. (1960). *The rhythmic structure of music.* Chicago: University of Chicago Press.

Foley, E. A. (1975). Effects of training in conservation of tonal and rhythmic patterns of second-grade children. *Journal of Research in Music Education, 23*(4), 240–248.

Fraisse, P. (1963). *The psychology of time.* New York: Harper & Row.

Friedman, W. J. (1982). *The developmental psychology of time.* New York: Academic Press.

Goodnow, J. J. (1971). Matching auditory and visual series: Modality problem or translation problem? *Child Development, 42,* 1187–1201.

Goodnow, J. J. (1972). Rules and repertoires, rituals and tricks of the trade: Social and informational aspects to cognitive and representational development. In S. Farnham-Diggory (Ed.), *Information processing in children.* New York: Academic Press.

Goodnow, J. J. (1977). *Children drawing.* Cambridge, MA: Harvard University Press.

Hildebrandt, C. (1984). Children's representations of time in music. *Arts and Learning SIG Proceedings: American Educational Research Association, 2,* 14–22.

Hildebrandt, C. (1985a). The effect of sustained and non-sustained sounds on adult's representations of simple rhythms. *Arts and Learning SIG Proceedings: American Educational Research Association, 3,* 100–110.

Hildebrandt, C. (1985b). *A developmental study of children's representations of simple rhythms.* Unpublished doctoral dissertation, University of California, Berkeley.

Hildebrandt, C., & Bamberger, J. (1980). *Claps and gaps: Adult's representations of simple rhythms.* Unpublished manuscript, D.S.R.E., Massachusetts Institute of Technology.

Hildebrandt, C., & Richards, R. (1978). *Children's representations of simple rhythms: A cross-sectional and longitudinal study.* Unpublished manuscript, Harvard University.

Jones, R. L. (1974). The development of the child's conception of meter in music. *Journal of Research in Music Education, 24*(3), 142–154.

King, C. D. (1972). *The conservation of melodic pitch patterns by elementary children as determined by ancient Chinese music.* Doctoral dissertation, Ohio State University.

Larson, R. L. (1973). Levels of conceptual development in melodic permutation concepts based on Piaget's theory. *Journal of Research in Music Education, 21*(3), 256–263.

Nelson, D. J. (1984). The conservation of rhythm in Suzuki violin students: A task validation study. *Journal of Research in Music Education*, *32*(1), 25–34.

Norton, D. (1979). Relationship of music ability and intelligence to auditory and visual conservation of the kindergarten child. *Journal of Research in Music Education*, *27*(1), 3–13.

Norton, D. (1980). Interrelations among music aptitude, IQ, and auditory conservation. *Journal of Research in Music Education*, *28*(2), 207–217.

Perney, J. (1976). Musical tasks related to the development of the conservation of metric time. *Journal of Research in Music Education*, *24*(4), 159–168.

Pflederer, M. (1964). The responses of children to musical tasks embodying Piaget's principle of conservation. *Journal of Research in Music Education*, *12*(4), 251–268.

Pflederer, M. (1966). How children conceptually organize musical sounds. *Council of Research in Music Education*, *7*(2), 52–62.

Pflederer, M. (1967). Conservation laws applied to the development of musical intelligence. *Journal of Research in Music Education*, *15*(3), 215–223.

Pflederer, M., & Secrest, L. (1968a). Conservation in musical experience. *Psychology in the Schools*, *5*(2), 99–105.

Pflederer, M., & Secrest, L. (1968b). Conservation-type responses of children to musical stimuli. *Council of Research in Music Education*, *13*, 19–36.

Piaget, J. (1952). *The child's conception of number*. (C. Gettegno & F. M. Hodgson, Trans.). London: Routledge & Kegan Paul. (Original work published 1941)

Piaget, J. (1964). Relations between notions of time and speed in children. In R. E. Ripple & V. N. Rockcastle (Eds.), *Piaget rediscovered: A report of the conference on cognitive studies and curriculum development* (pp. 40–48). Ithaca, NY: Cornell University.

Piaget, J. (1969). *The child's conception of time*. (A. J. Pomerans, Trans.). New York: Routledge & Kegan Paul, Inc. (Original work published 1927)

Piaget, J. (1970). Piaget's theory. (G. Gelleier & J. Langer, Trans.). In P. H. Mussen (Ed.), *Charmichael's manual of child psychology*. London: Routledge & Kegan Paul.

Piaget, J. (1970). *Structuralism*. (C. Maschler, Trans.). New York: Basic Books. (Original work published 1968)

Piaget, J. (1974). *The child's construction of quantities: Conservation and atomism*. (A. J. Pomerans, Trans.). London: Routledge & Kegan Paul. (Original work published 1942)

Piaget, J. (1980). The psychogenesis of knowledge and its epistomological significance. In M. Piatelli-Palmarini (Ed.), *Language and learning: The debate between Jean Piaget and Noam Chomsky*. Cambridge: Harvard University Press.

Serafine, M. L. (1979). Meter conservation in music. *Council of Research in Music Education*, *59*, 98–101.

Serafine, M. L. (1980). Piagetian research in music. *Council of Research in Music Education*, *62*, 1–21.

Sloan, W. B. (1973). The child's conception of musical scales. *Psychology of Music*, *1*(1), 10–18.

Smith, J. (1983). *Memory for musical rhythms: The effect of skill*. Unpublished doctoral dissertation, Macquarie University, Australia.

Torrey, R. W. (1975). *The growth in children of capacities for making selected music seriations*. Unpublished doctoral dissertation, University of California, Berkeley.

Turiel, E. (1983). *The development of social knowledge: Morality and convention*. Cambridge, England: Cambridge University Press.

Turiel, E., & Davidson, P. (1985). Heterogeneity, inconsistency, and asynchrony in the development of cognitive structures. In I. Levin (Ed.), *Stage and structure: Reopening the debate*. Norwood, NJ: Ablex Press.

Upitis, R. B. (1985). *Children's understanding of rhythm: The relationship between development and musical training*. Unpublished doctoral dissertation, Harvard University.

Webster, P. R., & Zimmerman, M. P. (1984). Conservation of rhythmic and tonal patterns of second through sixth grade children. *Council of Research in Music Education*, *73*, 28–49.

Wohlwill, J. (1981). *Music and Piaget: Spinning a slender thread*. Paper presented at the 89th Annual Convention of the American Psychological Association.

Zimmerman, M. P., & Secrest, L. (1968). *How children conceptually organize musical sounds*. Northwestern University. (ERIC Document Reproduction Service No. ED 028 200)

Zimmerman, M. P., & Secrest, L. (1970). Brief focused instruction and musical concepts. *Journal of Research in Music Education*, *18*(1), 25–36.

5
Toward a Theory of Music Syntax: Some Observations of Music Babble in Young Children

JOHN M. HOLAHAN

The idea that music is a language is neither new nor correct. The expression "music is the universal language" is often used to convey the fact that speakers of different languages may be members of a common music culture. Unfortunately, some musicians have taken the expression more literally to mean either that music is a language, or that music may be explained by principles of linguistics (Bernstein, 1976). Some scholars have attempted to explain music by "borrowing" principles from linguistics in conjunction with traditional music theory (Lerdahl & Jackendoff, 1983). Relatively little progress has been made with those proposed explanations. Nonetheless, the fact remains that language and music do share common characteristics. Because both language and music are experienced fundamentally as patterns of sound arranged in time, it seems reasonable to suggest that the cognitive capacity for language and the cognitive capacity for music are analogous, but not homologous, processes. That is, although language and music share similar sensory and motor systems in the human body, there is no substantive evidence to suggest that the two cognitive capacities stem from common biological, genetic, or evolutionary origins. At a sufficiently abstract level of analysis, however, it may be possible to derive fundamental analogies between the cognitive capacity for language and the cognitive capacity for music.

Throughout history, philosophers, linguists, and psychologists have developed theories of the nature of language and language acquisition. Both mechanistic (empiricist) and organismic (rationalist) theories have been created. In the latter half of the 20th century, Chomsky's rationalist theory of language, transformational-generative grammar, has given new direction to the understanding of language and language acquisition (Chomsky, 1957, 1965, 1975, 1979, 1980). Chomsky asserted that an adequate grammar of a language must determine the properties of each sentence of that language. The grammar must explain the orderly arrangement, the phonetic form or sound pattern, and the meaning of the words in a sentence. Those three aspects of a sentence are formally accounted for by the syntax, phonology, and semantics of the language.

The syntactic component of the grammar consists of a finite set of rules that define how words are combined into sentences. The phonological component of the grammar is a set of rules that define how syntactic elements are pronounced in speech. The semantic component of the grammar provides information about the meaning of sentences generated by the grammar. Taken together, those three components serve as a theoretical model of how the mind is capable of listening to (receptive) and speaking (productive) language. An interesting property of an adequate grammar is that it can account for the infinite variety inherent in a language with a finite and relatively small set of linguistic rules. A second important aspect of a linguistic grammar is that the rules and representations defined by the grammar reveal principles of language that are apart from the conscious knowledge of a speaker of the language.

Chomsky used the metaphor that language is a "mental organ" that grows in the mind of every human being. As such, the language faculty is partly genetically determined and partly environmentally determined. The genetic component of language consists of a set of principles of organization that exist in all human languages. Taken together, that set of principles constitutes a universal grammar. All human beings, regardless of their native language, are endowed with a universal grammar for language. From birth, young children are given exposure to their native language. Although much of that exposure consists of incomplete or imperfect excerpts of language, children demonstrate through speech and comprehension that they possess the majority of the rules of their native language before the age of 5. Given the imperfections in the language-learning environment, Chomsky believes that it is impossible, in principle, for traditional empiricist models of learning to explain how children are capable of mastering their native language.

Current research in psycholinguistics is being undertaken to create a formal explanatory theory of how the young child makes the transition from "language babbler" in infancy to knowledgeable and self-directed language user before the age of 5. It is generally accepted that a description of the development of the child's grammatical knowledge is an important component of an adequate theory of language development.

Philosophers and psychologists have developed theories of the nature of music. Historically, the psychology of music may be traced back to the origins of experimental psychology in the latter half of the 19th century. Carl E. Seashore became the dominant music psychologist during the first half of the 20th century. Since the turn of the century, the psychology of music has been a multidisciplinary subject matter. Much of the experimental research in the psychology of music and music education has been devoted to the measurement of students' potential to learn music (music aptitude) and their attainment of music learning (music achievement). Other research traditions in the psychology of music have been devoted to laboratory experiments in psychoacoustics, cognitive psychology, and neurophysiology. The majority of research in the psychology of music and music education has been based upon the mechanistic principles of empiricism. Gordon's research (1965, 1979, 1984) seems to be most closely associated with a rationalist or organismic viewpoint. (For a summary of current and past research perspectives in the psychology of music, see Hodges, 1980, and Shuter-Dyson & Gabriel, 1981.)

It is reasonable to assume, by analogy, that an adequate theory of music must explain the orderly arrangement of tonal and rhythm elements in music (syntax), and the sound pattern of individual tonal patterns and rhythm patterns in music (phonetic form). There are no music elements that are analogous to semantic meaning in language. Music syntax must explain the mental construction of music as a continuous experience over time (diachronically), whereas music phonology must explain the mental construction of discrete music elements from tone to tone or note to note in time (synchronically).

Although music is characterized by the orderly arrangement of patterns of tones and rhythms, those tonal patterns and rhythm patterns are not related to lexical categories in language, such as noun or verb. Nonetheless, tonal patterns and rhythm patterns are organized by the musical mind into musical categories such as tonalities and meters. There is consensus among psychomusicologists that "auditory imagery," "inner hearing," or "audiation" is a fundamental process of music cognition. "Audiation takes place when one hears music through recall or creativity, the sound not being physically present except when one is engaging in performance, and derives musical meaning" (Gordon, 1979, p. 7). Tonal syntax is embodied in the recognition that the pitch relationships among the tones in a series of tonal patterns collectively suggest a tonality such as major, minor, dorian, and so on. Rhythm syntax is embodied in the recognition that the relationships among the durations and accents in a series of rhythm patterns collectively suggest a meter such as duple, triple, and so on. When one audiates music with tonal and rhythm syntax, one is said to possess a sense of tonality and a sense of meter (Gordon, 1984). Like the speaker's knowledge of the "rules of grammar," a sense of tonality and a sense of meter are not part of the child's conscious knowledge of music. A formal theory of tonal syntax and rhythm syntax should explain what a person knows when he or she demonstrates a sense of tonality and a sense of meter. Such a formal description should make explicit the mental structures that give rise to the recognition of tonality or meter.

Music syntax, like language grammar, enables the child to comprehend familiar and unfamiliar music aurally, and to reproduce familiar music and to create novel music orally. In the psychology of music, or psychomusicology, there is relatively little research that bears on the preschool child's acquisition of music syntax from infancy to age 5. The preschool child's music behavior has been characterized as being "music babble" (Gordon, 1984; Moog, 1976; Moorhead & Pond, 1977; Shuter-Dyson & Gabriel, 1981). A formal explanatory theory of how the young child makes the transition from "music babbler" to self-directed music maker, in terms of a theory of music syntax, is not available. Perhaps this is because the child's music development is slow when compared to his or her language development. Nonetheless, it seems reasonable to suggest that a theory of music syntax is an important component of an adequate theory of music development.

The purpose of the research reported here is to gain insight into the nature of music syntax as it develops in young children.

Method

Sample

Two samples of preschool-age children were observed. One sample consisted of 125 five-month-old to 5-year-old children, in five homogeneous age groups, who were enrolled in the Temple University Day Care Center. The children represented diverse ethnic and socioeconomic groups living in metropolitan Philadelphia. The children in each age group were provided informal music activities and were observed in two 30-minute sessions each week for 4 months. Observations were obtained from large group interactions among the children 3 years of age and older, and small group and individual interactions with the children younger than 3 years old.

The second sample consisted of 25 predominantly white, middle-class, 3- to 5-year-old children who were enrolled in a parent cooperative nursery school in Lancaster, Pennsylvania. The children were provided informal music activities on 1 day each week for 2 academic years. The author participated in the children's play, work, and mealtime activities throughout the day, thus providing many opportunities to observe their music behaviors in large group, small group, and individual interaction.

Cross-sectional observations reported here were obtained from infants and children younger than 3 years old in the first sample and longitudinal observations were obtained from children 3 to 5 years old in the second sample. Observations were recorded in notebooks, and on some occasions, on audiotape recordings. The reported observations are representative of typical musical behaviors of the respective samples.

Informal Instruction

The children in the longitudinal and cross-sectional groups were provided informal exposure to music by the author. The exposure consisted of singing songs in major, minor, mixolydian, dorian, lydian, and phrygian tonalities, with and without harmonic accompaniment on a guitar or an autoharp. The children were given opportunities to sing familiar songs of their own choosing, and to create songs, if they so desired. The children were also encouraged to move to music, using large and small muscles. The song materials included duple, triple, and unusual paired meters. Unusual paired meter occurs, for example, in music written with a 5/8 measure signature in which the metrical structure is 3 + 2 or

2 + 3. The children were given opportunities to move to music in rhythmic responses suggested by the author and in movements of their own choosing.

The music activities were informal for the following reasons. First, songs and activities were not taught with a rote procedure. Children were free to listen to and participate in activities without restrictions or demands imposed by the author. Second, no attempt was made to "teach" specific musical or nonmusical concepts such as pitch matching, "beat," "high" and "low," "loud" and "soft," and "steps" and "skips," which are examples of formal music instruction and theoretical understanding. Third, the children were encouraged to respond to the music activities, but they were never told that a specific response was inadequate or incorrect. Fourth, recorded music and music instruments were never used as substitutes for use of the human voice and body in music activities.

Observations

The introduction of informal music activities provided a relatively unfamiliar form of multidimensional stimulation for the children in both groups. Listening to, singing, or moving to music as simple as a rote song is, in itself, a multidimensional experience. The complex whole of a rote song includes tonal elements, rhythm elements, a linguistic text, and in some cases, physical actions, such as the motions that accompany "The Wheels on the Bus." The child consciously or unconsciously may attend to parts of any one dimension, or combination of dimensions at any time. For many children, the song text seemed to dominate their conscious awareness. On some occasions, however, a given child demonstrated awareness of tonal or rhythm elements, usually a pattern of one to three tones, or a brief rhythm pattern.

First Spontaneous Performances

From the beginning of instruction, the infants and young children in the cross-sectional group engaged in one-to-one interactions with the author. Two 9-month-old infants often babble-sang discrete pitches in response to rote songs. When songs were being sung in the key of D major and minor, one of those infants repeatedly babble-sang A above middle C; when songs were being sung in the key of G major and minor, she babble-sang G above middle C. Although the pitches she sang were part of the ongoing musical stimulus, it cannot be inferred that the child's pitch sense included the syntactic relation that is sometimes referred to as a sense of tonic, however, that she attended to one pitch is indicative of a sense of pitch center.

The infants and young children in the cross-sectional group engaged in all types of movement responses to music. One 11-month-old boy was particularly fond of swaying to music while standing in a secluded corner of the room. With his hands and feet outstretched at his sides, he swayed from side to side, using the walls to support his weight. His swaying was not synchronized with the tempo of the music, however; he swayed only when music was being performed. Whenever the music stopped, he peered from around the corner in anticipation of moving to more music.

Many children in the longitudinal group participated in one-to-one interactions with the author. In those first interactions, a given child sang familiar songs that had recently been sung to him or her, but on some occasions, he or she created a novel song. A spontaneous performance of a rote or created song usually consisted of one or two phrases. Rarely did a child sing a rote song in its entirety, unless the author was asked to sing along. The tonal aspects of those spontaneous performances only vaguely resembled the tonal characteristics of the songs to which the children had been introduced. One pitch, if any, was consistent throughout a performance. Different children sang the same rote song in different ways, but any one child tended to sing the same song using similar tonal patterns from one performance to the next.

When engaged in spontaneous performance, most children seemed to be self-absorbed, if not self-conscious. On some occasions, however, a given child could be observed singing spontaneously, seemingly without self-awareness.

The children in the longitudinal group also engaged in all types of movement responses to music. They walked, ran, jumped, hopped, clapped, rocked, and swayed in response to music. As a group, there was no consensus demonstrated in the characteristics of their movement. Although the children moved seemingly without self-awareness or reservation, there seemed to be little relationship between the subjective characteristics of their movement and the objective rhythmic characteristics of the music to which they moved.

More Advanced Performances

As music became more familiar to the children, their musical performances became more advanced. In the cross-sectional group, the 9-month-old girl who babble-sang to music from the beginning of informal instruction continued to do so. Her musical babble-singing was extended to include singing individual pitches and pitch patterns without music being present physically. Her parents reported that "singing" and "dancing" became part of her daily activities. The emergence of child-directed music making suggests the presence of the capacity to "generate" music and not merely to imitate music. Likewise, a 15-month-old boy increased his active participation in music making; however, he sang only in conjunction with a musical stimulus. He frequently sang the song "Up and Down" (Figure 5.1).

He evidently sang along with only those parts of the song that he could approximate in speech. It is also interesting to note that each portion that he sang, with the exception of the last pitch, consisted of the same three-tone pattern of disjunct diatonic intervals in the same melodic rhythm. All portions that he sang included the tonic tone (G). It is interesting to note that the child's capacity to render both a consistent tonal pattern and a consistent tonic tone suggest the presence of at least a syntactic sense of tonic, if not a syntactic sense of tonality.

FIGURE 5.1. Response of a 15-month-old boy in the cross-sectional group to the song "Up and Down." Underlined portions were babble-sung by the boy as he listened to the song in its entirety. (Song composed by Doug Nichol.)

A 2½-year-old boy often spontaneously sang the song "Bingo." Contrary to the previous examples, he sang the song in its entirety, although the "words" and "music" of his performance could barely be recognized as being the song "Bingo." That this child's rendition of "Bingo" did not have recognizable tonal syntactic properties suggests that his memory for the song did not include a representation of the abstract syntactic characteristics of the melody.

The children in the longitudinal group also demonstrated more advanced levels of performance achievement. A 3½-year-old girl was observed to be walking and chanting the chant in Figure 5.2 in a consistent tempo. Her mother indicated that the girl had learned to chant that rhythm by being exposed informally to her older sister's Suzuki piano lessons. Although she repeated that pattern many times with precision, she was reluctant to chant other rhythm patterns or the same rhythm pattern with another text. Although this child was clearly capable of reproducing the rhythm pattern (the phonology of the rhythm pattern), she did not demonstrate a sense of meter for other patterns in duple meter.

On another occasion, a 4-year-old boy became interested in echo-clapping rhythms with the author. Among the duple meter patterns that he echo-clapped were the pair of patterns shown in Figure 5.3, which comprise the song "Up and Down" (notated in Figure 5.1). Although he could clap the individual patterns quite consistently, the boy could not clap the melodic rhythm of the song "Up and Down" consistently with the author. Again, the boy demonstrated a phonological understanding of the rhythm pattern in isolation (synchronically), but he was unable to comprehend the structure of duple meter over time (diachronically).

A 5-year-old girl spontaneously sang the first two phrases of a song to which she only recently had been introduced. The tonal patterns that comprise the two

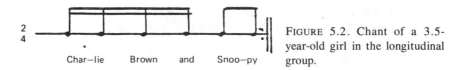

FIGURE 5.2. Chant of a 3.5-year-old girl in the longitudinal group.

FIGURE 5.3. Echo-clapping patterns of a 4-year-old boy comprising the song "Up and Down."

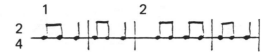

phrases of the song as they had been sung to the children (1) and as she sang them (2) are shown in Figure 5.4. The two renditions of the two phrases have the same melodic contour, but not the same interval content. Although not all of the note-to-note relationships are preserved in the spontaneous performance, it is perhaps most important that both renditions begin and end on the same pitch. In this case the child is demonstrating syntactic knowledge of pitch over a fairly wide (diachronic) time interval.

Creative Music Responses

Many children in both the cross-sectional and longitudinal groups created novel songs. In general, their creative acts were one of two types. The first, and most frequent, creations were modifications of familiar songs. In those creations the child improvised a song based on the melody, rhythm, and text of the familiar song. The second type of creative performances consisted of story-like or conversational texts, sung or intoned with brief melodic formulas in a free rhythmic structure.

A 5-year-old girl in the longitudinal group often created songs of the second type. On one occasion she created a song based on "The Three Bears" story. She was able to recreate that improvisation a second time, more than 2 hours after the first. Many melodic and rhythmic details of the two performances were similar, if not identical. It is unlikely that a theory of musical memory could account for the similarities in the two performances without including a syntactical representation of the musical information in the performances.

A 4-year-old girl became interested in echo-singing tonal patterns with the author while playing outdoors one day. After echoing four or five patterns on a neutral syllable, the patterns shown in Figure 5.5 were performed. She echoed the first pattern confidently, without self-awareness. When pattern 3 was performed by the author, the girl turned away, as if withdrawing from the dialogue, then she responded with pattern 4. Immediately after the performance, she ran

Approximate

FIGURE 5.4. Tonal patterns of a song (1) as sung to a 5-year-old girl in the longitudinal group and (2) as she sang them.

FIGURE 5.5. Echo-singing of tonal patterns by a 4-year-old girl in the longitudinal group and the author.

off and did not respond to any other tonal patterns sung by the author. She apparently was not upset, but somewhat bewildered by what she had performed. This child's creative performance is most interesting because it is limited to isolated (synchronic) tonal patterns. Although it is apparent that she possesses a phonological understanding of the first tonal pattern, she is also capable of restructuring that pattern in a novel way. Thus it is possible to suggest that young children are capable of creating at a level similar to their phonological or syntactic understanding.

Interpretation

It seems reasonable to suggest that three qualitatively different levels of music babble may be identified in the foregoing observations. At the first level of babble, the children perform discrete music elements—a pitch, a tonal pattern, a movement, or a rhythm pattern synchronically in conjunction with an external musical stimulus. Children in this level of development typically do not perform apart from musical stimulation.

At the second level of music babble, children perform combinations of discrete music elements arranged synchronically, but those discrete elements do not give rise to tonal or rhythmic organization. To the adult, those performances lack tonal and rhythm syntax. Children in the second level of music babble are capable of spontaneous performance of music apart from a musical stimulus. The emergence of spontaneous performance can be interpreted as being an objective indication that children are capable of representing musical sounds mentally—the children are beginning to audiate apart from concurrent perception of an external musical stimulus. The quality and quantity of preschool children's spontaneous musical performances may be the best predictor of their concurrent rote singing achievement and their later developmental music aptitude in kindergarten (see Gordon, 1979; Levinowitz, 1985).

At the third level of music babble, children's spontaneous performances become more coherent. Spontaneous performances of familiar songs resemble, but are not identical to, the characteristics of the songs as they had been sung to the children. Children in the third level of music babble also are capable of creating and improvising music apart from concurrent musical stimulation. Spontaneous and creative performances take on tonal and rhythmic syntax, as evidenced by a recurring pitch center and a consistent tempo. Organization of this type exists "across time" diachronically. Tonal and rhythm music syntax begins with the emergence of diachronic organization. When children at the third level of babble listen to or perform music, they are beginning to become aware of relationships among the sounds of the music that have occurred in the immediate past, and are occurring in the present. Young children's music syntax originates in the second and third levels of music babble and becomes more sophisticated through formal music instruction throughout the school years (Gordon, 1984).

That the development of music syntax is more than a function of memory is demonstrated by the organization of children's creative music responses. Although they are novel, and therefore not memorized, these creative responses are only as coherent as the children's rote singing and spontaneous performances. Moreover, because children can create music, it seems reasonable to suggest that music syntax, like language syntax, is a generative capacity.

Conclusions and Implications

There is little doubt that children learn a great deal from informal exposure to, and spontaneous performance of, music. The same can be said of children's exposure to, and spontaneous performance of, language. Chomsky (1975) observed that children's acquisition of linguistic competence is based on extremely little exposure to the "data" of language. One can only speculate about what the young child could learn if he or she were exposed to the "data" of music one half as much as he or she exposed to the "data" of language.

The emergence of the mental representation of musical sounds by young children tends to suggest that, like language, music can be considered to be a "mental organ" that may be studied in the organismic tradition of Chomsky's theoretical linguistics. A formal theory of the human cognitive capacity for music would have far-reaching implications for the cognitive psychology of music and for music education. For example, with an adequate theoretical foundation, it may be possible to explain how the young child represents songs mentally. If Chomsky's rational theory of language is correct, it seems reasonable to suggest that the task of learning the tonal, rhythmic, and linguistic information in a simple rote song cannot be explained easily, and possibly at all, by empiricist theories of learning. Moreover, the belief that laboratory studies of music cognition can explain how children acquire music understanding, or can lead to a valid theory of musical knowledge is increasingly suspect.

For music education, it seems reasonable to suggest that the practice of beginning to expose children to music only when they arrive at kindergarten also is increasingly suspect. The fact that preschool children can profit from informal music instruction may provide impetus for additional research investigations that bear on how and what the preschool child learns by listening to, and performing music. Effective informal exposure to music will be crucial for the future musical development of young children.

Acknowledgments. The observations reported here were made during the years 1980–1982 while the author was a Russell Conwell University Fellow at Temple University. The author wishes to express thanks to the staff, parents, and children of the Temple University Day Care Center for making their contribution to this research. The author also wishes to express thanks to the staff, parents, and children of the Unitarian Cooperative Nursery School for making this research possible.

References

Bernstein, L. (1976). *The unanswered question*. Cambridge, MA: Harvard University Press.

Chomsky, N. (1957). *Syntactic structures*. The Hague: Mouton.

Chomsky, N. (1965). *Aspects of the theory of syntax*. Cambridge, MA: M.I.T. Press.

Chomsky, N. (1975). *Reflections on language*. New York: Pantheon.

Chomsky, N. (1979). *Language and responsibility*. New York: Pantheon.

Chomsky, N. (1980). *Rules and representations*. New York: Columbia University Press.

Gordon, E. (1965). *Musical aptitude profile*. Boston: Houghton Mifflin.

Gordon, E. E. (1979). *Primary measures of music audiation*. Chicago: G.I.A. Publications.

Gordon, E. E. (1984). *Learning sequences in music: Skill, content, and patterns. A music learning theory*. Chicago: G.I.A. Publications.

Hodges, D. A. (Ed.). (1980). *Handbook of music psychology*. Lawrence, KS: National Association of Music Therapy.

Lerdahl, F., & Jackendoff, R. (1983). *A generative theory of tonal music*. Cambridge, MA: M.I.T. Press.

Levinowitz, L. M. (1985). *The comparative effects of two types of song instruction on the development of a sense of tonality in four-year old children*. Unpublished master's thesis, Temple University, Philadelphia, PA.

Moog, H. (1976). *The musical experience of the pre-school child* (C. Clark, trans.). London: Schott.

Moorhead, G. E., & Pond, D. (1978). *Music of young children*. Santa Barbara, CA: Pillsbury Foundation for the Advancement of Music Education.

Shuter-Dyson, R., & Gabriel, C. (1981). *The psychology of musical ability* (2nd ed.). London: Methuen.

6
Children's Rhythmic Development from Age 5 to 7: Performance, Notation, and Reading of Rhythmic Patterns

LYLE DAVIDSON and BERNADETTE COLLEY

Musicians speak about their memory of music in a variety of ways. Some mention the primary importance of their finger memory when learning a piece; some rely more on their visual memory of the printed score; still others suggest that an aural image of the piece guides their performance. The variety of responses to the memory tasks that musicians routinely face suggests that the memory of music takes place in at least three different modalities: sensorimotor, visual, and auditory.

The anecdotes and reports pertaining to musical memory made by mature musicians are useful when investigating musical development because they suggest a range of questions about what may be fruitful avenues of research. For instance, although musicians' memory for music may rely on at least three different modalities, they express music in only two ways: through the performance of a piece or through a notation of a piece. Mature musicians are able to both notate and perform musical events, but to date we have little information about instances of these two forms of expression during childhood.

Related Research

The literature on children's rhythmic development shows that the measurement of rhythmic ability has been influenced by a number of factors. In the broadest sense, there are four issues that these studies address, either singularly or in combination with related issues. Some authors focus on the inherent musical features of specific tasks. Others focus on the differences between types of psychomotor skills assumed to be necessary for musical performance. A third issue of research is the chronological stages of children's mental and physical development as a function of rhythmic perception and performance. Finally, there is some research that examines children's ability to make notations of musical patterns.

Musical Features

There is some controversy as to what constitutes the musical features of rhythm that need to be examined. For instance, some investigators require children to attend to meter and tempo or alternatively to meter or pulse (Foley, 1975; Norton, 1979; Serafine, 1979). Others separate the melodic rhythm from the beat (Thackray, 1972). Gordon's assessment (1980) is based on his own definition of rhythmic structure in which rhythm is delineated into "tempo beats," "meter beats," and "melodic rhythm." For example, in Gordon's system, the melodic rhythm ♫ ♫ ♩ is viewed as being "superimposed" on the meter beats ♫ ♫ ♫, which, in turn, is superimposed on the tempo beats ♩. ♩.. Gordon's departure from the standard time-signature definitions of rhythm, while initially cumbersome, does at least satisfy the need to define rhythmic events as they are heard rather than as they are notated. Central to his argument is that melodies in 3/8, 6/8, and 9/8 are all aurally perceived in the same way, even though their notations differ. He proposes that rhythm should be taught in terms that match our aural perceptions of it, instead of terms like "simple compound" which are visual perceptions dependent on standard musical notation. Gordon's categorization of rhythmic features is based on the perception abilities of 18,000 students in grades 4 through 12. It represents to date the most exhaustive systematic attempt to define and categorize rhythmic features according to their perceived difficulty.

Gordon's taxonomy of rhythmic complexity is founded on a hierarchical classification of various rhythmic patterns that include at least two, but no more than six notes. He establishes groups of patterns that he arranges in levels of difficulty according to their metric features. In addition, each of the basic patterns in the seven difficulty levels is further classified according to sixteenth-note subdivisions and tied elongations, totaling 20 to 35 patterns per level. Patterns range from the simple "usual duple"—♩ ♩, ♫ ♫, ♩ ♫, ♫ ♩—to the complex "unusual unpaired nonmetrical"—♫ ♫ ♪, ♫ ♩ ♩, ♪ ♩ ♫, ♫ ♩ ♪.

Gordon's approach to measuring musical understanding can be considered noncontextual in the sense that rhythmic and melodic patterns are viewed as idiosyncratic and isolated "chunks" of music, rather than as contributing parts of a musical whole such as a phrase or song. The question of whether the mind "chunks" rhythm into small bits warrants further research, but other studies with subjects of all ages do show that the musically untrained tend to hear rhythm in series of patterns, each containing a few sounds, rather than in proportion to a continuous series of equidistant pulses (Bamberger, 1980; Gabrielsson, 1979).

Gordon's taxonomy raises an interesting issue of whether rhythmic complexity in music is determined by the complexities of the symbolic features of the notation itself, or by the difficulty with which those features are perceived by the listener when the notation becomes sound. For example, Gordon classifies ♫ ♩. as easy, but ♩. ♫ as difficult (Gordon, 1980, p. 141), a difference that seems counterintuitive to a reader of music. However, if Gordon's results are applicable to subjects of all ages, and differences in relative difficulty of two items is a result of their aurally perceived difficulty rather than their notational difficulty, then the focus of perception research ought not necessarily to be on notation-based definitions of rhythmic complexity. For example, one research design might be to categorize test items according to the number of attacks in each—four taps versus six taps (Gardner, 1971), or to the total length of time the item requires for completion, regardless of the number of events within that duration (e.g., 5 seconds vs. 10 seconds).

Traditional, notation-based definitions of rhythmic structure may have contributed to a mismeasurement of rhythmic perception. Explaining rhythm in terms of mathemetical proportions may be counterintuitive to the manner in which we actually perceive the phenomena that musicians refer to as beat, pulse, rhythm, meter, and so on. When asked to maintain a steady beat with a given melody, even musically trained children who have reached the age of 11 seem to confuse the beat with patterns of melodic rhythm (Thackray, 1972). Perhaps, then, rhythm perception research would be stronger if it were based on simpler definitions of rhythmic structure.

Types of Skills

A number of researchers have tried to determine the specific skills that were the most appropriate indicators of rhythmic understanding, such as verbal performance, meter recognition, or notational discrimination. Investigators who have measured rhythmic ability with very young children have most often relied on the child's ability to imitate, chant, or recognize simple songs or song fragments. Since preschool-age children find tasks requiring gross motor coordination particularly difficult (Frega, 1979; Gilbert, 1981; Rainbow, 1977), verbalization seems to be a more appropriate measure of rhythmic ability than motor-rhythm tasks. Children, in fact, have demonstrated remarkable accuracy when chanting texts to songs even in complex meters such as 1/8, 5/8, 7/8, and 9/8 (Dittemore, 1970). Teaching even kindergarteners to sing songs in complex meters does not seem to inhibit their performance of songs in simple meters (DeYarman, 1972).

It is possible that the accuracy of performance by children in studies employing song or rhythmic speech may have been due more to memorization of the melodic rhythm as inseparable from its accompanying text than to an accuracy of rhythmic perception. Moog (1976) found that 4- and 5-year-old children responded to a rhythmically spoken text in the same manner as to the same text sung to a melody. When the text was extracted, however, 75% of the 5-year-olds failed to even recognize the rhythm of a familiar song. Given that singing constitutes a major portion of elementary school music instruction, it would be useful to know if the presence of a text continues to influence rhythmic perception beyond the age of 5. If so, is there a certain stage of development in which text no longer influences rhythmic acumen, or at which children can separate textual and rhythmic features? If text presence were found to be a hindrance for certain age groups, tasks would need to be devised that did not rely on memorization or verbalization of song texts.

Gordon (1980) tested his learning sequence of rhythmic patterns by comparing subjects' success on each pattern in three perception skill categories. He hypothesized that patterns that were easiest to hear would also be easiest to perceive aurally, read, and write. The aural perception test required subjects to respond to a same/different task in identifying meters as being either duple or triple. The second skill, reading recognition, was an aural-visual matching task that required subjects to match an aurally presented melodic pattern with its printed notation. The third skill, notational understanding, was measured by having subjects complete the notation of a given pattern by adding note heads, flags, beams, ties, and rests.

Gordon's results did not support the hypothesis that rhythmic task difficulty is consistent across skill-type conditions. Discrepancies often existed between two or more tasks on the difficulty ratings of the same item. For instance, ♩ ♩ and ♩. ♫ were difficult to perceive aurally, but easy to notate. Subjects found ♫♫ and ♫♫ easy to perceive aurally but difficult to identify on the printed page. It is our contention that these discrepancies may have been affected by the amount of training students had received in music notation. Notationally "naive" subjects might be able to hear the difference between ♫♫ and ♫♫ , but would see both notations as "patterns having four sounds," thus being unable to decipher the meaning of the differences in beaming. Furthermore, the applicability of Gordon's findings with fourth- through twelfth-grade subjects to younger subjects awaits investigation.

Mental and Physical Development

Piaget's principle of conservation, that is, the ability to recognize the invariance of one property of an object despite changes in related properties of the same object, has spawned the majority of research that assesses children's understanding of rhythmic concepts (e.g., recognizing that the rhythm of two examples may be the same despite melodic or tonal variations). Properties that have been varied by researchers while keeping rhythm and/or pulse constant have included tonal changes (Foley, 1975; Norton, 1979; Pflederer, 1967), visual score changes (Jones, 1976; Roberts-Gray & Yip, 1977), and changes in violin bowings (Nelson, 1980).

It is difficult to ascertain a clear picture of rhythmic-cognitive development from the body of Piagetian literature. The results are confounded by varying ages of subjects, inconsistencies of definitions of conservation as applied to rhythmic understanding (Pflederer, 1967), and the reliance on "same/different" tasks. Tasks that rely on "same/different" responses to two aurally presented musical examples are measures of musical memory and perception, not necessarily musical understanding. Furthermore, the comparability of musical objects (i.e., a time-ordered punctuated phenomenon such as rhythm) to the visual-physical objects used in the original Piagetian time and speed conservation tasks is questionable.

What is needed to supplement the Piagetian-based literature (Pflederer & Sechrest, 1968) are studies that measure rhythmic understanding in a variety of psychomotor contexts—perception, description, performance, and notation. The reading of symbolic representations, whether they are in standard music notation or a newly invented symbolic form, might contribute considerably to our understanding of cognitive development as it applies to music. A child who can imitate a rhythmic pattern, who can symbolize the same pattern in her or his own way, and moreover, can translate that symbolization into an accurate performance is more fully demonstrating an *understanding* of rhythmic concepts than the child who is asked only to echo-clap, keep a steady beat, distinguish between fast and slow tempi, or tell whether two items are the same or different. Most 5- to 8-year-olds do not have the vocabulary necessary to describe musical events accurately (Van Zee, 1976). It is the responsibility of researchers to develop more child-centered measures, perhaps such as invented notations (Bamberger, 1980), in order that children can convey their comprehension of musical events through a symbolic representation.

Longitudinal studies of children's rhythmic development are scarce. To date, Petzold's (1966) 6-year investigation of children in grades 1 through 6 is the major longitudinal work that examines the stability of children's musical aptitude as they pass through the elementary school years. Since all of Petzold's 500 subjects had received weekly music instruction during the course of the study, we cannot attribute their musical growth purely to cognitive or physical development. However, results of his study show two things: that individuals differ in their aptitude for music even at the age of 6, and that these differences are relatively stable over time. Specifically, periodic testing at 1-year intervals showed significant differences between high and low scorers throughout the 6 years. The children with high or low scores in their initial year of testing usually did not change their position in relation to their peers during subsequent years. Also, the rhythmic accuracy with which all subjects responded to the aural presentation of melodic fragments and maintained a steady tempo provided by a metronome did not change substantially once a child reached the third grade.

Gilbert's (1981) assessment of rhythmic coordination of preschool children revealed a significantly greater rate of improvement between the ages of 3 and 4 than for other years. Based on these two studies alone, it seems possible that there may be stages in child development in which rhythmic coordination develops more rapidly than at other times. The periods between the ages of 3 and 4, and 7 and 9, for example, appear to be times of significant growth. To complete the developmental picture, research dealing with children ages 5 to 7 is needed. A study of children during these years, in addition to adding to our knowledge of rhythmic development, might also shed some light on the influences of a school environment (i.e., formal music instruction, exposure to new types of music, etc.). Furthermore, the beginning of formalized schooling brings with it a plethora of pencil-and-paper tasks devoted to teaching the symbolization of mathematical and linguistic concepts. What does such a major change in the children's daily activities do to their ability to memorize and recall without visual prompts? As children are required to learn the symbolic representation for language, is some other memory capacity sacrificed, or does it fade for a while? Musically, will an ability to remember songs by rote decline as notation is introduced? Will children begin to attend to isolated features of a musical phrase rather than to perceive it as a whole?

Children's Notations

Bamberger (1980, 1982) contends that experience with standard musical notation influences rhythmic perception in that the invented notations of both children and adults show a marked difference between those made by subjects who
are musically trained and those who are not trained. Adults and children without
musical training, she finds, tend to hear rhythm "figurally" (i.e., in idiosyncratic
"chunks"). Those exposed to standard music notation, on the other hand, depict
rhythm "formally" (i.e., with symbols that depict a traditional view of rhythm
as having a constant recurring pulse over which other events are proportioned).
Bamberger reports to have found notationally naive children who invent surprisingly sophisticated notations. Igaga and Versey (1977) and Walker (1981)
have measured rhythmic understanding through subjects' notations by requiring
subjects to use a symbolic system that they assume to be representative of the
musical event, and easier to understand than standard music notation. The
technique used by these authors (i.e., depicting duration with long and short
dashes) is also suggested by practitioners for introducing children to rhythmic
notation (Osborn 1966; Stone, 1976). However, whether these "representative
symbols" make more sense to children than other forms of notation remains an
empirical question.

Summary

Each of these areas of study provides a portion of our understanding of the
development of children's rhythmic comprehension. On the basis of these studies
we do know that the features of rhythm can be delineated into measurable factors,
that differences in performance modes yield different results in ability levels, that
periods of rhythmic development feature different rates of growth, and that musically untrained subjects can show rather sophisticated musical understanding
through their invented notations. While these studies contribute much to our
knowledge of children's appreciation of rhythm, the picture remains somewhat
fragmented for many reasons.

That investigators have chosen to focus on either rhythmic production or
rhythmic perception may be an important reason for the fragmented state of our
knowledge of rhythmic development. The separation of the two abilities in terms
of research design in addition to differences in the ages of the subjects, types of
physical skills required to perform the test tasks, and the musical features of the
tasks themselves remain a hindrance to a fuller understanding of children's
appreciation of rhythm. On the basis of the foregoing review, four major issues
were raised that we felt warranted examination, and that could be usefully
brought together in one study.

First, we sought to find out whether the inherent contextual features of a rhythmic example played a role in children's performance and perception of it. In other
words, would items having certain features be easier or more difficult than those
which did not? Three contextual questions were posed:

1. What effect would the presence of a text have on performance and perception after the age of 5?
2. What effect would the total length of an item have on children's ability to remember it?
3. How would the rhythmic complexity of a task affect the children's ability to perceive and perform the task?

Second, we wanted to test Gordon's findings of discrepancies between skill types on identical items, and we wanted to make comparisons between perception tasks and performance tasks.

Third, we wanted to determing whether Petzold's findings regarding the stability of subjects' rank in relation to their peers in grades 1 through 6 was also true for students in kindergarten, first, and second grade. Would the transitional time during which children's environment is changing from the concrete to the symbolic also affect their perception and performance of music? Also, would any of these three years be a period of more rapid growth than the others?

Finally, we wanted to expand Bamberger's investigation of the degree to which children's invented notations could reliably stand as an indication of their understanding of rhythmic concepts. We wanted to find out the extent to which the notations depicted features of the musical events, and moreover, whether the children could use their notations as symbolic aids for performance.

Method

Subjects

The children of this study were enrolled in elementary schools in Cambridge, Massachusetts. They came from working and middle-class backgrounds. None were being especially trained in music, although some did start instrumental lessons during the three years in which the study was conducted. They had reached the age of 5 years before the first round of data collection, 6 years before the second round, and 7 years before the third round. Fifty-one children were tested during the first year of the study. Due to attrition, 46 children remained for the second year, and 39 children remained for the third year.

Procedure

Data were collected during a 4-week period in the spring of each of the three years of testing. The experimenter met the children individually in an area of the school separated from the child's regular classroom. The experimenter sat close enough to the subject to record the child's performance, while observing his or her written and kinesthetic response to the tasks. Each child was visited twice by the researcher with an average of 2 weeks elapsing between each visit. One session was devoted to testing the children's performance and perception of rhythmic domain patterns, and the other to testing the children's performance and perception of one familiar song and one newly learned song. Sessions were not allowed to last more than 20 minutes.

The materials for the tasks were simple. Two cassette tape recorders were used, one to play the prerecorded musical examples, and one to record the child's performances. For notating their responses, the children were each given a 12″ × 18″ piece of white construction paper and a choice of colored felt-tipped markers. The music for the first session consisted of four clapped rhythmic domain patterns that were derived from the song, "Row, Row, Row Your Boat." The second session used the songs "Row, Row, Row Your Boat" and "Hop, Hop, Hop" as test tasks.

There were several steps to each session. In the first session, to introduce the child to the scope of the task, the taped performance of all four clapped items was played (Figure 6.1). After the child had heard all the items, he or she was asked to recall each item after it was played a second time. This time, the child was asked to clap the pattern for the experimenter exactly as he or she had heard it. In order to get the child's best performance, a pattern was repeated, if necessary, but not more than three times. After the child had recalled each of the four items, he or she was asked to perform it a third time.

This time after each performance, the child was asked to notate it on the construction paper. During the third step, making the notation, the children were allowed as much time as they needed to write the notations in their "music book." The experimenter introduced the task by asking the children to "write the clapping down on your paper so that someone else could clap it back just by looking at what you've written," or "so that you could clap it back if you looked at it next week." The children were told that they could write anything they wished ("marks, words, pictures, lines, notes, shapes") to help them remember the sound of the clapping. They were asked to clap back each of the items immediately after they had completed their notation of it.

Finally, after all the patterns had been notated, each child was asked to "read" their notation (i.e., perform from their invented notations). The experimenter explained to the children that he wanted to "see if their music book really

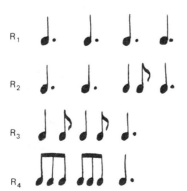

FIGURE 6.1. Domain patterns.

FIGURE 6.2. Song patterns.

worked." The responses to this performance were labeled "decodes." After all four items had been notated and decoded in their original order, the experimenter asked each child to read back his or her notation, this time randomizing the order of the patterns. The randomized decoding performance was included to determine whether or not the child could successfully read his or her own notation. At the end of the session, the experimenter asked each subject to explain how his or her notation was an aid in remembering the musical event (i.e., "to explain how the music book works").

The second session with each subject was devoted to assessing the child's ability to recall, notate, and decode phrases of the familiar song "Row, Row, Row Your Boat." In the second and third years of testing, an unfamiliar song "Hop, Hop, Hop" was also introduced to balance the effect that previous knowledge of a song may have had on both performance and memory (Figure 6.2). The experimenter began the session by asking the subject to listen to the entire song. The child was then asked to sing the song back to the experimenter exactly as it was heard on the tape, and then to write the song down in a music book, as had been done in the previous session. After the notation was completed, the

Item	Number of pulses	Number of surface attacks	Complexity score	Complexity type
 R₁	4	4	0	Simple
 H₁	3	3	0	Simple
S₂	4	5	1	Simple
 H₃	3	5	2	Simple
 R₃	3	5	2	Simple
 R₄	3	7	4	Complex
 S₄	4	12	8	Complex

FIGURE 6.3. Complexity and length.

researcher asked the subject to sing the entire song back to him, using the notation as a guide. He pointed to various segments of the notation that he had observed the child make in correspondence to individual phrases, and asked the child to sing back only those segments of the song.

In this report, we were interested in the children's responses to the conventional first and third phrases of the familiar song (S_2, S_4) and the first and third phrases of the unfamiliar song (H_1, H_3). These phrases, combined with selected patterns from the first session, produced a total of seven rhythmic items (see Table 6.1) to be used for analysis, four from the songs and three from the domain patterns.

Analysis of Data

Analysis of children's rhythmic ability was based on three skills: recall, notation, and decode. Within each skill, the seven rhythmic patterns were classified according to the presence or absence of a text, the item's complexity, and the item's length.

Musical Features

The *text presence* classification was used to distinguish those items which were presented with an accompanying text from those which were not. Therefore, patterns R_1, R_3, and R_4 were classified as *no text* items. Patterns S_2, S_4, H_1, and H_3 were classified as *text* items.

A *complexity* score was calculated for each rhythmic pattern. Complexity scores were derived by subtracting the number of pulses (or metrical stresses) in a pattern from the total number of surface events. For example, pattern R_1 was given a complexity score of zero (0) because its pulse and surface are identical and coincidental. Pattern S_4 was given a complexity score of eight (8), and consequently considered a more difficult pattern than R_1 because it contains 12 surface events that are divided among four pulses (Figure 6.3). Patterns having a rhythmic complexity of 5 or less (R_1, H_1, S_2, H_3, R_3) were classified as *simple*, and those having a rhythmic complexity of greater than 5 (R_4, S_4) were classified as *complex*.

The *length* of each pattern was determined by the total number of pulses it took to complete the pattern. Rests falling on a final beat were not counted as constituting a pulse, since children were asked to perform the song one phrase at a time, making it impossible to determine whether the rest had been performed. Hence, items R_3, R_4, H_1, and H_3 were considered *short* (i.g., having pulse lengths of 3. Items R_1, S_2, and S_4 were considered *long* (i.e., having pulse lengths of 4).

Skills

Each child received scores in each of the three skill types: recall, decode, and notation ability. The scores reflected the degree to which the subject's response matched the model target.

The recall and decode scores ranged from 0 to 3, according to the degree to which the subject accurately performed pulse and/or surface rhythm. A score of 0 indicated that the subject responded with neither accurate pulse nor surface. A score of 1 was given to children who demonstrated accurate pulse, but inaccurate surface. Children who clapped or sang the correct number of surface attacks but did not maintain a steady pulse were given a score of 2. Children who performed with both accurate pulse and surface were given a score of 3.

The notation score for each subject ranged from 0 to 1, based on the percentage of pulse and/or surface events that appeared in the child's invented notation. A high degree of accuracy was defined as having notated more than two thirds (66%) of the number of pulses and/or more than two thirds (66%) of the total number of surface attacks. Figure 6.4 gives an example of three notations and their scores.

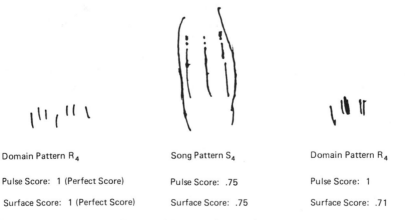

Domain Pattern R_4

Pulse Score: 1 (Perfect Score)

Surface Score: 1 (Perfect Score)

Song Pattern S_4

Pulse Score: .75

Surface Score: .75

Domain Pattern R_4

Pulse Score: 1

Surface Score: .71

FIGURE 6.4. Notation scoring.

Our expectations were that items having a text would present less difficulty than items without a text, and that simple items and shorter items would be easier for children to recall, notate, and decode than complex and longer items. First, the children's scores were calculated for each of the skills (recall, notation, and decode) for all three years. Chi-square tests of independence determined the relationship between ability and musical features on three skills in three conditions: presence of text, complexity of item, and length of item. The analyses were based on the numbers of "perfect-scoring" versus "non-perfect scoring" and "high-scoring" versus "low-scoring" children in each category. Perfect scorers were those children who demonstrated 100% accuracy of pulse and surface dimensions (i.e., children who received recall and decode scores of 3 and notation scores of 1). High scorers were those children who demonstrated either accurate surface rhythm or accurate pulse and surface rhythms (i.e., children who received scores of 2 or 3 in recall and decode, and scores greater than 67% in notation). All other children were considered "low scorers." The comparisons were separated into three conditions for each skill type and two levels of assumed difficulty for each condition.

Second, chi-square tests of independence were used to analyze the relationship between skills (i.e., notation with recall, and notation with decode). Third, the scores were compared on the basis of single items and skill types across years, by computing the percentage of high-scoring subjects for each item in each year. Fourth, stability of the group's rhythmic ability was assessed across years by comparing the numbers of subjects who received high or perfect scores under each condition for all three years.

Results

Analysis by Musical Features

RECALL SCORES

Table 6.1 shows the results of children's recall ability under all conditions for all three years. Recall ability among the 5-year-olds was dependent on each of the three conditions: presence of text ($p < .05$), rhythmic complexity ($p < .01$), and item length ($p < .05$). Specifically, items with text were easier to recall than items without text, simple items were easier than complex items, and longer items were easier than shorter items. The children who achieved high scores at the age of 5 achieved them in all issues in recall. However, at the age of 6, none of these conditions differentiated among the children. By the time children had reached the age of 7, their recall ability was dependent only on the length of an item ($p < .01$); that is, longer items remained easier than shorter items.

NOTATION SCORES

Results of the children's notation ability were first analyzed separately on the basis of their attentiveness to pulse and surface under the three conditions of text,

TABLE 6.1. Chi-square test for independence of item difficulty—recall

	Round 1			Round 2			Round 3		
	$N=51$, df=1	χ^2	ϕ	$N=46$, df=1	χ^2	ϕ	$N=39$, df=1	χ^2	ϕ
High scorers									
Text presence, (text×no text)	$p<.01$	11.9	.5	ns*			ns		
Complexity, (simple× complex)	$p<.01$	10.1	.4	ns			ns		
Length, (long×short)	$p<.05$	5.0	.3	ns			$p<.01$	6.7	.4
Perfect scorers									
Text presence, (text×no text)	ns			ns			ns		
Complexity, (simple× complex)	ns			ns			ns		
Length, (long×short)	ns			ns			ns		

*ns: not significant.

complexity, and length. Table 6.2 shows the notation by condition results for all three years. A significant relationship was found for all years ($p < .01, p < .05$, $p < .05$) between an item's rhythmic complexity and the accuracy of children's notation of its pulse rhythm. However, the direction of the relationship was not consistent for all three years. For the first two years, the children failed to notate the pulse of either simple or complex items. By the third year, children could notate the pulse of both the simple and the complex items. By the third year of testing, a significant relationship existed between the accuracy of children's notation of surface rhythm and three factors: the presence of a text ($p < .05$), the item's rhythmic complexity ($p < .01$), and the item's length ($p < .05$). Children could notate the surface rhythm of items with and without text, and of simple and complex items. The children who were unable to notate long items also failed to notate short items.

After the pulse and surface notation scores had been combined into one notation score (i.e., a high pulse *or* high surface notation score), chi-square tests of independence were performed on the basis of the three conditions. Table 6.3 shows the combined notation scores. A dependent relationship was found for the 5-year-old children under conditions of text presence ($p < .01$), complexity ($p < .05$), and length ($p < .01$). This was caused by their inability to notate either the pulse or the surface pattern of the items. No significant effect occurred in the second year. Significant effects were found for 7-year-olds between complex and simple items ($p < .05$) and long and short items ($p < .05$) for those achieving high scores.

TABLE 6.2. Chi-square test for independence of item difficulty—pulse and surface notation

	Round 1			Round 2			Round 3		
	$N=51$, df$=1$	χ^2	ϕ	$N=46$, df$=1$	χ^2	ϕ	$N=39$, df$=1$	χ^2	ϕ
Pulse notation									
High scorers									
Text	ns*			ns			ns		
Complexity	$p<.01$	1.4	.5	$p<.05$	4.7	.32	$p<.05$	5.8	.39
Length	ns			ns			ns		
Perfect scorers									
Text	ns			ns			ns		
Complexity	ns			$p<.05$	6.9	.39	ns		
Length	ns			ns			ns		
Surface notation									
High scorers									
Text	ns			ns			$p<.05$	5.1	.36
Complexity	ns			$p<.01$	7.2	.39	$p<.01$	9.6	.5
Length	ns			ns			$p<.05$	6.6	.41
Perfect scorers									
Text	ns			ns			$p<.01$	6.7	.41
Complexity	ns			$p<.01$	13.0	.54	ns		
Length	ns			$p<.05$	4.0	.3	$p<.01$	9.1	.48

*ns: not significant.

TABLE 6.3. Chi-square test for independence of item difficulty—collapsed pulse/surface scores

	Round 1			Round 2			Round 3		
Collapsed notation	$N=51$, df$=1$	χ^2	ϕ	$N=46$, df$=1$	χ^2	ϕ	$N=39$, df$=1$	χ^2	ϕ
High scorers									
Text	$p<.01$	12.0	.49	ns			ns		
Complexity	$p<.05$	5.5	.33	ns			$p<.05$	4.1	.33
Length	$p<.01$	12.0	.49	ns			$p<.05$	4.4	.33
Perfect scorers									
Text	ns			ns			$p<.05$	4.4	.33
Complexity	ns			$p<.01$	19.9	.66	ns		
Length	ns			ns			$p<.05$	4.7	.35

*ns: not significant.

TABLE 6.4. Chi-square test for independence of item difficulty—decode

	Round 1			Round 2			Round 3		
	$N=51$, df$=1$	χ^2	ϕ	$N=46$, df$=1$	χ^2	ϕ	$N=39$, df$=1$	χ^2	ϕ
High scorers									
Text presence, (text×no text)	$p<.05$	4.	.28	ns*			ns		
Complexity, (simple× complex)	$p<.01$	10.4	.45	ns			ns		
Length, (long×short)	ns			ns			ns		
Perfect scorers									
Text presence, (text×no text)	ns			ns			ns		
Complexity, (simple× complex)	ns			ns			ns		
Length (long×short)	ns			ns			ns		

*ns: not significant.

DECODE SCORES

Table 6.4 shows the results of the comparisons of conditions based on children's decoding ability. A significant number of 5-year-olds were unable to accurately decode items classified in either the condition of text presence ($p < .05$) or complexity ($p < .01$).

Analysis Between Skills

To determine whether a dependent relationship existed between notation and the other types of skills, the collapsed notation scores were compared with the recall and decode scores.

NOTATION WITH RECALL

Table 6.5 shows the results of comparisons between notation sophistication and recall ability in each of the conditions. When all items were combined, the relationship between recall ability and notational sophistication was significant for year 1 ($p < .05$) and year 3 ($p < .01$). The children who could notate items could also recall them. The relationship between these two skills was also found to be significant when measured on the basis of simple items for the first year, while for the second year both conditions of text and shorter and more complex items were found to be significant.

TABLE 6.5. Chi-square test for independence of skills ability—notation × recall

Recall	Round 1 $N=51$, df=1	χ^2	ϕ	Round 2 $N=46$, df=1	χ^2	ϕ	Round 3 $N=39$, df=1	χ^2	ϕ
All items	$p<.05$	3.9	.3	ns			$p<.01$	7.7	.45
Text	ns*			$p<.01$	6.7	.38	ns		
No text	ns			$p<.01$	8.5	.43	ns		
Simple	$p<.05$	4.0	.28	ns			ns		
Complex	ns			$p<.05$	4.9	.34	$p<.01$	11.0	.47
Long	ns			ns			ns		
Short	ns			$p<.01$	10.1	.47	$p<.05$	4.5	.34

*ns: not significant.

NOTATION WITH DECODE

Comparison between children's decoding skills and the degree of their notation sophistication shows less of a relationship than do comparisons with their recall skills. None of the decode comparisons was consistent for more than 1 year on any measure, nor for more than one measure in any single year (Table 6.6).

Analysis of Items by Age and Skill

In order to ascertain the relative difficulty of a specific item in each age group, the number of children who achieved high scores on each skill was converted into a percentage of the total sample. Table 6.7 shows the percentages of children receiving high scores on five items for each skill type for three years of testing. Pulse and surface notation percentages for item R_1 are not given since nearly all of the children achieved nearly 100% accuracy during all three years. Table 6.7 is depicted in graph form in Figures 6.5 through 6.8.

TABLE 6.6. Chi-square test for independence of skill ability—notation × decode

Decode	Round 1 $N=51$, df=1	χ^2	ϕ	Round 2 $N=46$, df=1	χ^2	ϕ	Round 3 $N=39$, df=1	χ^2	ϕ
All items	$p<.05$	4.9	.31	ns			ns		
Text	ns*			ns			ns		
No text	$p<.01$	7.0	.39	ns			ns		
Simple	ns			ns			ns		
Complex	ns			$p<.01$	7.9	.4	ns		
Long	ns			ns			ns		
Short	$p<.01$	7.0	.39	ns			ns		

*ns: not significant.

TABLE 6.7. Percentage of subjects receiving high scores

Item	R_1			R_3			R_4			S_4			S_4		
Year	1	2	3	1	2	3	1	2	3	1	2	3	1	2	3
N	51	46	39	51	46	39	51	46	39	51	46	39	51	46	39
Recall	.84	.78	.89	.66	.67	.98	.14	.24	.75	.62	.74	.93	.72	.80	.80
Decode	.40	.52	.59	.24	.37	.47	.16	.11	.38	.40	.37	.88	.28	.37	.52
Notation pulse	—	—	—	.18	.27	.49	.15	.25	.47	.23	.35	.19	.20	.39	.39
Notation surface	—	—	—	.23	.47	.70	.21	.36	.49	.15	.39	.70	.00	.14	.18

RECALL

In recall comparisons there was an increase in the numbers of high scorers during the three years. On all of the items except for R_1, more 6-year-old children recalled items accurately than did 5-year-old children. By the time the population had reached age 7 a larger percentage of children approached mastery than had done so the previous year.

The most dramatic increase in recall accuracy occurred between the ages of 6 and 7 with the exception of item S_4 ("Merrily, merrily, merrily, merrily"), which appeared to be as difficult at age 7 as it had been a year earlier. The most difficult item to recall accurately was item R_4, particularly for the 5- and 6-year-olds.

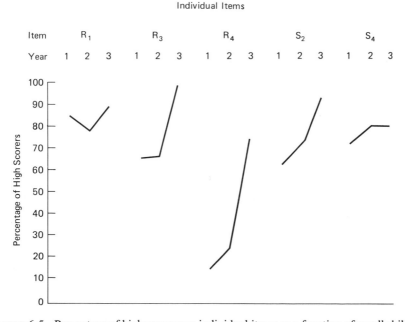

FIGURE 6.5. Percentage of high scorers on individual items as a function of recall ability.

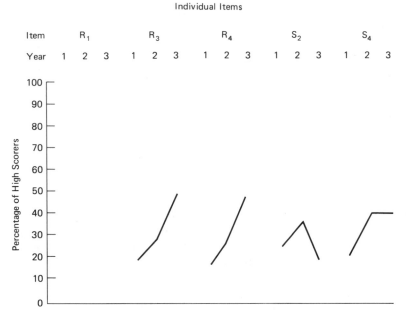

FIGURE 6.6. Percentage of high scorers on individual items as a function of pulse notation.

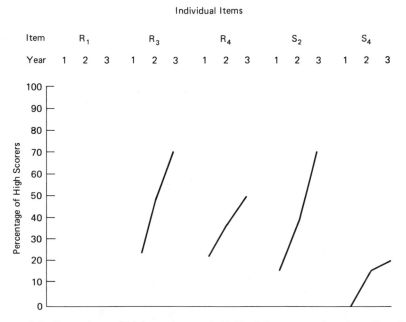

FIGURE 6.7. Percentage of high scorers on individual items as a function of surface notation.

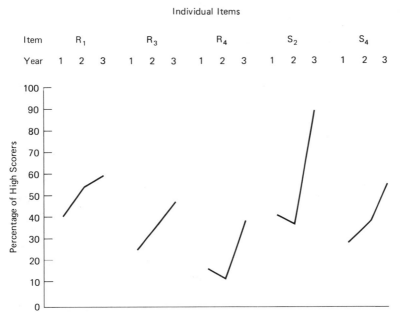

FIGURE 6.8. Percentage of high scorers on individual items as a function of decode ability.

NOTATION

There was a general increase in the accuracy with which children notated pulse events as they matured. This was especially true for the items without text. The sharp decline in "pulse attenders" for item S_2 may indicate either a shift in attentiveness from pulse to surface, or a more accurate attentiveness to surface in general. Many children omitted one of the "Row's" in "Row, Row, Row Your Boat" during the first round of testing. Since this item had four pulse events and five surface events, it was difficult to be certain whether notations having four marks on the page were indicative of surface attentiveness or pulse attentiveness.

Except for items S_2 and S_4, the notation of pulse and surface events was nearly parallel from year to year. For item S_4, the percentage of children attending to pulse was 20 points higher than those attending to surface up through the age of 6. By the age of 7, however, the gap between "pulse attenders" and "surface attenders" on phrase S_4 had narrowed.

While the number of children achieving high scores increased on all measures, the most striking skill development occurring during the three years appears to be children's ability to accurately depict surface rhythms through their invented notations.

DECODE

Comparing the decoding scores across years shows a less conclusive picture than do the notation scores. There was a steady increase from year 1 to year 3 on three of the items. The scores for items R_4 and S_2 dropped during the second year and then increased significantly during the third year.

Stability of Skills Across Years

Figures 6.9, 6.10, and 6.11 show the percentages of high-scoring subjects in each year and under each condition. On the basis of the number of high-scoring subjects, notational sophistication appears to be a more reliable indicator of pulse or surface perception than either recall or decode skill. Under all conditions, there was a steady increase in notational accuracy within the sample population from year 1 to year 3.

To examine the stability of scores within the high-scoring group of children, the number who maintained high or perfect scores for all three years was calculated. The change in the total number of subjects in years 2 and 3 reflects the attrition rate during the course of the study. A comparison of stability in terms of skill type is shown in Table 6.8. These figures reflect the average number of high scorers and perfect scorers who maintained their level of ability for a 3-year period. This assessment shows that the predictability of children's standing in relation to their peers from year to year is stronger for responses in which children are asked to recall and imitate rhythms than for those that require them to notate the same rhythms. As a group, the children were much more stable in the recall condition than in either notation or decode.

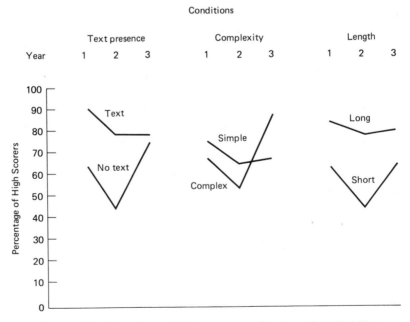

FIGURE 6.9. Percentage of high scorers as a function of recall ability.

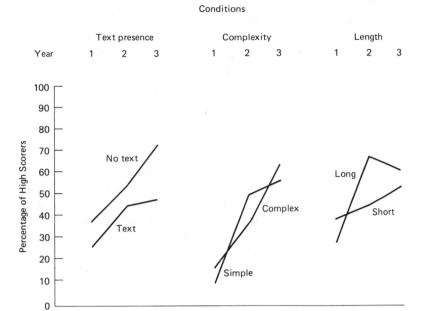

FIGURE 6.10. Percentage of high scorers as a function of notation ability.

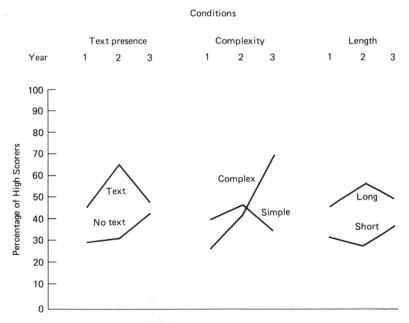

FIGURE 6.11. Percentage of high scorers as a function of decode ability.

TABLE 6.8. Mean numbers of subjects maintaining high scores and perfect scores for three years

	Recall $(n=39)$	Decode $(n=39)$	Notation $(N=39)$
High scorers	17.10	4.80	2.16
Perfect scorers	8.00	0.16	0.83

RECALL

Table 6.9 gives the number of children receiving high recall scores and perfect recall scores in all conditions for all three years. The ability to recall items with 100% accuracy consistently for all three years appears to have been less difficult for items having an accompanying text, a simple rhythmic structure, and a length of four pulses than for items having the alternate conditions. However, the percentage of high scorers who achieved 100% recall accuracy increased dramatically for the alternate conditions (no text, complex structure, and short items) between the ages of 6 and 7.

NOTATION

The cross-year stability of children's notation skills is shown in Table 6.10. A consistent annual increase in the number of children who accurately depicted pulse and surface rhythms was evident for those items that do not have an accompanying text as well as those items having a complex rhythmic structure. In addition, there was a noticeable shift in attentiveness from pulse to surface rhythm on

TABLE 6.9. Stability across years—recall

	Year 1 $(n=39)$	Year 2 $(n=39)$	Year 3 $(N=39)$	All years
No text	26*	20	29	14
	6**	6	27	1
Text	36	34	30	22
	26	24	24	16
Complex	27	22	34	18
	6	9	28	1
Simple	30	29	26	15
	20	21	23	12
Short	32	19	25	11
	7	5	23	2
Long	34	33	31	23
	25	26	27	16

*Indicates number of higher scorers.
**Indicates number of perfect scorers included in high-scorer total.

TABLE 6.10. Stability across years—notation

	Year 1 (n=39)	Year 2 (n=39)	Year 3 (N=39)	All years
No text				
Pulse	6*	11	18	2
	4**	6	15	1
Surface	10	16	20	6
	7	15	18	4
Text				
Pulse	11	18	5	1
	3	4	1	0
Surface	4	10	13	1
	0	5	5	0
Complex				
Pulse	5	12	14	0
	2	4	10	0
Surface	1	6	11	1
	0	3	6	0
Simple				
Pulse	4	13	3	0
	4	4	1	0
Surface	7	15	20	4
	3	9	15	2
Short				
Pulse	6	10	6	1
	4	3	4	1
Surface	10	15	16	6
	7	11	12	2
Long				
Pulse	11	23	9	3
	3	8	6	0
Surface	4	11	15	1
	0	5	6	0

*Indicates number of high scorers.
**Indicates number of perfect scorers included in high-scorer total.

items that do have an accompanying text, as well as on those items that have a simple rhythmic structure.

DECODE

Table 6.11 shows the stability of decoding skills for all three years. Considering the small numbers of subjects who were consistent in their decoding ability over a 3-year period, the children appear to have been relatively unstable on this skill. Nevertheless, there was a substantial increase in the number of children who could accurately decode their notations of complex rhythmic items from year 2 ($n=2$) to year 3 ($n=16$). On the other five measures, the number of children with strong decoding skills increased only somewhat from year 1 to year 3.

TABLE 6.11. Stability across years—decode

	Year 1 (n=39)	Year 2 (n=39)	Year 3 (N=39)	All years
No text	11*	12	16	4
	3**	7	3	0
Text	18	27	18	9
	7	1	8	0
Complex	10	15	27	4
	3	2	16	1
Simple	16	19	13	4
	3	5	5	0
Short	12	11	14	2
	7	0	7	0
Long	18	23	19	6
	6	6	7	0

*Indicates number of high scorers.
**Indicates number of perfect scorers included in high-scorer total.

Discussion

There were four central issues that this study sought to investigate. First, we wanted to consider the role that contextual musical features might play in children's production, notation, and reading of rhythms. Second, we wanted to test Gordon's (1980) finding that differences exist between items across different skills or modes of response. Third, we wanted to look at the development of rhythmic ability of children as they pass from kindergarten into the early years of school. Finally, we wanted to compare the rhythmic knowledge that children demonstrated in their notation to that demonstrated in their performance. For summative purposes, important developmental findings are discussed as they relate to the musical features of tasks, the types of skills used in this study, and children's notations.

Musical Features

We were interested in the effect that three features of the rhythmic examples had on the children's responses: the effect of text, the effect of complexity, and the effect of length. Each feature was subdivided into two levels of hypothesized difficulty.

TEXT

The presence of text plays a strong role in the responses of 5- and 6-year-olds, but not in those of the 7-year-olds. Older children were better able to separate a text from its rhythm than the younger children. The results confirm Moog's (1976) finding in that, through the age of 6, when children are given rhythmic tasks that involve a rhythmically spoken or sung text, they have great difficulty separating the text from its musical setting, or vice versa.

The nature of the text itself may play a role in the ability to recall rhythms accurately. For example, 93% of the 7-year-olds accurately recalled phrase S_2 ("Row, row, row your boat") while only 80% recalled S_4 ("Merrily, merrily, merrily, merrily"). The most typical recall error for S_2 for 5-year-olds was to shorten the text to "Row, row your boat." By the age of 7 more children accurately recalled S_2, but still shortened the length of S_4 to "Merrily, merrily, merrily." The differences in recall skills on these two items may be due either to the semantic differences in the two phrases, or to the repetition of a multisyllabled word in S_4 that the children may have found confusing, even though most of the children knew the song.

The differences in subjects' surface notations of these two items is more marked. The accuracy of children's notation of five syllables distributed over four pulses (S_2) grew substantially from age 5 (15%) to age 7 (70%), but notation of 12 syllables within four pulses (S_4) was still considerably more difficult than five syllables for even the 7-year-olds (18%).

Items without a text were notated more accurately than those with a text, when the aggregated scores of text and no-text items were compared. This finding, however, is confounded by the substantial number of children who notated the song phrases by writing the words, thus making the scoring of the rhythmic features depicted in the notations difficult. In contrast to notating, the decoding of items with a text was easier than without a text for 5- and 6-year-olds. The differences diminished considerably as children reached the age of 7. This could certainly have been due to the knowledge of the song that children brought to the task. Since we did not systematically test for the effect of familiarity of a song on decoding ability, we cannot say whether the difference is a function of decoding skills or memory of the song. However, since as they matured more children used the words of the song in their notations, more of their decodes consisted of linguistic rather than musical features. That is, the younger children perhaps relied more on their memory of the song while "reading" their notations, whereas more of the older children "read" the words of their notations, causing the rhythmic performance to be less accurate.

Text influence, then, appears to be a function not only of the absence or presence of a text in a rhythmic task, but also of the rhythmic syllabification of the entire phrase, and perhaps even of the individual word (e.g., "merrily"). Further studies are needed to determine the features of words, phrases, and texts that might inhibit or enhance rhythmic perception. Researchers and teachers might test these effects by presenting children with rhythmic speaking tasks that require children to chant both a series of nonsensical (but enjoyable) phrases and those with semantic referents to determine whether the semantic component interferes with the musical features in the mind of the child. If semantic richness were found to play an adverse role in affecting children's attentiveness to musical features of a song, the popular practice of song-singing for the purposes of teaching musical concepts might warrant reevaluation.

COMPLEXITY

Measuring the complexity of rhythm items by subtracting the number of pulses from the number of surface events proved to be a useful means for explaining differences in children's performances in this study. The most complex items were those in which there was a large difference between the number of accented events (pulses) and the total number of events in the pattern (surface), whereas the least complex were those that had smaller differences between the pulse and the surface events.

The simple-complex dichotomy was found to be useful in assessing rhythmic development when children are expected to simply recall rhythmic patterns or song phrases. The 5-year-olds had the most difficulty with those items labeled "complex" by this definition. By the time they were 7 years old, however, the complex items no longer were challenging. When rhythmic development is assessed through invented notations, the improvement rate in notation sophistication is roughly the same for simple and complex items. That children attend to the number of events in their visual depictions of rhythm, be it the total number or the number of accented events, is apparent. Whether this attentiveness to numerosity is a function of environmental influences of newly learned concepts in mathematics or of rhythmic-cognitive development awaits further study. In terms of decoding of notations, the simple-complex dichotomy does not appear to be a useful tool for analyzing rhythmic features until children have reached the age of 7.

Unfortunately, there were only two complex items in this study, one with a text, and the other without. While the interaction with the text–no-text condition is possible, it is at least clear from the results of the single-item analysis that a rhythmic pattern having seven surface events proportioned over three pulses (R_4), without the aid of an accompanying text, is quite difficult for children under the age of 7. Furthermore, when one considers the improvement in decoding ability on this item (R_4), it is likely that the children's invented notations acted as a symbolic aid. That 7-year-olds found symbolic representation to be an aid to memory on this task suggests a developmental shift between ages 6 and 7 after which memory alone no longer suffices for decoding a rhythmically complex task. Before this conclusion can be confirmed, it will be necessary to test children's ability on items like R_4 with and without an accompanying text.

LENGTH

The grouping of the items by number of pulses proved not to be as useful as the categorizations by text or complexity. The findings were counterintuitive in that, under all skill conditions and for each year, children found longer items easier to recall, notate, and decode than shorter items. One explanation for this might be that the total duration of an item may not be as important as the relative complexity of an item. Another might be that the difference between a three- and four-pulse item is too slight to affect significant differences in performance or perception. Furthermore, the obvious effects shown by the results of the comparisons along text and complexity conditions indicate that these features were more salient in producing differences across all conditions than was the total duration of the items.

Skill Differences

RECALL AND DECODE

As was expected, recall of a rhythmic pattern was found to be an easier skill for children through the age of 7 than decoding of the same pattern. The exception to this trend for decoding scores, on item S_2, is most likely due to the phrase being the first in the song. Therefore, we attribute the "decoding" improvement on this item more to memory than to actual encoding of symbols. The number of children receiving high recall scores increased steadily with each year on every item, except for item S_4 ("Merrily, merrily, merrily, merrily"), which reached a plateau during the second year of testing.

A breakdown of "high scorers" into "pulse" or "pulse and surface" attenders showed that children may shift their attention from pulse events (accented beats) to surface events at different ages before ultimately becoming able to attend to two rhythmic features simultaneously. For example, on item R_4, 28% of the 5-year-olds attended accurately to its pulse, 53% to its surface, and only 14% to both. One year later, 20% more recalled the item with accurate pulse, 25% fewer with accurate surface, and 10% more did both. By the time the group had reached the age of 7, 75% recalled R_4 with both accurate pulse and surface.

Comparisons of recall or decode scores with children's notations were problematic in that scoring equivalencies between a temporally bound performance and a static visual representation was impossible. For the recall and decode tasks, the pulse and surface distinction was a measure of accuracy in the child's motor-rhythmic coordination over time (pulse), the accuracy of the number of events reproduced (surface), and the combination of the two (perfect score). On the other hand, "accuracy" in notation, by necessity, could only depend upon the number of, and visual differentiation between, marks on the page. When scoring, we were not willing to make interpretations of proportional spatial placement unless it was undoubtedly clear through questioning that the child had systematically and consciously made a decision to make the distinction, and had used such a strategy consistently. The notation scores were therefore interpreted as a reflection of the child's attentiveness to volume and numerosity as visual equivalents of pulse and melodic rhythm, respectively. As such, they are useful means of assessing rhythmic development in children ages 5 to 7, and we recommend that researchers interested in children's cognitive rhythmic development give children's invented notations further attention.

NOTATION

The results of our study suggest that, when notation is used as a measure of rhythmic perception, surface attentiveness is more salient than pulse attentiveness for monitoring rhythmic development. If surface accuracy were to be used as a testing measure, however, it would be imperative that test items include patterns that use the same number of events, but each proportioned over a different number of pulses, or perhaps over the same number of pulses in different ways (e.g., items R_3 and S_2). The results from this study show that, regardless of text influence, children's accuracy of rhythmic perception decreases as the number of surface events increases.

The case for surface attentiveness as an indicator of rhythmic perception becomes even stronger if one compares the cross-years stability of children's pulse notations to their surface notations. In all six task-type conditions, there was a steady increase in the number of subjects achieving 100% accuracy in their surface notations, whereas for pulse notations there was a decline in the three conditions of text, simple, and long. The surface notations of the items having no text were considerably more reliable than for those items with a text.

Clearly, there is a difference in the relative ease with which young children can perform each of these three skills in that recall was found to be an easier skill than notating items, and notating items easier than decoding them. We investigated the possibility that success on the notation task might predict high achievers on the recall or decode measures. Chi-square tests of independence between notation ability and recall ability showed a significant relationship for the first year and third year, but neither association was strong enough to be conclusive ($\phi = .3$ and $\phi = .45$, respectively). A significant relationship ($\phi = .31$) between decoding and notation ability was found in the first round of testing, but not for the second and third years.

The chi-square results are not strong enough to indicate that notation skills are necessarily related to memory or decoding skills. Therefore, Gordon's (1980) finding that rhythmic acumen varies with the type of task used for measurement must be maintained. Since rhythmic ability does not remain constant across various types of skills, children who capture rhythmic features in their notations will not necessarily be the most advanced performers of rhythmic games and exercises. Likewise, children who are expert performers of rhythmic patterns may be at a loss when asked to symbolize or explain their performances.

In closing we must emphasize that an ability to perform does not carry with it the ability to reflect on the dimensions articulated by the performance. Nor does an ability to perceive and reflect indicate an ability to perform. We recommend that children's notations be used as an additional, not a substitute, means for assessing rhythmic development. Recall, performance, symbolization, and decoding are equally important skills in the growth of the musically educated person. It is therefore essential that these skills carry equal import in future assessments of children's musical development.

Acknowledgments. This research was supported in part by grants from the Carnegie Corporation, Rockefeller Foundation, and the Spencer Foundation. The work was carried out in the Cambridge Public Schools and at the Cambridge Friends School. We are grateful to the teachers, children, and parents who helped us to persue our interest in musical cognition, and to Joan Meyaard for her assistance in preparing the manuscript.

References

Bamberger, J. (1980). Cognitive structuring in the apprehension and description of simple rhythms. *Archives de Psychologie, 48,* 171–199.

Bamberger, J. (1982). Revisiting children's drawings of simple rhythms: A function for reflection-in-action. In S. Strauss (Ed.), *U-shaped behavioral growth* (pp. 191–226). New York: Academic Press.

DeYarman, R. M. (1972). An experimental analysis of the development of rhythmic and tonal capabilities of kindergarten and first grade children. In E. Gordon (Ed.), *Experimental Research in the Psychology of Music* (Vol. 8, p. 1–44). Iowa City: University of Iowa.

Dittemore, E. E. (1970). An investigation of some musical capabilities of elementary school students. In E. Gordon (Ed.), *Experimental Research in the Psychology of Music* (Vol. 6, pp. 1–44). Iowa City: University of Iowa Press.

Foley, E. (1975). Effects of training in conservation of tonal and rhythmic patterns on second-grade children. *Journal of Research in Music Education, 23*(4), 240–249.

Frega, A. L. (1979). Rhythmic tasks with three, four, and five year old children: A study made in the Argentine republic. *Bulletin for the Council of Research in Music Education, 59,* 32–34.

Gabrielsson, A. (1979). Experimental research on rhythm. *The Humanities Association Review, 30,* 1–2, 69–91.

Gardner, H. (1971). Children's duplication of rhythmic patterns. *Journal of Research in Music Education, 19*(3), 355–361.

Gilbert, J. P. (1981). Motoric music skill development in young children: A longitudinal investigation. *Psychology of Music, 9*(1), 21–24.

Gordon, E. E. (1980). *Learning sequences in music: Skill, content, and patterns.* Chicago: G. I. A. Publications.

Igaga, J. M., & Versey, J. (1977). Cultural differences in rhythmic perception. *Psychology of Music, 5*(1), 23–27.

Jones, R. (1976). The development of the child's conception of meter in music. *Journal of Research in Music Education, 24*(3), 142–155.

Moog, H. (1976). The development of musical experience in children of pre-school age. *Psychology of Music, 4*(2), 38–45.

Nelson, D. J. (1980). The conservation of meter in beginning violin students. *Psychology of Music, 8*(1), 25–33.

Norton, D. (1979). Relationship of music ability and intelligence to auditory and visual conservation of the kindergarten child. *Journal of Research in Music Education*, *27*(1), 3–13.

Osborn, L. A. (1966). Notation should be metric and representational. *Journal of Research in Music Education*, *14*(2), 67–84.

Petzold, R. G. (1966). *Auditory perception of musical sounds by children in the first six grades*. Madison: University of Wisconsin (ERIC Document Reproduction Service No. ED 010 297).

Pflederer, M. (1967). Conservation laws applied to the development of musical intelligence. *Journal of Research in Music Education*, *15*(3), 215–223.

Pflederer, M., & Sechrest, L. (1968). Conservation-type responses of children to musical stimuli. *Bulletin of the Council for Research in Music Education*, *13*, 19–36.

Rainbow, E. L. (1977). A longitudinal investigation of the rhythmic abilities of pre-school aged children. *Bulletin of the Council for Research in Music Education*, *50*, 55–61.

Roberts-Gray, C., & Yip, J. (1977). A musical conservation problem. *Perceptual and Motor Skills*, *44*(1), 96–98.

Serafine, M. L. (1979). A measure of meter conservation in music based on Piaget's. *Genetic Psychology Monographs*, *99*(2), 185–229.

Stone, K. (1976). New notation for new music (parts 1 & 2). *Music Educator's Journal*, *63*(2), 48; *63*(3), 54.

Thackray, R. (1972). *Rhythmic abilities in children*. London: Novello.

Van Zee, N. (1976). Responses of kindergarten children to musical stimuli and terminology. *Journal of Research in Music Education*, *24*(1), 14–22.

Walker, R. (1981). The presence of internalized images of musical sounds and their relevance to music education. *Bulletin of the Council for Research in Music Education*, *67*, 107–111.

7
The Development of Music Preference in Children

ALBERT LeBLANC

Music preference, often called "musical taste" in the older research literature, has long held the interest of researchers in aesthetics, philosophy, psychology, and music. Kate Hevner (1930, 1935a, 1935b, 1936, 1937a, 1937b) is responsible for much of the early experimental work in music preference, although it should be noted that she was by no means the first person to conduct experiments involving preference. To her great credit, she conducted enough sequential studies to derive benefit from her own earlier work. Farnsworth (1950) summarized in his monograph much of the experimental work undertaken to that date.

Wapnick (1976) published a comprehensive review of research in music preference, while Abeles (1980) reviewed the human response to music and Haack (1980) examined the behavior of music listeners. The chapters by Abeles and by Haack each contain material that is distinctly of interest to students of music preference. Kuhn (1980) presented an extremely thorough survey of instrumentation available for the measurement of music attitudes, while LeBlanc (1984) discussed the philosphical and practical tradeoffs that the researcher is forced to make when choosing a response mode to measure individual music preferences.

The study of music preference received a significant impetus with the founding of the Special Research Interest Group: Affective Response in 1980 as a unit of the Society for Research in Music Education of the Music Educators National Conference.[1] A programmatic series of studies in the development of individual music preference is being conducted by researchers from the School of Music at

---

[1] Special Research Interest Group: Affective Response publishes an occasional newsletter reporting current research activities in the field of music preference. To inquire about the newsletter, write Harry E. Price, Chair of SRIG Affective Response, School of Music, University of Alabama, P.O. Box 2876, University, AL 35486. The chair will change from time to time, but the SRIG may always be contacted by writing to the chair of the Society for Research in Music Education, Music Educators National Conference, 1902 Association Drive, Reston, VA 22091. The Society publishes the *Journal of Research in Music Education*, which is a primary source of authoritative research articles in the field of music preference.

Michigan State University, and the Special Research Interest Group: Affective Response has become a clearing house for North American researchers who are active in this topic area. In the United Kingdom, the Aesthetic Research Group in the Department of Psychology of Leicester University has done experimental work in this topic area.[2] It is encouraging to note that research undertaken in music preference continues to claim the interest of both music educators and psychologists on an international scale.

Some scholarly journals have become fairly consistent publishers of reports of research in music preference. The most noteworthy and consistent source is the *Journal of Research in Music Education*, and excellent material also appears in the *Journal of Music Therapy* and *Contributions to Music Education*. Interested readers should remember that music preference is a matter of central importance to the music therapy profession, and many articles appearing in the *Journal of Music Therapy* will have some relevance to the study of music preference even if their titles do not reveal it. The *Bulletin of the Council for Research in Music Education* sometimes reports preference research, and the British journal *Psychology of Music* has also published research in this area, especially the reports of studies conducted by the Aesthetics Research Group at the University of Leicester. Historically, the psychology journals have been a notable source of reserch involving music preference. They are much less important now because of a declining interest in this topic among psychologists, and a corresponding increase in music preference research among the music-oriented disciplines.

While the overall topic of music preference has long held the attention of researchers, comparatively few of them have ventured to advance a theory that attempted to even partially explain how people learn to like the music they like. Much of the early writing about "musical taste" was devoted to an exposition of what kind of music the writer considered to be intrinsically best, followed by an attempt to convince others that the writer was correct, followed by a critique of those who did not choose to agree with the writer. In other words, this early writing was more a matter of polemics than of philosophical or empirical inquiry. It is most revealing to note the sometimes apologetic way in which Farnsworth (1950) asserted that no single style of music is intrinsically better than its competitors (see especially his Preface and page 81).

Farnsworth did not go on to enunciate a theory of how music preference develops in an individual, although he did a thorough job of presenting the variables that he and other researchers considered influential in the process (see Chaper 6, Farnsworth, 1950). Hevner and Farnsworth stand as a bridge between the polemicists of music preference, who advocated specific musical values, and the contemporary empiricists of music preference, who simply want to learn something about the variables and processes through which people learn to like the music they like. In their deference to empirical method, however, the con-

---

[2]The group may be reached through Dr. David J. Hargreaves, Aesthetic Research Group, Department of Psychology, Leicester University, Leicester, LE1 7RH, England.

temporary researchers have been reluctant to venture the assumptions and do the synthesis necessary to create a comprehensive theory of how the music preference of an individual develops.

Prince (1972) expressed dismay over the "irregular and unsystematic" approach that had been taken to the study of music listening, and he pointed out the desirability of having such studies conducted by "a combination musician-psychologist" rather than by researchers whose education came from only one of these areas (p. 445). He went on to offer a formal paradigm for research into music listening, which he hoped would serve as a first step in organizing research in this area. Prince presented a graphic schema to illustrate the variables in his paradigm and their interrelationships (p. 447). It must be noted that music preference was only an incidental element within the paradigm.

Prince's article represented an important step beyond the work of Farnsworth, but his failure to make specific predictions through his paradigm prevents his article from functioning as a theory. There is nothing specific for a researcher to test. Scholars continued to call for a theoretical framework to structure research into the affective response to music (McMullen, 1980).

The Interactive Theory of Music Preference (LeBlanc, 1982) that will be described here was developed in a historical context of philosophical and aesthetic theory that was so generalized as to be untestable, and in the context of Prince's proposed paradigm, which was a distinct advance.

The LeBlanc theory benefited from some tightly focused experimental studies that were published in the years it was being formulated. Prominent among these studies is the work of R. Douglas Greer and associates (Greer, Dorow, Wachhaus, & White, 1973; Greer, Dorow, & Randall, 1974). In contrast to the atheoretical nature of much previous research into music preference, Greer and his associates were working to measure the reinforcement value of specific styles of music, and they intended to use the results to test specific principles of behaviorism. Greer (1981) has published a summative chapter on behaviorist research into music affect, but the development of individual music listening preferences is only an ancillary issue in the chapter.

The Interactive Theory of Music Preference

The entire theory may be summarized as follows:

Music preference decisions are based upon the interaction of input information and the characteristics of the listener, with input information consisting of the musical stimulus and the listener's cultural environment.

The model in Figure 7.1 shows that the theory is hierarchical, with each level of the hierarchy identified by a reference number in the left margin. The bottom of the hierarchy is the point of entrance for input information, which will be processed by the listener, and which can ultimately cause a music preference decision leading to observable behavior. Arrows in the model indicate that the

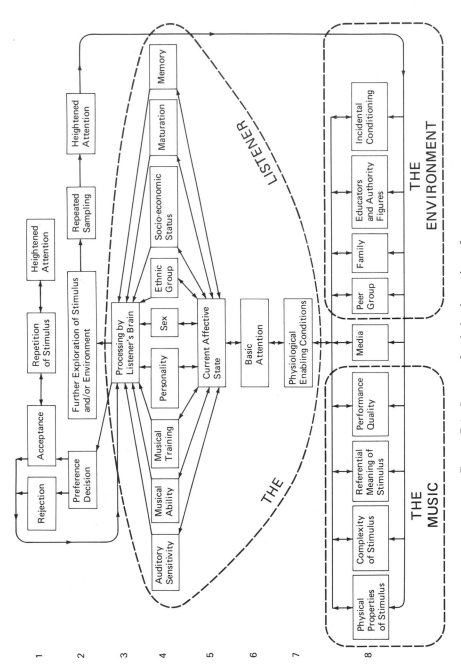

FIGURE 7.1. Sources of variation in music preference.

flow of information is generally upward, whereas double-headed arrows indicate the many possible interactions. Variables included within the model and theory are considered plausible influences upon music preference because of their logical relationship with music preference outcome behavior, and because they have been isolated in previous research studies or could be isolated and tested in well-designed future studies.

Input Information (Level 8)

The input information that is so vital to the functioning of the theory is represented in Level 8 of the model. Two classes of variables (influences) are available for input into the decision-making system. The four variables on the left represent stimulus (music) input, while the four on the right show the influence of the listener's cultural environment. The media are placed midway between musical and cultural environment input variables to graphically indicate the mediating influence they wield with most listeners in the contemporary American culture. They wield this influence by selectively sampling certain information that is available from the universe of music and cultural influences present within society. They then present this selectively sampled content to be processed by the individual music listener.

The effect of the Level 8 variables may be summarized as follows:

The physical properties, complexity, and referential meaning of the music stimulus, as well as the quality of the performance through which it is heard, influence the music preference decision. Incidental conditioning of the listener, as well as the opinions of the listener's peer group and family, influence the music preference decision. Educators, authority figures, and the media influence music preference decisions. These influences will vary in intensity and direction at different stages of the listener's life.

The Level 8 variables will now be examined in detail, with special attention given to the effect they will have on the developing child.

INPUT INFORMATION FROM MUSIC

Physical Properties

Physical properties of the music stimulus would include its frequency, intensity, duration, and waveform, but these objective characteristics would mainly interest psychoacousticians as opposed to the average music listener. Melody, harmony, timbre, texture, rhythm, and form are the physical properties noted by musicians when they listen to music, and there is good reason to believe that nonmusicians also attend to these properties. What is lacking in the case of nonmusicians is sufficient education to know what aspect of the music they are attending to, and the technical vocabulary needed to communicate this to others.

Most of the programmatic studies conducted at Michigan State University during the past several years have focused upon various physical properties of the sound stimulus. LeBlanc (1981) investigated the effect of style, tempo, and performing medium on children's music preference, LeBlanc and Cote (1983) measured the effect of tempo and performing medium on preference, and LeBlanc and McCrary (1983) studied the effect of tempo alone on preference responses.

This sequence of studies is informative because it demonstrates the interactive nature of the different facets of a single variable in the theory: physical properties of the music stimulus. LeBlanc (1981) found that style, tempo, and performing medium all had measurable influences upon children's music preference, but the three variables designed into this study interacted with each other in a way that made it impossible to isolate the specific effect of each one. That was the reason for designing the LeBlanc and Cote study (1983) to deal with only two of these variables, but a significant interaction was still encountered. Finally, LeBlanc and McCrary (1983) conducted a study to measure the effect of tempo alone, and it was shown to have a powerful effect upon the music preferences of fifth- and sixth-grade students. Knowledge about the preference effect of tempo continues to accumulate, with Sims (in press) testing its effect on preschool through fourth-grade listeners, and LeBlanc, Colman, McCrary, Sherrill, and Malin (in press-b) probing the effect of tempo in grades 3 through college senior. Unfortunately, space limitations will not permit as full a discussion of the research efforts being made with each variable of the theory.

Complexity of Stimulus

The next of the Level 8 variables is the complexity of the music stimulus. This variable is based upon the principle that a stimulus that is too simple will be disliked because it leads to boredom, a stimulus that is too complex will be rejected because it leads to frustration, and a stimulus of optimum complexity for the person perceiving it will be liked because it avoids the problems associated with stimuli of either extreme.

The complexity of stimulus variable is one that has fascinated experimental aestheticians, and Walker (1980) has advanced an entire theory of preference acquisition based upon psychological complexity. In a paper delivered at the Ann Arbor Symposium (1981) he applied his theory to music education, and Radocy and Radocy (1983) have extended this application to music therapy, using certain elements of the LeBlanc theory to help develop specific therapeutic applications.

Referential Meaning of Stimulus

The referential meaning of stimulus variable deals with the extramusical meaning that may become attached to a piece of music. An obvious example of this would be the referential meaning of the lyrics that go with a song. A not so obvious example would be the associations of color, imagery, or mood that some listeners pair with certain pieces of music. The referential meaning that a piece of music holds for a listener can influence that listener's preference decision with regard to that music.

Performance Quality

Performance quality has seemed so important in music that many people have taken it for granted in their analytical thinking about the human response to music. Yet there is no assurance that competing pieces of music will always have the luxury of getting equally good performances. When performance quality is uneven, the music that receives the better performance, or that is performed in a style that most appeals to the listener, will have an advantage when it comes to the preference decision.

Interaction of Music Stimuli

It is possible for the Level 8 variables to interact with each other as well as with variables at other positions in the hierarchy. One example would be that of an opera singer who alters the timbre of his or her voice (a physical property) while pronouncing certain words (the referential meaning) to bring about a distinctive interpretation (performance quality).

Changing Music Input to Influence Children's Music Preference

Taken as a group, these first four of the Level 8 variables constitute the input information from the music stimulus. How might they apply in the development of children's music preference, especially from the earliest days of childhood? It is quite likely the complexity variable will be the most important of the four, assuming that reasonable care is given to the other three. A multivoiced fugue by Bach or one of Webern's best planned examples of serial composition might both qualify as one of this culture's highest achievements in art music, yet both are very likely to go unappreciated by the young child, owing to their sheer complexity. (The term "art music" will be used throughout this chapter to represent the serious concert music usually called "classical music" by the general public. This is done to avoid confusion with the classical period in music history.)

It will be difficult for parent or teacher to select music of optimum complexity for the very young child, but it is safe to say that the child will not be able to deal effectively with music stimuli of a complexity suitable for adults. The gap becomes greater if the adults involved are musically educated. The first step for a parent or teacher who wants to shape the young child's music preference will be to select music that is simple enough for the child to enjoy, but not so simple as to bore the child after the first few hearings. Once the complexity level has been optimized, the parent can begin to think about other aspects of the music.

One of these other aspects, referential meaning, is widely appealed to by those who market children's music. This can be seen in the lyrics of the songs that commemorate gifts, favorite foods, parties, or trips to the zoo. It is noteworthy that so much of the music marketed for young children is vocal as opposed to instrumental, and the reason may be that the merchandisers of this music simply want each piece to carry a pleasant referential meaning for the child. Without lyrics, it becomes much harder to assure that a piece of music will have referential meaning to a reasonably wide sample of people.

Unfortunately, performance quality is often a lower priority in the production of music intended for children. This problem can be avoided by the astute parent who provides his or her child with some music that was not specifically created for children. It is important to offer the child a musically varied diet, and this will be difficult or impossible if the only music used is that intended for children.

How does the physical properties variable relate to this discussion? In selecting music, the teacher or parent should simply avoid obvious monotony or extremes. When the music is reproduced in the home, however, there is a more subtle problem to avoid. Many parents will want to give their child his or her own cassette player as soon as the child is old enough to handle it. While this is a reasonable way to encourage children's music listening, the sound quality of these machines is seldom up to a par with their visual appeal. It is important for the parents to make sure the child gets to hear good music played back on a good sound system. Moreover, this kind of music listening must not be a rarity in the child's daily life.

INPUT INFORMATION FROM THE MEDIA

The next influence charted in Level 8 of the theoretical model is the media. They are located symbolically in the middle of the input variables, where they literally mediate between the music stimulus and the cultural environment input variables. The mechanism through which they mediate is by selecting from the huge amount of music stimulus input that is available in our culture, and passing it on to their listeners while adding the values, opinions, and cultural context of that segment of the culture with which they identify. Large cities are noted for the diversity of their radio broadcast offerings, with stations identifying with ethnic groups (for example black or Hispanic), age level (for example teenage, usually favoring rock music), and sociocultural orientation (for example stations programming country music or art music, music styles that typically appeal to adults).

To listen predominantly to a country music radio station is to associate oneself with that style of music, and the values (for example, conservatism and patriotism) and demographic characteristics (typically white, working class, and middle aged) of the people who usually form the audience of country music. There is a danger that this example is an oversimplification, but broadcast industry studies have shown that on the average it is possible to pinpoint the demographic characteristics of a listening audience at least as much as has been suggested above.

Although the examples cited above focus upon the broadcast media as the mainstay in terms of influencing music preference, they are not the only component of the media that can do this. The print media can draw the attention of readers to the kinds of music they support or criticize, and can have considerable influence upon the careers of composers and performers. It is doubtful, however, that the print media influence the young listener nearly as much as do the broadcast media.

Few would argue against the idea that the broadcast media are immensely important in the socialization of teenagers, but the influence wielded upon younger listeners is not so obvious. It is essential to remember that the very young child will not control the choice of radio station, nor will the child make the decision of when to turn it on or off. Through their opportunity to select listening experiences and determine how much time is spent listening, parents and child care professionals have a potent tool for influencing the child's developing music preference. It is ironic that so many parents fail to realize this, and the choice of listening experience is very often made through habit alone.

INPUT INFORMATION FROM CULTURAL ENVIRONMENT

When the Level 8 variables of peer group, family, educators and authority figures, and incidental conditioning experiences are considered as a whole, they represent the combined influence of the listener's cultural environment. The cultural environment represents the societal influences that impart the tendencies for listeners to respond in certain ways when presented with information from a music stimulus. The influence of society is all-pervasive, and it has already begun to shape the response patterns of most listeners quite early in life. That is why the cultural environment variables are located in Level 8 of the model, where they begin to exert their influence upon the listener as soon as a specific music stimulus is heard. The effect of the cultural environment upon music preference is treated in detail in LeBlanc (in press-a).

Peer Group

While its influence becomes extremely powerful in the adolescent years, the child's peer group will not attain an influence equal to that of the family in the early years of childhood. After peaking in adolescence, the influence of the peer group typically declines as music listeners progress toward adulthood and a greater reliance upon their own judgment in deciding what kinds of music they like.

If parents and child care professionals want to influence the child's developing music preference, they would be well advised to try to get the child to affiliate by the time he or she enters adolescence with a peer group that shares their own musical values. In the typical school system, this would usually be the school chorus, orchestra, or band. Because the influence of the adolescent peer group is so great, any other affiliation group that hopes to challenge its influence needs to be close-knit and to maintain fairly constant contact with its members. If all other factors remain equal, a smaller affiliation group will usually exert more influence over an individual than a larger one. During the high school years, a select performing group such as a wind ensemble would be the kind of peer group that could successfully challenge the influence of the adolescent peer group at large. It is also possible for the family to support the values of one peer group and not another, and this would help to swing the balance in the direction desired by the family.

Family

In contrast to the peer group, the family will have its greatest influence over the child's music preferences in the earliest years of the child's life. From the baby's first days at home, the family will control the music that the baby hears. The family's influence is very great during the early years because the child is unlikely to spend much time away from the home, except in the case of families in which both parents work and there are no other family members available to provide child care. Here the child care center would share some of the family's influence.

While the family exerts virtually total control over the kind of music the young child gets to hear, it is doubtful that many families make much of an effort to shape the child's music preferences in a systematic way. What is more likely is a situation in which the family maintains its established music listening habits despite the presence of a new baby. A favorite radio or television station may be left on all day, and that station would end up selecting most or all of the child's listening material. The family's influence is felt here through its choice of broadcast station and the decision to turn it on.

When the child has teenage siblings present in the home, the listening experience may be sharply different from what would be the case if the parents were alone with a young child. This makes it possible, and indeed likely, that successive children will have a very different listening experience within the same family. The first child would probably hear adult-oriented music, while those who follow are increasingly likely to hear the music preferred by teenagers. Children of any age can influence the music heard in the home, but teenagers are the ones most likely to exert a strong influence, and they are also the ones most likely to have preferences that contrast strongly with those of the rest of the family.

Parents and children are not the only family members who can influence the music heard in the home. Any relative who lives with the family or spends a great deal of time with the family can influence what is heard, and employees such as housekeepers or baby sitters can also exert influence in proportion to the amount of time they spend listening to music within earshot of the child. Grandparents or great-grandparents can inject an influence from an earlier era if they have access to recordings of the music of their own youth.

Perhaps a member of the family is an amateur or professional musician (see Kelley and Sutton-Smith, Chapter 2, this volume). The child will then be likely to hear that person's practice, and any music lessons that are taught in the home.

The potential of home listening experience to influence the music preference of the developing child should be obvious, yet there is a lack of careful research to measure the precise experience that the child has and to evaluate its influence on the child's concurrent and future music preference. Such studies will be time consuming, and may be viewed as trivial by people outside this field of interest, but they are absolutely necessary if we are to learn what we need to know about the musical aspects of child development.

Educators and Authority Figures

In our culture, the family will usually be the first agent of society to make its influence felt in the development of children's music preference. Educators and authority figures will typically come next in the temporal sequence of influences. It is very likely that the people in charge of day care will be the first educators or authority figures to come into contact with the young child. Parents can try to influence the type of music heard in day care centers, and they can also arrange private music lessons for the child. The Suzuki method of string instrument instruction is intentionally targeted to begin with the young child, and one of its most basic principles is the parent's close involvement with the child's music instruction and home practice. Parents who value art music would be well advised to consider enrolling their child in a Suzuki program.

The influence of educators becomes considerably stronger when the child enters elementary school, but educators in the United States tend to do comparatively little to influence the music preferences of their students. Teachers who are music specialists will usually try to do more in this area than classroom teachers. The best way for a parent to enlist the influence of a specialist music teacher, outside of arranging for private music lessons, is to enroll the child in the school's music performing groups such as band, orchestra, or chorus.

Teachers are not the only educators who can influence the child's music preference, at least indirectly. College professors teach the people who become classroom teachers, boards of education and accreditation agencies determine curricular policy, and school administrators carry out this policy, which can mandate higher or lower levels of importance to music instruction. Educational evaluators are charged with measuring how well a school system's policy is being carried out, as well as assessing the effect of this policy upon student learning.

Church authorities may be the first authority figures to have an impact on what kind of music the young child hears. Most faiths have a distinct policy on music, which will usually address the amount of emphasis given to music and the kind of music to be used in a worship service. Changes in church policy can have a wide-ranging effect upon the musical experiences of the congregation; the most striking example during this generation would be the changes in Roman Catholic liturgical music wrought by the policy decrees of the Second Vatican Council.

The authority figures who are capable of influencing music preference tend to be a much more diverse group than educators. They include the members of advisory panels who make recommendations to government agencies that fund the composition and performance of music, as well as the legislators who determine the level of funding for these agencies and the agency staff members who carry out actual projects. Private philanthropists play a parallel role when they support music.

Once a piece of art music has been created, conductors and soloists will influence when and how often that music is performed. In the field of popular music, the record companies will play this role. Music critics and the media will influence the reception given to a new piece of music.

American educators and authority figures tend to be comparatively mild in their endorsement or rejection of specific kinds of music. One must look to other countries for examples of more aggressive behavior on the part of educators and authority figures, and totalitarian governments will provide the most striking examples.

Incidental Conditioning

Incidental conditioning, the last variable of the cultural environment group from Level 8, is a psychological process through which music can be paired with pleasant or unpleasant associations. When the associations linked with the music are pleasant, that kind of music tends to be liked. The psychological link is formed when a certain type of music is heard in situations that already carry a pleasant or unpleasant meaning for the listener.

The most typical example of incidental conditioning from everyday life is the married couple that has "their song." Usually, this is a song that was popular at the time of their courtship, and it was often brought to their attention by the broadcast media. The pleasant experience of courtship became linked with this song because they often heard it during their courtship.

Incidental conditioning could be a powerful tool in the hands of parents or teachers who want to influence the child's developing music preference. All that is needed to invoke this influence is the deliberate pairing of the desired type of music with situations that are already pleasant to the child. If the home is a happy one, there will already be a tendency to associate pleasant connotations with the music that is heard in the home. It should be noted in passing that incidental conditioning can also work to impart a negative preference to music. This would seldom be the intention of the people presenting the music, but it could happen accidentally, as in the case of music heard in the dentist's office during a particularly painful treatment.

Listener Processing Influences (Levels 4 through 7)

The theory states:

Input information from the musical stimulus and the cultural environment must pass through the intervening variables of physiological enabling conditions, basic attention, and current affective state before it can interact with the listener's personal characteristics and be processed by the listener's brain. The intervening variables may completely block the passage of input information, or may allow it to pass while adding their own influence to the information. Their influence can range from extremely subtle to quite pronounced, but it is always capable of altering future processing and the music preference decision.

INTERVENING PROCESSING VARIABLES

At this point, the theoretical model narrows down to a single succession of influences through which the input information from Level 8 must pass. Levels 7, 6, and 5 are occupied by intervening variables that function as filters or gates.

While a closed gate will block all further processing of input information, a filter will permit input information to pass through, while influencing everything that passes through it. Some of these variables can function as either a filter or a gate.

Physiological Enabling Conditions

The variable labeled physiological enabling conditions represents the conditions in the listener that are necessary for the optimum processing of input information. When these conditions are particularly unfavorable, all processing can be blocked. One example would be hearing impairment—a listener could be deaf to sounds above a certain frequency level, or the listener could be totally deaf. Sleep is a more common example of information blockage through this variable. Pain would represent the potential of this variable to act like a filter. A listener in pain could still perceive input information, but would be unlikely to give full attention to it.

Basic Attention

In contrast to physiological enabling conditions, the basic attention variable of Level 6 is essentially an act of the listener's will. The input variables of Level 8 are all dependent upon a certain basic level of listener attention in order for further meaningful processing to occur. This variable provides a good example of the interactions possible between levels of the processing hierarchy. A performer, for example, might be distressed because his or her audience appeared to be ignoring him or her (withholding basic attention as listeners). His or her performance quality might suffer, or it might improve to meet the challenge.

Current Affective State

Current affective state, located at Level 5, is best visualized as the listener's current mood. It will function more as a filter than a gate, but it will always have some influence upon the listener's reaction to input information.

PERSONAL CHARACTERISTICS

At Level 4 of the model, input information begins to be influenced by comparatively stable personal characteristics of the listener. The theory states:

The personal characteristics of the listener influence further processing of input information and the music preference decision.

Auditory Sensitivity

The first of these Level 4 variables, auditory sensitivity, is a higher order refinement of the basic hearing acuity represented at Level 7 by physiological enabling conditions. A person who is deaf to frequencies above 400 Hertz, for example, is missing much of the basic information in the music of this culture. On the other hand, one who is deaf to frequencies above 4,000 Hertz is getting most of the basic information in ordinary music, and is missing only the acoustic richness provided by music that contains meaningful information in frequencies above that level. This milder form of hearing impairment could still influence the listener's reaction to certain kinds of music.

Musical Ability

The musical ability variable in Level 4 stands for a seemingly inherited ability to make the most of music instruction, and to do better on musical tasks in the absence of instruction than the general population might be expected to do. In defining this variable, it is not this author's intent to enter the debate over the relative importance of inheritance versus education, but rather to point out the fact that some people are more successful in music than others if all other things are held constant. This musical ability can influence their music preference.

Musical Training

The musical training variable of Level 4 represents the effect of music training upon the individual. In the area of preference, the most likely result of this training will be the strategy that the listener uses in processing musical information. As one example of this, the trained musician is far more likely to focus upon musical form or harmony than is the untrained listener.

Personality

The listener's personality is likely to make that person more or less subject to outside influences such as the peer group, the media, or educators. It can also help a person to identify more closely with certain themes presented in the referential meaning of music.

Sex

The listener's sex can make a person more likely to identify with same-sex or opposite-sex performers. Because of differing rates of sexual maturation, male and female adolescents can display a differing pattern of preference for same-sex or opposite-sex performers.

Ethnic Group

The listener's membership in a certain ethnic group can influence music preference decisions through its influence on which radio station a person is more likely to listen to, and through the ethnic group's identification with its own style of music and patronage of performers from their own ethnic group. Ethnic radio programming is much more evident in the larger cities.

Socioeconomic Status

The listener's socioeconomic status creates a social expectation that this listener will align himself or herself with the style of music most preferred by others of the same status. The clearest example of this is the case of very wealthy individuals who tend to publicly espouse and support art music regardless of their listening preferences in private life.

Maturation

The listener's maturation exerts a complex influence upon music preference, and one that tends to interact with the other influences portrayed by the model. The young child, for example, tends to value the opinions of family and educators, while the adolescent will actively reject family and educators' values in favor of the adolescent peer group. People entering old age will almost always lose some of their hearing acuity (auditory sensitivity) to the onset of presbycusis. Young adults will not ordinarily enjoy the economic independence (socioeconomic status) of people who are well into middle age. Throughout the school years, musical training is likely to increase in direct proportion to the listener's age (maturation). All of these situations are typical examples of the influence of listener maturation, and they also demonstrate some of the many possible interactions.

Memory

Both cognitive and musical memory are embraced by the listener's memory variable in Level 4. Cognitive memory enables the listener to recall previous knowledge about the kind of music being heard. This might include traditional factual information, but it will also include the influences this listener has noticed from the cultural environment. Musical memory is a much more specialized concept, enabling the listener to recall a theme and observe its variations, and to mentally follow the musical form of a piece. Both kinds of memory will influence the processing of input information from Level 8.

Listener Action Variables

PROCESSING BY LISTENER'S BRAIN

Level 4 marks the end of the influence variables, and Level 3 presents the first of the listener action variables, the actual processing of input information by the listener's brain. The theory states:

All input information from the musical stimulus and the cultural environment, as influenced by intervening variables and the personal characteristics of the listener, is processed by the listener's brain. The listener may decide to seek additional information or to make a preference decision at that time. If the decision is one of acceptance, the listener is likely to repeat the stimulus under heightened attention until reaching a point of satiation. Whatever the decision, the listener will be inclined to make similar decisions in the future when presented with similar input information.

It is important to note that the only information that gets processed at Level 3 is that which has successfully come up through the hierarchy of the model. The specific strategies used in processing are beyond the scope of the theory, but other writers have speculated that the formulation and testing of expectations, development of fantasy or imagery, and signaling and experiencing of physiological and motor responses are important aspects of a listener's processing of music input information.

DECISION BETWEEN PREFERENCE JUDGMENT AND FURTHER EXPLORATION

A decision point occurs at Level 2, with the listener deciding to make a preference judgment or to seek additional information about the stimulus, the cultural environment, or both. Listeners who decide to seek more information will carry out a *repeated sampling* process, and they are likely to do this in a state of *heightened attention*. The model has a feedback loop to illustrate this repeated sampling, and it goes all the way back to the input variables of Level 8. Any combination of these variables may be sampled again.

Listeners who carry out repeated sampling will often do it with specific questions in mind. "Was that an electric organ or a synthesizer?" "I thought the strings were out of tune, but maybe not." "I wonder what my music teacher will think of this performance." Any information taken in through repeated sampling will have to make its way through the influence hierarchy again, but it is unlikely to lose any of its impact to the filter and gate variables of Levels 7, 6, and 5 because of the heightened attention that usually accompanies repeated sampling.

PREFERENCE DECISION

Level 1 of the model represents the making of a clearcut preference decision by the listener. This decision will come as soon as the listener feels that enough information is at hand. The model's feedback loop going back to Level 3 from the *acceptance* or *rejection* decision made in Level 1 represents the tendency of listeners to behave in a consistent way once they make an initial preference decision about a certain kind of music. If they accept it once, they become more likely to accept similar examples of music in the future. The same tendency holds true for rejection.

Repetition has been a topic of intense interest to the scholars of music preference, and the model accounts for repetition in two different ways. The repeated sampling feedback loop going from Level 2 back to Level 8 does not embody a preference decision; it is a quest for more information. This feedback loop would also account for repetition forced by a music teacher, but it should be remembered that a teacher will have great difficulty in getting a student to pay either basic or heightened attention to the forced repetition of music, and forced repetition is not likely to put the student listener in a more favorable current affective state. If the student is commited to music, and the forced repetition involves rehearsal to perform this piece of music or a student's voluntary preparation for an examination, the repetition is more likely to be received in a friendly way.

The other type of repetition is symbolized by the variables of Level 1. It is the voluntary repetition carried out by a listener who has decided that he or she likes the music to which he or she is listening. This repetition will also be carried out under heightened attention, and it is likely to continue until the listener reaches a point of satiation with the music.

Summary

The model symbolizes a single music preference decision made by a listener at one point in time. An individual's music preference or "musical taste" will be a product of many of these decisions made at many points in time. By studying many preference decisions across many points in time, researchers can hope to learn more about the development of individual music preference.

Several variables that have been popular with music preference researchers over the years have been subsumed within other variables in the model rather than given an independent identity. The author feels they are a by-product of the variables that are shown, or that all of their effect is accounted for already by the variables shown. Readers who are interested in a more complete discussion of subsumed variables should consult LeBlanc (1982, pp. 40–41).

Future Research

Future studies of music preference would benefit greatly if their staffing were drawn from several disciplines. While professional music educators have produced an impressive body of research in this area, it tends to be focused upon school-age subjects, and much of it seems to be intellectually oriented toward the production of immediate practical outcomes. We need to add the perspective of other disciplines, and these other disciplines need to supply substantive input focused upon the subjects being studied as well as technical input concerning research methodology. In other words, we need help from child development professionals as well as from statisticians.

Successful Parent and/or Teacher Intervention

Parents and teachers are faced with a basic question of values in the area of music preference. Is it fair and ethical for them to intervene in the process through which the child's music listening preference is formed? The answer to this question is as varied as the basic values of our own pluralistic society. One thing that is certain is the fact that every other aspect of our cultural environment will intervene heavily and at will as the child's preference evolves.

The parent has an obvious stake in the child's well-being, and the teacher is society's chosen agent to impart the values of our culture to its young. Why shouldn't parents and teachers participate on an equal footing with disk jockeys and rock stars in the child's cultural education? This author feels that parents and teachers should be an unabashed part of the child's cultural education, freely advocating their own musical values. The only caveat offered is that children should be free to make their own ultimate decisions about what music to value, and it is probably better to advocate preference for a variety of musical styles rather than to espouse a narrow view of what is worthwhile. It must be remembered that, with the arrival of adulthood, the child will eventually make his or her own preference decisions regardless of the values of others.

If the decision is made to intervene actively in the child's development of music preferences, the theory presented in this chapter can serve as the framework for specific advice on intervention strategies. A sampling of that advice follows.

1. Choose music listening examples with moderate physical properties—not music that is extremely loud or slow, or with extreme pitch levels. By the same token, provide a diet of music listening that gives variety in its physical properties. Remember that a scratchy record or a tape deck that produces wow and wobble during playback inserts very objectionable physical properties into any music listening experience.

2. Select music listening examples of a complexity level appropriate for your child. Since the precisely appropriate level will be difficult to determine, "triangulate" by presenting some examples that would seem to be a little more complex and some a bit less complex than you would consider appropriate for your child.

3. Provide music listening examples that have a pleasant referential meaning. While this is helpful, parents and teachers do not need to avoid all vocal music that treats of unpleasant subjects, nor should they avoid good instrumental music.

4. Select music listening examples of the very best performance quality. It would be better to avoid a great piece of music rather than to introduce it to the child through an inferior performance.

5. Listen to broadcast media that support the same kind of music that you would like your child to prefer. Provide records or tapes for home listening that exemplify the type of music you value. Consider subscribing to a magazine that supports the kind of music you value as soon as your child is old enough to read it or to view its pictures with understanding. If you value art music, remember that public radio and television stations need your financial support.

6. Encourage your child to associate with peer groups (affiliation groups) that value the same kind of music that you value. In the early years the parents will have a great deal of influence over the child's affiliation groups. The Suzuki string program is one example of an organized music experience available to very young children. The influence of the peer group will become greater as the child gets older, and it is particularly important during the adolescent years. If you want your child to value art music, it is desirable that he or she become involved in a high-quality school music program, where other students will be likely to value such music and a music teacher will be present as a role model.

7. Openly demonstrate your support of the kind of music you value. It is important that the child see you actively enjoying the music you like and that you want your child to like. Especially with the younger child, you must take pains to make sure that your enjoyment of your kind of music is observed and understood. Remember that you can demonstrate your enjoyment of your kind of music through verbal and nonverbal communication.

8. If you are an educator, openly demonstrate your support for the kind of music you value, as described in point 7 above. Your influence upon the child will probably be quite strong until the child enters adolescence. By the time the child grows to college age, your influence will probably be in ascendancy again. Use it. If you are a parent, encourage the educators with whom your child is associated to value the kind of music you value. Parents and educators should also call upon the influence of authority figures to support the kind of music they value.

9. Arrange pleasant experiences for your child to be accompanied by the type of music you value. Use music to go along with any experience that you expect your child to enjoy.

10. Have your child tested early in life to make sure that he or she has the physiological capability to perceive and enjoy good music. If deficiencies are discovered, try to treat the child's condition and at the same time provide music listening enhanced in a way that may help to overcome your child's physiological deficiency.

11. Try to make sure that your child is paying attention to the music when an important music event is taking place. This will require you to sometimes postpone a music event (such as playing a new record) or elect to keep the child away from it (such as avoiding expensive nighttime concert tickets if the hour is one when your child is likely to be sleepy). Sometimes (and this is often the case with educators) you will simply have to insist that the child pay attention to what is going on.

12. Try to arrange music experiences to coincide with the child's better moods. If, for example, the young child is inclined to be grouchy before supper, don't select that time for a major music experience. Do not be reluctant to cancel or postpone a music experience if the child's current mood is unfavorable.

13. Do what you can to optimize your child's auditory sensitivity. The child should be kept away from long periods of exposure to very loud noise, and the child's ears should be kept free from excessive buildups of earwax.

14. Have your child tested for musical ability and make the most of what the child has. Edwin Gordon (1965, 1979) has developed a series of published tests of musical ability, and these are recommended as reliable and valid measures.

15. Make every effort to obtain musical training for your child. The Suzuki string program is one example of an organized musical experience available for the very young child. If your child is musically gifted, training becomes even more important. For the child with limited musical ability, musical training will still influence the development of music preference.

16. Try to select music examples that fit in with the developing personality of the child.

17. Acquaint the child with musical role models of the child's own sex. That would include both famous musicians featured in the media and local practitioners. Try to break down any perception of sex stereotyping as to which musical roles are open to which sex.

18. In music listening experiences, feature musical styles characteristic of the child's own ethnic group and performers from the child's own ethnic group. In

some cases this will be greatly facilitated through the use of other (popular) styles in addition to art music.

19. As the child becomes older, present a more challenging diet of music examples. The maturing child will be able to deal with higher levels of complexity.

20. When working with the child in a music listening experience, ask questions and invite comments to encourage processing of the input information that you have presented.

21. Arrange listening experiences so that the child will hear the music you support more than once. Repeated sampling is always desirable up to a certain point, when it will begin to generate a negative reaction. It is fairly easy for a parent or teacher to determine the point of diminishing return in the area of repetition and stop the repetition before it goes too far.

22. Show pleasure when the child makes a preference decision in favor of the music you advocate, but don't show excessive displeasure if the child does not agree with you.

With patience, good judgment, and a consistent application of the principles explained in this chapter, parents and teachers have an excellent chance of influencing the child's developing music preference.

References

Abeles, H. F. (1980). Responses to music. In D. A. Hodges (Ed.), *Handbook of music psychology* (pp. 105–140). Washington, DC: National Association for Music Therapy.

Farnsworth, P. R. (1950). *Musical taste: Its measurement and cultural nature* (Stanford University Publications, University Series, Education-Psychology, Vol. 2, No. 1). Stanford, CA: Stanford University Press.

Gordon, E. (1965). *Musical aptitude profile*. Boston: Houghton-Mifflin.

Gordon, E. (1979). *Primary measures of music audiation*. Chicago: G. I. A.

Greer, R. D. (1981). An operant approach to motivation and affect: Ten years of research in music learning. In *Documentary report of the Ann Arbor Symposium* (pp. 102–121). Reston, VA: Music Educators National Conference.

Greer, R. D., Dorow, L. G., & Randall, A. (1974). Music listening preferences of elementary school children. *Journal of Research in Music Education, 22*, 284–291.

Greer, R. D., Dorow, L. G., Wachhaus, G., & White, E. R. (1973). Adult approval and students' music selection behavior. *Journal of Research in Music Education, 21*, 345–354.

Haack, P. A. (1980). The behavior of music listeners. In D. A. Hodges (Ed.), *Handbook of music psychology* (pp. 141–182). Washington, DC: National Association for Music Therapy.

Hevner, K. (1930). Tests for the aesthetic appreciation in the field of music. *Journal of Applied Psychology, 14*, 470–477.

Hevner, K. (1935a). Expression in music: A discussion of experimental studies and theories. *Psychological Review, 47*, 186–204.

Hevner, K. (1935b). The affective character of major and minor modes in music. *American Journal of Psychology, 47*, 103–118.

Hevner, K. (1936). Experimental studies of the elements of expression in music. *American Journal of Psychology, 48*, 246–268.

Hevner, K. (1937a). The affective value of pitch and tempo in music. *American Journal of Psychology, 49*, 621–630.

Hevner, K. (1937b). The aesthetic experience: A psychological description. *Psychological Review, 44*, 257.

Kuhn, T. L. (1980). Instrumentation for the measurement of music attitudes. *Contributions to Music Education, 8*, 2–38.

LeBlanc, A. (1981). Effects of style, tempo, and performing medium on children's music preference. *Journal of Research in Music Education, 29*, 143–156.

LeBlanc, A. (1982). An interactive theory of music preference. *Journal of Music Therapy, 19*, 28–45.

LeBlanc, A. (1984). Selecting a response mode in music preference research. *Contributions to Music Education, 11*, 1–14.

LeBlanc, A. (in press). Elements in the development of individual music preference: The culture as educator. In J. T. Gates (Ed.), *Music, society, and education in the United States*. University, AL: University of Alabama Press.

LeBlanc, A., Colman, J., McCrary, J., Sherrill, C., & Malin, S. (in press-b). Tempo preferences of different-aged music listeners. *Journal of Research in Music Education*.

LeBlanc, A., & Cote, R. (1983). Effects of tempo and performing medium on children's music preference. *Journal of Research in Music Education, 31*, 57–66.

LeBlanc, A., & McCrary, J. (1983). Effect of tempo on children's music preference. *Journal of Research in Music Education, 31*, 283–294.

McMullen, P. T. (1980). Music as a perceived stimulus object and affective responses: An alternative theoretical framework. In D. A. Hodges (Ed.), *Handbook of music psychology* (pp. 183–193). Washington, DC: National Association for Music Therapy.

Prince, W. F. (1972). A paradigm for research on music listening. *Journal of Research in Music Education, 20*, 445–455.

Radocy, R. E., & Radocy, J. A. (1983, November). *Clients' musical preferences: May the hedgehog be a guide?* Paper presented at the meeting of the National Association for Music Therapy, New Orleans, LA.

Sims, W. L. (in press). Effect of tempo on music preference of preschool through fourth grade children. In C. K. Madsen & C. Prickett (Eds.), *Applications of research in music behavior*. University, AL: University of Alabama Press.

Walker, E. L. (1980). *Psychological complexity and preference: A hedgehog theory of behavior*. Monterey, CA: Brooks/Cole.

Walker, E. L. (1981). Hedgehog theory and music education. In Music Educators National Conference (Ed.), *Documentary report of the Ann Arbor Symposium: Applications of psychology to the teaching and learning of music*. Reston, VA: Music Educators National Conference.

Wapnick, J. (1976). A review of research on attitude and preference. *Bulletin of the Council for Research in Music Education, 48*, 1–20.

8
Conceptual Bases for Creative Thinking in Music

PETER R. WEBSTER

J. P. Guilford's 1950 keynote address to the American Psychological Association is often cited as the beginning of modern-day interest in the formal study of creative behavior. His message centered on the need to expand thinking about "intelligence" to include creative abilities such as divergent thinking skills. Research expanded throughout the 1960s and has continued until this time. In the field of psychology, behaviorists, humanists, and developmentalists have all addressed this topic with their respective theories and research procedures. In the introduction to *Art, Mind, and Brain*, Gardner (1982) wrote:

The greatest psychologists—from William James to Sigmund Freud, from B. F. Skinner to Jean Piaget—have all recognized the importance and appeal of a study of the creative processes. They have all sought to explain how human beings can fashion comprehensive theories in science or powerful works of art. And if they have not fully succeeded in providing a coherent and cogent account of this most puzzling of areas, it is not for want of trying. (p. xi)

Formal study of creative behavior in music by musicians has been slow to benefit from this work. Although a number of writers have commented in a personal sense about the creative process in music and have speculated about ways to encourage creative behavior, carefully designed studies that have sought to explain just what creative thinking in music is have not been plentiful. Nearly all of the literature is in the form of short, speculative articles and exploratory research efforts by doctoral students. There are a few monographs (Lasker, 1971; Schafer, 1979), but they are devoted almost exclusively to methodology in the classroom or music studio and have little theoretical or empirical research base. (For a more detailed account of the literature on creative thinking in music, see Webster [in press-b], which contains a literature model and a listing of over 100 articles on the subject.)

Fortunately, there is recent evidence that the small amount of substantive research directed at creative thinking in music is beginning to grow larger. Music researchers, particularly those concerned with educational matters, are beginning to expand the conceptions of music aptitude and achievement by constructing methods for evaluating creative thinking potential (Flohr, 1979; Gorder,

1976; Kratus, 1985; Webster, 1977, 1983). Psychologists and educators interested in matters of music cognition and artistic development are continuing to study creative abilities but with greater intensity (Bamberger, 1977; Gardner, 1982). It is in this spirit of growing, interdisciplinary interest that the following remarks are based.

This chapter presents a conceptual model of creative thinking in music. This model is based on what research we do have, plus some speculation about how creative thinking in music might occur. It should be made clear that this is a *conceptual* model and not a detailed representation of the many interacting variables that constitute the creative process. It is presented in the hope that it will stimulate more focused research so that a much more refined model will result. The chapter will close with a brief look into the future of research in this field, particularly in terms of measurement and technological advances.

The Conceptual Model

Related Literature

Rhodes (1971) explored the relationships of various writings by noted philosophers, psychologists, and musicians on the subject of creative thinking and behavior. She organized her study around the manifestation of creativity in the "person," "process," and "product," and the educational setting. Comparative data included the writings of Whitehead, Bergson, Maritain, Beardsley, and Dewey (philosophers); Freud, Kris Maslow, Koestler, Wertheimer, Barron, Torrance, and Guilford (psychologists); and Schoenberg, Stravinsky, Sessions, Copland, Hindemith, and Mursell (musicians), among others. A number of similar viewpoints emerged that hold particular significance for theory:

1. Creative behavior is a normal human response as opposed to an expression of mental illness.
2. The source of creative power is of natural origin as opposed to supernatural origin.
3. Some relationship exists between creativity and cognitive intelligence, and definite groups of cognitive abilities are involved in creative thinking.
4. Factors guiding the creative process spring largely from rational choice under the guidance of a pervading creative idea rather than from some form of inspiration.
5. The form of the final creative expression is communicable in a material result.
6. Stages of creative process are characterized by the recognition of the problem, accumulation of facts and materials, and the development of the problem through manipulation.
7. In terms of mental activity during creation, the process is an interaction between conscious and nonconscious states.

Greenhoe (1972) suggested a theoretical model of creative musical perception based, in part, on the three dimensions of Guilford's Structure of Intellect Model

(Guilford, 1967). The dimension of Content was defined in terms of the elements of music: timbre, frequency, duration, and dynamics. The dimension of Operations included processes of perception that were defined as a hierarchy (hearing, attention, memory, expectation, and evaluation). Products ranged from blurred impressions to high-level thoughts of musical implication. Greenhoe offered no data to support her adaption, but did argue consistently for the inclusion of music listening as part of the creative experience in music.

As part of her overall view of the creative thinking process in music, Greenhoe also endorsed Wallas' (1926) stage theory (preparation, incubation, illumination, and verification) and applied each stage to a musical context. The role of the *musical imagination* is stressed during the illumination stage, as Greenhoe argued for "deliberately rehearsing certain sounds in the imagination—intervals, scales, melodies, entire pieces committed to memory; and by practicing free imagery in sounds, letting the mind go as it will, but attempting, always to think in sound images" (Greenhoe, 1972, p. 181).

Other authors in music have suggested that the Wallas stage theory is workable as a way of generalizing about the progress of musical ideas from initial inception to refinement as part of a musical whole. For example, Feinberg's view of creative thinking in music as a multilevel, problem-solving process is closely tied to the stages that Wallas proposed (Feinberg, 1973).

In addition to these more conceptual studies, there are findings from direct observation of the creative process in music that aid in model construction. Much of this work is based on children's musical efforts. In his review of literature on original songs, Kratus (1985) made a distinction between research that has focused on the *musical* content of the songs versus studies that have evaluated the constructs of musical flexibility, fluency, originality, and the like (creativity factors borrowed from the psychological literature). This latter approach has been applied largely to children after the age of 10, whereas the former approach has concentrated on younger children. Both sets of data help us to understand the developmental process of creative thinking in music and contribute to theoretical speculation.

Moorhead and Pond (1941–1944), Doig (1941), Freundlich (1978), Flohr (1979), Prevel (1979), Gardner (1982), and Kratus (1985) have all studied the musical content of improvisations and compositions of children. Results have been variable and depend largely on the methods of data collection and researcher bias (Kratus [1985] contains an excellent review of this literature.) One clear trend that has implications for a conceptual model of creative thinking in music is the dominance of environment. Until the age of 5 or 6, children seem to exhibit very individualistic approaches to tonal, rhythmic, and motivic patterns and tonal center. Motor coordination seems to play an important role in this early stage, and a sense of overall musical syntax is absent in original song production. In children between the ages of 6 and 9, rhythmic and tonal patterns become much more predictable and seem to be closely related to music the children have heard as part of their culture. Changing meters are more common during this stage, and a feeling for tonality is more pronounced, although feeling for musical cadence and phrase structure is not clear. After the age of 10, children become much more conscious of "correctness" of musical structure and tend to create music that is more organized in terms of musical "rules," but not necessarily more original. There is a tendency to imitate more closely the sounds of commonly heard music. Kratus (1985) found a steady rise in children's use of rhythmic and melodic motives until the age of 13, at which time a drop occurred. It is interesting to speculate on whether this drop is a result of a real lack of ability or an increase in the desire to break with the traditional melodic and rhythmic motives heard in the culture.

Using measurement techniques that have their basis in the Guilford model, Vaughan (1971), Gorder (1976), and Webster (1977) have investigated creative thinking in music with children between the ages of 10 and 18. Webster, (1983, in press-a) has used similar techniques with younger children as well. Although the products of musical improvisation, analysis, and composition have been the focus of study, the emphasis is less on the musical properties than on the creative expression as a function of the thought process. In each of these studies, criteria such as "musical flexibility," "musical fluency," and "musical originality" were carefully defined in terms of observed behavior and musical content. Tasks were constructed to engage children in the creative process and, in most cases, performances were audio- or videotaped for later study. Both subjective and objective measurement techniques were applied, and panels of experts were used. The results of validity and reliability data in these studies are encouraging, although none of the measures have been used extensively enough for major claims. One of these measures (Webster, 1983, in press-a) has been used in more than one study and will be summarized in more detail later in this chapter. A few tentative findings from this research hold particular importance for a model of creative thinking in music:

1. Musical divergent production skills are measureable and may play an important role in the creative thinking process.
2. Musical divergent production skills are not significantly related to traditional measures of musical aptitude (the discrimination of similar and different tonal and rhythmic patterns) and seem to play an independent role in the definition of musical intelligence.
3. Musical achievement (training in the knowledge of musical content) does affect the performance on musical divergent production skills.
4. Neither cognitive intelligence, academic achievement, nor gender seem significantly related to musical divergent production skills.

Model

There are no comprehensive, published models of creative thinking in music that serve as the basis for research and professional debate. The literature outlined above is helpful in forming such a model. Figure 8.1 represents an attempt to draw together both the results of this research and some careful speculation.

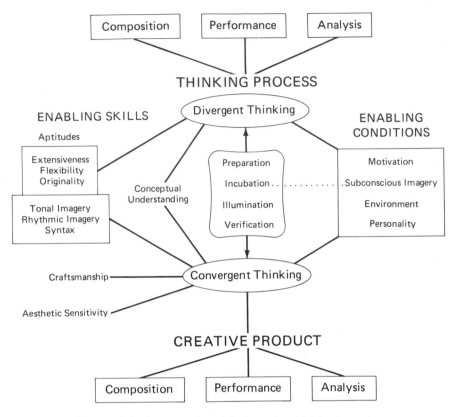

FIGURE 8.1. Conceptual model of creative thinking in music.

PRODUCT INTENTION

Few would argue that there are three principal ways that people involve themselves with music as art:

1. Composition—the conception and recording of sound structures for presentation at a later time.
2. Performance/Improvisation—the transmission of sound structures that are either composed previously or actually conceived by the performer at the time of performance.
3. Analysis—the process of understanding and explicating sound structures in written, verbal, or (in the case of active listening) mental form.

Many who have studied and written about creativity in general argue for a distinction between creativity as "process" versus "product." This is a legitimate distinction particularly if one is concerned with more singular matters of measurement, teaching strategy, or aesthetics. In generating theory, this distinction also plays a role, although the distinction is more blurred. Composition, performance/improvisation, and analysis can be considered at the outset of creative thinking as goals or as "intentions" of the creator. At the same time, they represent the final product of creation. These intentions also help to define entrance and exit points in the model as seen in the top and bottom portions of Figure 8.1. Subtle differences in the process result from each product intention; however, the inner workings of the process are thought to be quite similar.

ENABLING SKILLS

With the intention established, the creator must rely on a set of skills that allow for the thinking process to occur. These skills form the basis of a musical intelligence and interact with the thinking process in very rich ways. Figure 8.1 displays these skills as a group of four:

1. Musical Aptitudes—individual skills that are likely to be subject to great influence by the environment during the early years of development and possibly into early adult life. They include skills of tonal and rhythmic imagery (Gordon, 1979), musical syntax (sensitivity to musical whole), musical extensiveness, flexibility, and originality (Webster, in press-a).
2. Conceptual understanding—single, cognitive facts that comprise the substance of musical understanding.
3. Craftsmanship—the ability to apply factual knowledge in the service of a complex musical task.
4. Aesthetic sensitivity—the shaping of sound structures to capture the deepest levels of feelingful response; achieved over the full length of a musical work.

These enabling skills are used in slightly different ways, depending on the intention of the creator. The composer, performer, and listener must all possess an understanding of the materials of music—rhythmic, melodic, harmonic, and timbral concepts. In turn, this knowledge is built on an innate core of aptitudes that has been nurtured by the environment. As the creator begins to gain a storehouse of experiences based on the interaction of aptitudes and learned information, the application to solve musical problems begins to reveal craftsmanship. This skill involves sensitivity to complex musical relationships. For example, it is common to hear of the composer's craftsmanship in the writing of a fugue or in the scoring of a particular vocal passage. The performer is often evaluated on the technical mastery (craftsmanship) of a musical performance. The ability of a person to hear the return of a theme or the juxtaposition of harmonic content are additional examples.

When this craftsmanship is accompanied by the creator's ability to communicate meaningful musical substance over a long time span, then aesthetic sensitivity is in evidence. This skill is seen in the ability to sustain a sense of musical growth and direction over a long period of time. This is often the ultimate goal of a creative musician and can spell the difference between the mundane and the very great.

ENABLING CONDITIONS

In addition to personal skills that drive the creative thinking process, there are a number of variables to be considered that are *not musical*. These influences vary greatly from person to person and mingle with musical skills in delicate, complicated, and certainly profound ways. These "conditions" are listed on the right of the model in Figure 8.1 and are explained below:

1. Motivation—those drives (both external and internal) that help keep the creator on task.
2. Subconscious imagery—mental activity that occurs quite apart from the conscious mind and that may help to inform the creative process during times when the creator is occupied consciously with other concerns.
3. Environment—the host of characteristics of the creator's working conditions that contribute to the creative process, including financial support, family conditions, musical instruments, acoustics, media, societal expectations, and many others.
4. Personality—factors such as risk taking, spontaneity, openness, perspicacity, sense of humor, and preference for complexity that seem to exist in many creative persons and that may hold some significance for enabling the creative process.

There are many obvious examples of these enabling conditions at work. Composers are externally motivated by commissions or deadlines, and internally motivated by an overwhelming desire to compose. Listeners who engage in active and creative musical study are often internally motivated by a deep desire to understand musical structure. Certainly for performers who wish to rise to the top of their chosen profession, combinations of both internal and external motivation are vital for success.

Other enabling conditions are less obvious and need careful study. Subconscious imagery has not been investigated in any formal way in music, although it is part of a number of anecdotal accounts by creative musicians. It clearly plays a role in problem solving over time, a task that is common in composition and analysis. It may play a role in performance as well.

Personality assessment in terms of its relationship to musical behavior is a fascinating, but difficult area. Kemp (1981–1982), Lang (1976), Trollinger (1981), and Swanner (1985) have all investigated such factors as preference for complexity, introversion, aggressiveness, verbal imagination, and many others. Results are mixed, especially with younger subjects. Although no clear pattern emerges from these studies, the findings that we do have from music and other sources argue for the placement of personality in the model.

In terms of child development in creative thinking in music, environment must be singled out as a major factor. To date, there have been few controlled, comparative studies of creative thinking development among different environments or cultures. There is evidence that certain convergent listening skills such as tonal and rhythmic imagery can be influenced by teaching and exposure to musical experiences before the age of 9 or 10. There is every reason to believe that this is also true for other aptitudes. Certainly an encouraging environment for the skills of conceptual understanding, craftsmanship, and aesthetic sensitivity is vital. For creative adults, hostile environments can be a great detriment to creative thinking. A supportive work environment for a composer or performer is obviously desirable, although history has shown that this is not always an absolute requirement.

THINKING PROCESS

Much of what has been noted thus far about the model is relatively well known, at least intuitively. In fact, the education enterprise in music has been devoted almost exclusively to improving certain enabling skills and providing enabling conditions. *What has not received much study or attention by educators is the* process *by which these skills and conditions are connected to creative production*. The center of Figure 8.1 indicates movement between two types of thinking (Guilford, 1967), facilitated by stages of operation (Wallas, 1926). Connections between this process and the enabling skills and conditions are also noted.

Divergent thinking involves the generation of many possible solutions to a given problem—a kind of personal brainstorming. Convergent thinking, on the other hand, involves the weighting of those several possibilities and "converging" on the best possible answer. In divergent thinking, imagination plays an important role and is fueled by the individual's conceptual understanding of the material itself. The obvious is noted, then placed "on hold" in favor of other possibilities—often without regard for tradition or common practice. At some point, however, this thinking process must cease in favor of a more convergent filtering. The mind must sift through the mass of possibilities in order to "create" a final solution.

Direct relationships between these modes of thinking and the enabling skills and conditions are noted on the model. The aptitudes of tonal and rhythmic imagery and musical syntax are most clearly connected to convergent thinking. Tonal and rhythmic imagery concern the ability to perceive sound in relation to change and involve the representation of sound in short-term memory (Gordon, 1979). Musical syntax is the ability to shape musical expressions (usually during improvisation activities) in a logical manner according to patterns of musical repetition, contrast, and sequencing (Webster, 1983). In this sense, syntax is closely related to aesthetic sensitivity and is an early indication of this skill before extensive formal training.

The aptitudes of extensiveness, flexibility, and originality are clearly connected to divergent thinking. Extensiveness is a measure of a person's ability to generate a number of musical ideas or solutions to problems. Flexibility can be seen in the skill necessary to move within the musical parameters of tempo (fast/slow), dynamics (loud/soft), and pitch (high/low). Originality can be viewed as a function of uniqueness of musical expression, not necessarily associated with internal logic (syntax). (These factors are extensively discussed in Webster, 1983 and in press-a.)

Conceptual understanding directly impacts both divergent and convergent thinking. Since divergent thinking requires the mind to survey its "databanks" for possible musical content, it is reasonable to assume that the more that is there the better. It is impossible to expect individuals to think creatively if nothing is there to think creatively with—a common error in creative teaching strategy! It is also true that convergent thinking requires the continued development of a knowledge base. Craftsmanship and aesthetic sensitivity are also connected to convergent thinking because they require careful manipulation of musical material in sequential ways. Of course divergency plays a role here as well, but to a lesser degree.

Enabling conditions play important roles in all stages of the creative process and in each of the thought modes. A direct link between subconscious imagery and incubation is obvious.

Movement Between Modes of Thought: Stages

The movement back and forth between divergent and convergent thinking is not the same at all times. There are "stages" in this process that begin first with a preparatory phase. It is here that the creator first becomes aware of the problems at hand and for the dimensions of the total work that lies ahead. For the person who seeks to creatively analyze a composition, this preparatory time might involve initial sketches of the harmonic structure or possibly a first hearing in order to determine overall formal structure. For a performer, it might involve an initial reading and a quick analysis of the more troublesome passages. In terms of composition, this phase often takes the form of rhythmic, melodic, or harmonic sketches, or perhaps early decisions regarding formal content.

Regardless of the nature of this first set of creative experiences, there is likely to be resistance to immediate closure. In fact, a number of problems may result that force abandonment of the project for a time. Incubation may take the form of subconscious imagery (note the direct connection to this enabling condition) or some "informal" or "part-time" thinking of the problems at hand. It is during this phase that divergent thinking may play a crucial role, for it is here that a number of musical solutions are considered.

Movement to the third stage of illumination has been referred to in rather romantic terms as the "light bulb" or "Eureka!" stage. In fact, solutions to problems might come suddenly and provide the creator with a flood of energy that drives thinking ahead to the final stages of completion. More realistically, however, this stage comes in controlled segments, perhaps in a number of small solutions that begin to point the way for the final version. It is at this time that the creator may be "taken over" by the music—he or she may become "one" with the art and the sounds begin to form themselves as formal work continues at a much faster rate. Movement between convergent and divergent thinking becomes more weighted toward convergent processing. Craftsmanship and aesthetic sensitivity become very important here and the motivation to continue toward closure becomes internal.

For musical creative thinking, this stage often blends imperceptively with the final plateau of verification. As final drafts of a composition are completed, the composer may search for as many opportunities to hear the composition as possible, often seeking the opinions of fellow musicians. Performers work to refine their interpretations, seeking to share their efforts with as many listeners as possible. Those analyzing scores will continue to listen and study the music in hopes of verifying the fine points of their analysis, always looking for additional subtleties that were not heard before.

It should be noted that in music, as in other art, the process is really never finished. Although a particular product is created and finally communicated to society, the creator is compelled to begin again and again with other product intentions until the motivation for creative thinking—or the "spirit" of creativity—is no longer present.

The Model and Children's Creative Development

There is little controlled research on the creative process in music. We gain some perspective by talking with people about the process after the creative product is completed, but this is not completely satisfactory because of the idiosyncratic nature of the data. Often these discussions are with creative adults, and so even less is known about how this process works with children as they grow in their aptitudes, conceptual understanding, craftsmanship, and aesthetic sensitivity and as their thinking is influenced by environment and motivational drives.

Although the model in Figure 8.1 is not designed in developmental terms, there is no reason to suspect that any of the major aspects of the model are different for the young child engaged in creative thinking. The product intentions of the child are usually limited to performance/improvisation intuitively, and in all three domains if the child is in an educational environment that encourages written composition or analysis. There is no evidence in the educational literature that supports the notion that structured experience in all three of these domains is harmful, so long as the physical and intellectual development of the child is taken into account.

Enabling skills develop with age and experience. Aptitudes are likely to be present from birth and continue to develop with age. Stabilization of these aptitudes may well occur at some point between the ages of 9 and 11. There is statistical evidence for this in terms of tonal and rhythmic imagery (Gordon, 1979), but not as yet for the other aptitudes listed. Conceptual understanding obviously grows with age and experience, but *transfer* of this conceptual information into the mosaic of creative thinking experience does not often occur naturally and might well be an important goal of formal music education. This is certainly true of craftsmanship and aesthetic sensitivity as well. One way to view the enabling skills developmentally is to assume that they represent a hierarchy of abilities that can be encouraged as the child grows. Care should be taken not to discourage some exploration of craftsmanship and aesthetic sensitivity at a young age, but one must be aware that these skills will appear more slowly in young children and should be treated with this in mind in planning curricula.

The enabling conditions of motivation and environment are important for musical development in children. Various theories of motivation do suggest that younger children are naturally curious, with much of their motivation coming internally. This natural curiosity requires external encouragement at key times during the middle school years (ages 10–13) and during adolescence. In the general creativity literature, there is evidence of "creative slumps" during the transitionary periods in schooling (entrance into elementary, junior high, and high school). These may be times when external motivation becomes very important to the continued development of creative thinking ability. There is no evidence to suggest that this is any different in terms of music.

One of the major implications of the model for child development in music is that environments that encourage divergent thinking in music are just as important as environments that encourage convergency of thought. It seems quite clear that many children have the benefit of rich opportunities to develop musical skills at home or in formal schooling (music lessons with instruments and voice, performance opportunities in large groups, and instruction in music theory). These experiences are very important, of course, and fit nicely into the model for the development of enabling skills. However, little is done that encourages divergent thinking in music as it interacts with the more convergent aspects of musical thought. In other words, there is little development of environments that support the very core of the model.

An astonishing fact is that we have few or no data to support the role of creative thinking in music in the overall musical development of children. If this model is to be retained as a workable explanation of the creative thinking process in music for children and adults, we simply need more evidence. If this model is verified through careful study, the implications for how we structure environments both at home and in school are enormous.

Future Research

In addition to questions about child development, the model presents a number of other issues that should be considered:

1. What specific differences would one postulate based on different product intentions? In other words, what differences are there between the creative process employed by composers versus performers versus listeners?

2. What role does formal education play? Can divergent thinking in music be taught?
3. Preliminary research has shown that divergent thinking in music is possible to measure in young children. Is this true for older children? What is the predictive validity of such measurement?
4. There is mounting evidence that traditional measures of musical aptitude (the ability to discriminate differences in tonal and rhythmic patterns) are not significantly related to divergent music skills when measured across large samples. Does this indicate the need for an expanded view of music potential—considering both kinds of abilities? Are those few individuals who possess both sets of skills best thought of as "gifted"?
5. Is the ability to think creatively in music related to creative thinking in other fields? In other words, is there a kind of "g" factor for creative thinking?
6. Is it possible to have more meaningful data about the musical creative process itself? What new methods can we employ to understand the highest levels of artistic creation?

To answer these and other questions prompted by the model, there are three possible avenues of research that hold special promise: (a) further development of a useful measurement tool such as the *Measures of Creative Thinking in Music*, (b) continued use of ethnographic research techniques, and (c) increased use of technology as a tool for musical creation and measurement.

Development of *Measures of Creative Thinking in Music*

The *Measures of Creative Thinking in Music* (MCTM)[1] (Webster, in press-a) deserves special note here because of the promise it holds for measuring creative thinking in music for children in the 7- to 10-year-old age group. Its scoring factors are also candidates for use with older children and adults and for experimentation with preschool children. Extended use by a number of researchers may help to answer some of the questions posed above.

MCTM uses three sets of instruments: (a) a round "Nerf" ball about 4 inches in diameter that is used to play tone clusters on a piano (either in a rolled fashion or as individual clusters; (b) a microphone that is suspended in front of the piano and is attached to an amplifier, speaker, and small reverberation unit to cause an "echo" effect; and (c) a set of five wooden resonator blocks (temple blocks) that produce different pitches when struck by a mallet. The instruments are all in easy reach and can be played easily by children who have had no musical training. There is a brief warm-up period that is not scored and is designed to familiarize the children with the simple techniques necessary to play the

---

[1]MCTM is available on loan from the author for examination and possible use in research projects. Contact: Department of Music, Case Western Reserve University, Cleveland, Ohio 44106.

instruments. The entire measure is administered in a private room with only the child and the administrator. All tasks are videotaped unobtrusively and scored at a later time.

The measure consists of a series of 10 scored tasks, divided into three parts: *exploration*, *application*, and *synthesis*. The tasks begin very simply and progress to higher levels of difficulty in terms of divergent behavior. The atmosphere is game-like in nature, with no indication that there are any right or wrong answers expected. The text used by the administrator is standardized for each child and few models of instrument performance are given.

The *exploration* section is designed to help the children become familiar with the instruments used and how they are arranged. The musical parameters of "high/low," "fast/slow," and "loud/soft" are explored in this section, as well as throughout the measure. The way the children manipulate these parameters is, in turn, used as one of the bases for scoring. Tasks in this section involve images of rain in a water bucket, magical elevators, and the sounds of trucks.

The *application* tasks ask the children to do more challenging activities with the instruments and focus on the creation of music using each of the instruments singly. Requirements here ask that the children enter into a kind of musical question-answer dialogue with the mallet and temple blocks and the creation of songs with the round ball and the piano and with the voice and the microphone. Images used include the concept of "frog" music (ball hopping and rolling on the piano) and of a robot singing in the shower (microphone and voice).

In the *synthesis* section, the children are encouraged to use multiple instruments in tasks whose settings are less structured. A space story is told in sounds, using colored line drawings as a visual aid. The final task asks the children to create a composition that uses all the instruments and that has a beginning, a middle, and an end.

The scoring of the videotapes involves both objective and subjective techniques. The factors of Musical Extensiveness (ME) and Musical Flexibility (MF) are measured objectively either by counting the actual seconds of time a child is involved in a task (ME) or by observing the manipulation of musical parameters and the number of instruments used in combination (MF). Musical Originality and Musical Syntax are evaluated by a panel of judges using carefully developed criteria. Subjective evaluations based on rating scales are used for these factors. Each factor yields individual scores that can be used as such or converted to standard scores, summed, and used to create a total score.

Reliability and validity data have been collected in three separate studies (Swanner, 1985; Webster, 1983, in press-a) involving over 150 children, and the results appear promising. In terms of interscorer reliability, coefficients ranged from .57 to .78 with an average of .70. Internal reliability, measured in the form of Cronbach Alpha coefficients, ranged from .45 to .80 with an average of .65 (.69 for the most recent version). Measures of test-retest reliability have yet to be established.

Content validity was established with a panel composed of music educators, composers, and psychologists who met on four different occasions to review the measure, audit pilot tapes, critique scoring procedures, and offer suggestions for improvement. To help establish construct validity, the scoring factors from the first administration of the measure were studied to determine feasibility of factor reduction. Factor analysis showed that each factor significantly contributed to two global factors that represented the theoretical existence of convergent and divergent thinking. Some empirical validity exists in the form of significant correlations between music teacher ratings of divergent thinking and scores on the MCTM, although this has not been investigated extensively. All of the studies have shown a lack of correlation between measures of musical aptitude and achievement and the MCTM, thus establishing a certain inverse validity.

Although the measure offers a workable approach to the measurement question, continued work is necessary to improve its useability and technical quality. Future research must address the problems of lengthy scoring, specialized instruments, and incomplete reliability and validity data.

Ethnography

A second future direction that is important for research on creative thinking is ethnographic study, especially techniques surrounding protocol analysis. (For an interesting description of protocol analysis in cognitive research, see Hunt, 1982.) Ethnographers immerse themselves in a single or small number of settings for an extended period of time, collecting as many data as possible about what is observed. There are few preconceived ideas about what is supposed to be observed and there are often no stated hypotheses established before data collection. The system for data collection varies and is sometimes unspecified until the initial stages of observation. Typically the researcher uses a log or journal, audio and videotape recordings, or photographs. In protocol analysis, subjects are encouraged to "talk through" the process under investigation. The researcher keeps careful record of this and studies the result at a later time to detect a pattern. Theoretical implications for the research are considered as part of the ongoing process and are compared with existing theory on the topic.

The disadvantages of this type of study are clear for the rationalist: lack of control, fuzzy methods of evaluation, no apparent basis for inductive logic, and little chance for exact replication. For the ethnographer, these shortcomings are understood, but seen as acceptable in light of the advantages: (a) more "humanistic" approaches to describing phenomena because of the nature of the actual experience being observed, preserved, and explained; (b) the immediacy of the behavior observed—the reliance on first-hand observation of natural actions rather than performance on a written measure that might be obtrusive; and (c) compatibility with the diversity (complexity) of the arts experience (stated another way, that ability to explain the richness of aesthetic response in a descriptive manner).

These advantages hold special importance for research in creative thinking and behavior. Moorhead and Pond's work (1941–1944) is probably the best example of this methodology in action for this literature. Using classic ethnographic techniques during a time when such strategies were not codified, Pond observed children improvising music in a natural, unstructured setting. The chronicles of these observations still provide a rich source of hypotheses for other forms of research today. Other examples include the more recent studies by Flohr (1979), Webster (1983, in press-a), and Kratus (1985). Although these later projects do not employ all of the ethnographic procedures that are noted above, they are concerned with natural settings, nontraditional measurement techniques, and complex artistic response.

This line of investigation holds promise for the careful study of the creative process and for the verification of many elements within the model in Figure 8.1. Especially cooperative subjects are necessary, as are technological enhancements such as videotape and computers.

Computers and Synthesizers

Certainly computers have aided the researcher in numerical analysis for years, but this is only one use for this technology. With the advent of powerful microprocessors that are also affordable, the researcher interested in creative thinking can program the computer to: (a) present the user with creative problems to solve, (b) record the reactions to and the solutions for the problem, (c) suggest alternative solutions, and (d) analyze the results of the work of a number of users.

Within the last few years, a method for linking a computer with a music keyboard synthesizer has been developed, largely for the purposes of specialized performance and electronic music composition. This link, known as MIDI (musical instrument digital interface), holds particular significance for creativity research.

Imagine a subject seated at the music keyboard with a computer screen as the score. The subject is encouraged to compose a brief fragment of music. This fragment is displayed on the screen and is played through speakers. The subject continues to expand the fragment, working with it until a longer composition is created. The subject may save the work, take a break for a time, and return later to the saved composition and continue work until a final version is ready. Throughout this process, the "electronic sketches" have been saved, together with the final version of the composition. These sketches can be studied further at a later time.

Similar experiments might be envisioned for the performer and the listener. Because of the computer's ability to capture complicated data, store it, sort it, and retrieve it at a later time, the researcher is able to study rich, objective evidence about the creative process in music. These techniques are expanded even further by the developments in laser technology that provide vast amounts of storage and retrieval space for this kind of research.

Summary

The challenge in all of this is to recognize the strengths and weaknesses of the research and place what is of value together with other data as we advance theories and working models of musical ability. Music researchers and teachers must *themselves* be creative thinkers as they work with children and adults. This is not an easy task for many. The risks are great and the rewards may not always be clear. What is clear is that few issues in our profession deserve a higher priority. It is at the very core of what music is—of what art is.

References

Bamberger, J. (1977). In search of a tune. In *Arts and cognition*. Baltimore: Johns Hopkins University Press.

Doig, D. (1941). Creative music: I. Music composed for a given text. *Journal of Educational Research, 35*, 262–275.

Feinberg, S. (1973). *A creative problem-solving approach to the development of perceptive music listening in the secondary school music literature class*. Unpublished doctoral dissertation, Temple University.

Flohr, J. (1979). *A longitudinal study of music improvisation*. Unpublished doctoral dissertation, University of Illinois.

Freundlich, D. (1978). *The development of musical thinking: Case studies in improvisation*. Unpublished doctoral dissertation, Harvard University.

Gardner, H. (1982). *Art, mind and brain*. New York: Basic Books.

Gorder, W. (1976). *An investigation of divergent production abilities as constructs of musical creativity*. Unpublished dissertation, University of Illinois.

Gordon, E. (1979). *Primary measures of musical audiation*. Chicago: G. I. A. Publications.

Greenhoe, M. (1972). *Parameters of creativity in music education: An exploratory study*. Unpublished doctoral dissertation, University of Tennessee.

Guilford, J. (1967). *The nature of human intelligence*. New York: McGraw-Hill.

Hunt, M. (1982). *The universe within: A new science explores the human mind*. New York: Simon and Schuster.

Kemp, A. (1981–1982). The personality structure of the musician. *Psychology of Music, 9*(1), 3–14; *9*(2), 69–75; *10*(1), 48–58.

Kratus, J. (1985). *Rhythm, melody, motive and phrase characteristics of original songs by children aged five to thirteen*. Unpublished doctoral dissertation, Northwestern University.

Lang, R. (1976). The identification of some creative thinking parameters common to the artistic and musical personality. *British Journal of Educational Psychology, 46*, 267–279.

Lasker, H. (1971). *Teaching creative music in secondary schools*. Boston: Allyn and Bacon.

Moorhead, G., & Pond, D. (1941–1944). *Music of young children*. Santa Barbara, CA: Pillsbury Foundation for Advancement of Music Education.

Prevel, M. (1979). Emergent patterning in children's musical improvisations. *Canadian Music Educator, 15*, 13–15.

Rhodes, E. (1971). *A comparative study of selected contemporary theories of creativity with reference to music education in the secondary schools.* Unpublished doctoral dissertation, Louisiana State University.

Schafer R. (1979). *Creative music education.* New York: Schirmer.

Swanner, D. (1985). *Relationships between musical creativity and selected factors including personality, motivation, musical aptitude and cognitive intelligence as measured in third grade children.* Unpublished doctoral dissertation, Case Western Reserve University.

Trollinger, L. (1981). Responses of high and low creative women musicians to undergraduate music courses: Anxiety, boredom, avoidance, and pleasure. *Journal of Creative Behavior, 15*(4), 257–264.

Vaughan, M. (1971). *Music as model and metaphor in the cultivation and measurement of creative behavior in children.* Unpublished doctoral dissertation, University of Georgia.

Wallas, G. (1926). *The art of thought.* New York: Harcourt, Brace and World.

Webster, P. (1977). *A factor of intellect approach to creative thinking in music.* Unpublished doctoral dissertation, University of Rochester, Eastman School of Music.

Webster, P. (1983). An assessment of musical imagination in young children. In P. Tallarico (Ed.), *Contributions to symposium/83 the Bowling Green State University symposium of music teaching and research* (Vol. 2). Bowling Green, OH: Bowling Green State University.

Webster, P. (in press-a). Refinement of a measure of creative thinking in music. In C. Madsen (Ed.), *Research in music behavior: Application and extensions.* Tuscaloosa: University of Alabama Press.

Webster, P. (in press-b). Creative thinking in music: Approaches to research. In T. Gates (Ed.), *Music, society and education in the United States.* Tuscaloosa: University of Alabama Press.

Part III
Music and Education

9
Music and the Learning of Language in Early Childhood

C. RAY GRAHAM

Music has long been a favored medium for teaching languages. A cursory examination of the literature reveals numerous articles discussing the benefits of using music in language teaching, both for native language instruction (e.g., Blos, 1974; Doepke, 1967; Eastlund, 1980; Schmidt, 1976) and for second language teaching (e.g., Beardsley, 1957; Coe, 1972; Gatti-Taylor, 1980; Jolly, 1975). The tacit assumption of much of this literature seems to be that the sentence patterns and vocabulary learned through song will automatically become a part of the productive linguistic system of the learner.

The purpose of this paper is to examine different levels of processing of language and to suggest that not all language learned through music contributes significantly to the process of acquiring a second language. Tentative suggestions will be made of ways in which music may be used more effectively to enhance the acquisition of a second language by young children.

The Process of Language Learning

The scientific study of language, and especially of the development of language in young children, over the last few decades has contributed enormously to our understanding of how language is processed in human beings and how a mature linguistic system is acquired by them. In particular, there are two characteristics of human language and its development that are relevant to our discussion here. First of all, it has been shown that language is generative in nature, that is, that through the use of several subsystems (phonology, morphology, syntax, etc.), each with a rather small set of discrete units, large numbers of utterances can be created through the combining and recombining of elements. Second, it has been shown that the actual process of acquiring a language not only entails the learning of sentence patterns that repeat themselves, but also involves the analysis by the learner of each of the language subsystems and the synthesis of processes for recombining the elements properly to form utterances that are acceptable to the learner's speech community (Moskowitz, 1978, p. 94).

The actual mechanism that enables the child to perform this complicated task of analysis and synthesis is not well understood. The two essential prerequisites necessary for their performance appear to be exposure to the language or, as Krashen (1981) has referred to it, comprehensible input, and the opportunity for interaction with speakers of the language (Moskowitz, 1978, p. 94).

Hearing the language used in a communicative context enables the learner to map linguistic form to meaning and provides the material necessary for the processes of analysis and synthesis to occur. Interaction provides the means by which learners can test their "hypotheses" about the language and get both internal and external feedback regarding their success in synthesizing the forms.

In the process of acquisition there are identifiable stages and infrastages of development through which learners appear to pass in their assimilation of a language. One of these infrastages of particular interest here is that observed in the very initial periods of contact of a learner with novel linguistic forms. It has been observed that when a learner first encounters a new linguistic form, there is often far too much information contained in the form for the learner to be able to perform an immediate analysis of the structure of the form. If the learner is faced with the necessity of producing the form before it can be adequately analyzed, he or she will "imitate" or reproduce the form in its entirety, at least insofar as the immature neural system will permit, as an unanalyzed unit. As a matter of fact, the learner often learns to use the form in a functional way with almost adult-like proficiency. Subsequently, however, as the form begins to get integrated into the rest of the linguistic system, the learner begins to analyze the form into its component parts. As this happens, the apparent "correctness" of the form deteriorates and the learner goes through a stage in which his or her use of the form appears less mature than before. Kellerman (1985) has called this phenomenon "U-shaped behavior."

An excellent example of this phenomenon on the phonological level can be seen in Leopold's (1939, 1947) careful analysis of his daughter's acquisition of English and German. In his diary notes he indicated that at 10 months of age, Hildegard first learned the word "pretty" from some relatives. She pronounced the word "slowly and distinctly,... the [r] being a briefly rolled tongue-tip [r], which had never occurred before" (1947, p. 119). Leopold made the point that she produced the word with surprising accuracy in spite of the fact that the retroflexed [r] is a rather late acquisition by native English-speaking children. She continued to produce this word with the retroflexed [r] for 3 or 4 months. As she began to get more and more words in her vocabulary and the relationship between elements in her phonological system began to be worked out, the retroflexed [r] disappeared and she began saying [pɪtɪ] or [pwɪtɪ]. It was not until much later that she began producing the retroflexed [r] again, this time as an integrated unit in a more mature phonological system.

A similar phenomenon can be observed in English-speaking children's acquisition of irregular plurals of nouns (Moskowitz, 1978, p. 94). Upon hearing the word "feet," for example, a child will employ it with apparent correctness (although at this stage he or she will not consistently distinguish it from "foot").

A while later the child will begin appending an [s] to "foot" or "feet" to form the plural. Only much later will the child again use "feet" with no inflection as the plural form. In the interim, the child has learned the system of plural formation for nouns and has identified "feet" as an exception to the general pattern.

Another striking example of this chunking phenomenon that takes place in the early stages of developing a new form can be found in Bellugi's (1967) study of the development of negation in English-speaking children. In what she called stage two of this development the three children in her study used four different negative markers, which they placed adjacent to the verb: *no, not, can't*, and *don't*. At this stage, *don't* and *can't* were used an unanalyzed wholes with much the same function and meaning as *no* and *not*. *Can* and *do* did not appear in the children's repertoires at all. It was not until stage three that the children developed the auxiliary system and consequently the analyzed forms of *don't* and *can't*.

A similar process has been observed in second language acquisition. Wong-Fillmore (1976) has examined the acquisition of English by five native Spanish-speaking children. The prevalent pattern of acquisition in the early stages was for the children to learn literally hundreds of "frozen" forms or, as she called them, "formulaic utterances," which they used as unanalyzed wholes. As time went on the learners began to break these utterances into their constituent parts and to recombine elements to form novel utterances.

Thus, we can see that the normal acquisition of language often entails the initial chunking of new linguistic material for immediate use in communication, the analysis of this material into its component parts, and the eventual synthesis of "rules" for recombining these parts into novel and productive utterances.

Neurological Correlates of Language Processing

These processes of chunking and analysis and synthesis appear to have neurological correlates in brain research. It has long been known that young children are much less lateralized for language functioning than are older children or adults (Krashen, 1975; Lenneberg, 1967). Bever (1983) argued that cerebral asymmetries in processing material, whether visual or auditory, are due to the mode of processing of the material and not to the nature of the material itself. He claimed that the fact that the left hemisphere is dominant in processing language in most adults is because they process linguistic material "relationally" rather than "holistically." If this claim is accurate, it would suggest an explanation for the differences between adult and young children's processing of language, which correlates with observed linguistic behavior in children who have not yet acquired a mature linguistic system.

In dichotic listening studies of second language learners, Obler (1981) has found that right hemispheric participation is particularly great during the early stages of second language acquisition. She suggests that this may indeed be due to the fact that "formulaic utterances will comprise more of the speech of beginning second language learners, to be replaced by more creative, or elaborated, speech as they become more proficient" (p. 58).

The question might be asked, then, as to whether or not linguistic material can be learned holistically and never become integrated into the regular creative linguistic system. While this question cannot be answered with confidence from the current literature, studies of patients with their left cerebral hemispheres incapacitated but with active right hemispheres suggest that it is possible. In a summary of literature on this subject, Jakobson (1980) has indicated that, even when patients have entirely lost the capacity to speak normally, they may be able to produce ritualistic or memorized speech with perfect fluency. Likewise a number of reports have documented cases of persons whose normal language capacities have been impaired by left hemispheric lesions but who have retained the ability to sing previously memorized songs (Benton and Joynt, 1960; Head, 1963).

While these studies are suggestive of the fact that material that has been learned by rote may be stored differently in the brain than material that has been through the process of analysis and synthesis discussed earlier, no study has been done to date that examines actual syntactic patterns and lexical items learned by rote to see at what point and through what processes these items become a part of the normal creative linguistic system of the learner. Mayo (1979a, 1979b) has shown that with adult singers, the amount of left hemispheric processing of stimuli where both lyrics and melody are present increases with increased musical training of the subjects and with increased attention to the lyrics.

Use of Music in Language Learning

Extensive practical experience in teaching songs to young children, both in their native language as well as in a second language, has led me to hypothesize that there are different levels of involvement of the linguistic system in the process of learning and performing these songs. I will propose that there is a continuum of involvement ranging from the totally rote learning of material, such as when kindergarteners or first graders learn "The Star Spangled Banner" and perform it while standing at attention during circle time, to the learning of songs and using them for manipulating the behavior of others, as exemplified in the performance of the song "Hokey Pokey." I shall illustrate the early linguistic consequences of different modes of presentation of songs to young children in a foreign language class.

In a class of 3- and 4-year-old English speakers learning Spanish as a foreign language through a partial immersion program, I observed children learning a song by rote. The teacher was using no visual aids or gestures to indicate the meaning of the lyrics. The melody was appealing to the children and the lyrics were simple enough to be memorized quite readily. By the end of a 15-minute period, the children had learned to sing the song rather well, although there were phrases that were slurred together, suggesting that the children were unaware of word divisions. After the singing period was over I asked two of the girls who had seemed to perform best in the singing what the song was about. Their hesitant answers confirmed my suspicions that they were quite unaware of the meaning of the lyrics. I continued to observe over a period of several weeks as the children sang the song almost every day. Their articulation of the words improved and as I questioned them I discovered that they were beginning to get a general idea of what the song was about, but they were still unable to answer any detailed questions about the lyrics. The children performed the song without a flaw in a special program for parents and the parents were very impressed.

This level of processing of linguistic material in the lyrics of the song is clearly toward the lower end of the continuum of involvement of the linguistic system. While the material may have some effect on the children's development of such lower level speech phenomena as rhythm, syllable timing, and articulation of certain segmental features of the language, it is unlikely that any of the syntactic or morphological features of the language will be assimilated. It is even doubtful that any of the lexical items in the piece will become productive vocabulary in the spontaneous speech of the learners.

Another teacher in the same partial immersion preschool program used quite a different strategy in teaching songs. I observed him teaching a song that was quite a bit longer and more complex than the previously mentioned one. This song was about five little elephants, each of whom had something happen to him. The teacher had five pictures of elephants on tagboard attached individually to Popsicle sticks. He had five of the children from the class come up in front of the group, take one of the tagboard elephants and act out the parts of the song as he sang it. He then had the children sing the song along with him as the children acted out the meaning of the lyrics. After 15 or 20 minutes the children were singing the lyrics acceptably and all of the children in the group had had the opportunity to act out the part of one of the elephants. After the activity I asked several of the children in English what the song was about and was pleased to find that they could answer detailed questions about the contents of the lyrics. A couple of the actions had been misapprehended and had produced a slightly erroneous interpretation of the words (e.g., one of the elephants "got lost" and the children interpreted the action as "went away"), but they had, for the most part, learned the meaning of the lyrics.

I observed as the class continued to sing this song over a period of several weeks. Much of the vocabulary became a functional part of their linguistic repertoire. On a couple of occasions I heard children use some morphological pattern out of the song; for example, one child used the phrase se cayó ("he fell down") in reference to the falling of another child. It is difficult to assess fully without a careful investigation the extent to which the material in the song was assimilated. This second example, however, clearly represents a much more thorough processing of the linguistic material in the song than did the first.

One final example that comes from an English as a Second Language class will represent an even higher level of assimilation of language material through song. The song being learned was entitled "I'm Being Eaten by a Boa Constrictor," and was one of the culminating activities in a unit on reptiles in a kindergarten class. The children had visited a local science museum where they had seen live reptiles, including a special show where the museum director had allowed them to handle a boa constrictor. The teacher had prepared visual aids of different parts of the body and had a picture of a large boa. She had also decorated a large pillowcase to look like a snake. She had one of the children come up before the group and as she sang the song, she had the pillowcase "swallow" the child, bit by bit. She had the children sing along with her as she showed pictures of different body parts mentioned in the song. She then gave the pictures out to the children and had them hold up the body parts as they were mentioned in the song.

On subsequent days as the children sang the song they would have one child be "swallowed" as another manipulated the pillowcase boa. Each day for several days they had a follow-up activity after performing the song. On one occasion each child drew a picture of a boa swallowing a different part of the body and the teacher went around and wrote the relevant part of the song below the picture. The pictures were then sequenced properly and pasted onto a movie box scroll. The teacher had a child scroll the pictures by as she asked questions about each. The children then sang the song as a child scrolled the pictures by on the movie box. After several days of performing the song, the teacher assisted the children in creating new verses to the song, following the pattern of the original verses. By that time the words and syntactic patterns in the song appeared to be thoroughly intergrated into the children's productive linguistic repertoire. They could respond to questions about the song using sentences from the lyrics; they could identify and name all the parts of the body that were included in the song; and they could create new sentences using the sentence patterns (e.g., "What's happening to him?" "He's being swallowed by a boa constrictor.").

The key to the more in-depth processing of the linguistic material in the songs is the same as the key to language acquisition in general: comprehension of the text by the learner and interaction in which the learner has the opportunity to test his or her "hypotheses" about the language. An attractive melody contributes greatly to the memorability of the text of a song, but at the same time it makes it possible to perform the text in a holistic way without integrating the text into the productive linguistic system of the learner. If we are to use music effectively in teaching foreign languages to children we must be careful to make the lyrics comprehensible and to provide plenty of opportunities for meaningful interaction using the text.

References

Beardsley, T. S., Jr. (1957). Music in the classroom. *Modern Language Journal, 41*(1), 48.
Bellugi, U. (1967). The acquisition of negation. Unpublished doctoral dissertation, Harvard University, Cambridge, MA.
Benton, A. L., & Joynt, R. J. (1960). Early descriptions of aphasia. *Archives of Neurology, 3*, 205–222.
Bever, T. G. (1983). Cerebral lateralization, cognitive asymmetry, and human consciousness. In E. Perecman (Ed.), *Cognitive processing in the right hemisphere*. New York: Academic Press.

Blos, J. W. (1974). Rhymes, songs, records, and stories: Language learning experiences for preschool blind children. *The New Outlook*, *68*(7), 300–307.

Coe, N. (1972). What use are songs in FL teaching? *International Review of Applied Linguistics in Language Teaching*, *10*(4), 357–360.

Doepke, K. G. (1967). Retarded children learn to sing. *Music Educator's Journal*, *54*(3), 89–91.

Eastlund, J. (1980). Working with the language-deficient child. *Music Educator's Journal*, *67*(3), 60–63.

Gatti-Taylor, M. (1980). Songs as a linguistic and cultural resource in the intermediate Italian class. *Foreign Language Annals*, *13*(6), 465–469.

Head, H. (1963). *Aphasia and kindred disorders* (Vol. 1). New York: Haffner.

Jakobson, R. (1980). *Brain and language: Cerebral hemispheres and linguistic structure in mutual light*. Columbus, OH: Slavic Publishers.

Jolly, Y. S. (1975). The use of songs in teaching foreign languages. *Modern Language Journal*, *59*(1), 11–14.

Kellerman, E. (1985). If at first you do succeed . . . . In S. M. Gass & C. G. Madden (Eds.), *Input in second language acquisition*. Rowley, MA: Newbury House.

Krashen, S. (1975). The development of cerebral dominance and language learning: More new evidence. In D. Duto (Ed.), *Developmental psycholinguistics: Theory and applications* (pp. 209–233). Georgetown Round Table on Language and Linguistics. Washington, DC: Georgetown University.

Krashen, S. D. (1981). *Second language acquisition and second language learning*. New York: Pergamon Press.

Lenneberg, E. (1967). *Biological foundations of language*. New York: Wiley.

Leopold, W. F. (1939). *Speech development of a bilingual child: A linguist's record* (Vol. 1). Northwestern University Series in the Humanities, No. 6. Evanston, IL: Northwestern University.

Leopold, W. F. (1947). Speech development in a bilingual child: A linguist's record (Vol. 2). Northwestern University Series in the Humanities, No. 11. Evanston, IL: Northwestern University.

Mayo, W. S. (1979a). *An investigation of auditory laterality effects in the perception of words and music in singing*. Paper presented at the research Symposium on the Psychology and Acoustics of Music, University of Kansas.

Mayo, W. S. (1979b). *An investigation of auditory laterality effects for song stimuli: Influence of musical training and complexity of stimulus presentation*. Paper presented at the Research Symposium in Music Education, University of Western Ontario.

Moskowitz, B. A. (1978). The acquisition of language. *Scientific American*, *239*(5), 92–108.

Obler, L. K. (1981). Right hemisphere participation in second language acquisition. In K. C. Diller (Ed.), *Individual differences and universals in language learning aptitude*. Rowley, MA: Newbury House.

Schmidt, L. (1976). Music as a learning mode. *Music Educator's Journal*, *63*(1), 95–97.

Wong-Fillmore, L. (1976). The second time around: Cognitive and social strategies in second language acquisition. Unpublished doctoral dissertation. Stanford University, Stanford, CA.

10
Approaches to Classroom Music for Children

AMY BROWN

The first pedagogical argument that took place among music educators has become known as the "note versus rote" controversy. At the end of the 19th century music educators could not agree upon whether children should learn to read music or simply sing "by ear" with no regard for the relationship of sound to music on the printed page. The discussion was healthy, of course, because it focused attention upon the necessity for methodology in music teaching. It became increasingly clear, however, that the problem of "how" music should be taught could be treated meaningfully only after careful consideration had been given to "why" music should be taught. If the function of music education was to prepare children to sing together in Sunday School and later as adults in the church choir, the weekly choir rehearsal rote drill would suffice. Preparation to participate in performances of complex choral literature, on the other hand, would require the ability to read music notation. Samuel Cole spoke to this issue at a meeting of the National Education Association in 1903:

The real purpose of teaching music in the public schools is not to make expert sight singers nor individual soloists. I speak from experience. I have done all these things and I can do them again; but I have learned that, if they become an end, and not a means, they hinder rather than help, because they represent only the abilities of the few. A much nobler, grander, more inspiring privilege is yours and mine; to get the great mass to singing and to make them love it. (Birge, 1966)

In this address Coleman set the stage for the decades of philosophical discussion concerning music education that were to follow.

The Tanglewood Symposium is widely accepted as the landmark event that provided unifying purpose for the profession and led the way toward the acceptance of clearly defined "how to" classroom music learning experiences. The Symposium took place in the summer of 1967 under the sponsorship of the Music Educators National Conference, the Theodore Presser Foundation, the Boston University School of Fine and Applied Arts, and the Berkshire Music Center, and was held in Tanglewood, Massachusetts. Over a 10-day period "Music in American Society" was discussed and evaluated, and recommendations for more effective teaching were made. The participants were educators, musicians,

sociologists, philosophers, theologians, labor leaders, music educators, industri-
alists, philanthropists, and representatives of government. The Tanglewood
Declaration summarized the philosophical views upon which the Symposium
based its recommendations and provided a model through which music teachers
might better appreciate the importance of values clarification before music lesson
planning (i.e., "why" before "what"). The following excerpt expresses the principal tenets of the philosophy:

> We believe that education must have as major goals the art of living, the building of per-
> sonal identity, and nurturing creativity. Since the study of music can contribute much to
> these ends we now call for music to be placed in the core of the school curriculum.
>
> The arts afford a continuity with the aesthetic tradition in man's history. Music and
> other fine arts, largely nonverbal in nature, reach close to the social, physiological and
> psychological roots of man in his search for identity and self realization.
>
> Educators must accept the responsibility for developing opportunities which meet man's
> individual needs and the needs of a society plagued by the consequences of changing
> values, alienation, hostility between generations, racial and international tensions, and
> the challenges of a new leisure. (Choate, 1968)

Through this strong challenge the Tanglewood Symposium defined the task of
music education for some, clarified it for others, and indicted those who failed
to demonstrate expressed purpose in the classroom. In 1970 the Music Educators
National Conference (MENC) published its Goals and Objectives (GO) Project,
which initiated the implementation of the Tanglewood recommendations. Alongside such lofty goals as the building of a vital musical culture and an enlightened
musical public stood the goal to use the most effective techniques and resources
for music instruction (MENC, 1970). One MENC board member concluded that:

> The GO Project provided a forum for "brainstorming" in consideration of the needs of
> American society and our youth in particular, related to aesthetic enrichment through
> music. Whereas Tanglewood was the germinal definition of direction, the GO Project
> became the catalyst for reaction—a pragmatic focus. (Middleton, 1980)

Early in this century Samuel Cole identified a meaningful purpose for music
education; more recently the Tanglewood symposium defined a purpose for our
time, and the GO Project honored its recommendations. This refining of Samuel
Cole's 1903 proclamation that "why" supercedes "how" is largely responsible
for the national acceptance and success of the four major approaches discussed
below as effective techniques for teaching music.

Each of these learning systems, Orff, Kodaly, Dalcroze, and Comprehensive
Musicianship, holds the basic view that music is life-enhancing and that every
human being is endowed with musical capacities that can and should be developed. The paths through which they approach this development differ widely and
are attributed to irreconcilably disparate ideas concerning such basic components
as reading and writing music, singing, playing instruments, and choice of music
material. The strength of Orff, Kodaly, Dalcroze, and Comprehensive Musicianship lies in the fact that each represents a precise pedagogy for teaching every
aspect of a well-defined philosophy of music education. "How" consistently

reflects "why." The discussion of each system will begin with the philosophical underpinnings upon which it is built and continue into implementing activities, particularly for children in the lower grades.

The Orff Approach

Carl Orff (1895–1982) was a German composer whose contribution to music education for children has come to be known as the Orff Schulwerk. His appointment to compose music for adult dance classes and the opportunity to observe dancers and gymnasts stabilized the beliefs that would ultimately lead to his international fame as teacher. Orff was an avid gardener and nature enthusiast. He believed that in the same sense that wild flowers thrive naturally and cultivated flowers often do not thrive, children might also thrive if encouraged to grow through their own natural resources. Plants and children alike flourish with a careful balance of outside intervention. Orff perceived both nature and human evolution as processes of growth and flow from simple to complex with enigmatic beginnings. It seemed reasonable to him that children should be given the freedom to express their innate inclinations and to grow through their own sense of feeling. He referred to this idea as "elemental."

The use of instruments, which is an important component of the Orff approach, came about as a result of his experimentation with this "elemental" theory in the dance theatre. Responding to the desire to combine dance movement with music performance, he elevated music from the accompanying role of orchestra in the pit to an onstage, integral part of the presentation. The first scores were rhythmic only, composed for percussion instruments such as drums and cymbals, and were played by musicians. Orff later assigned the playing of these instruments onstage to the dancers themselves. This idea demonstrated his belief that novice musicians should be led to capitalize upon the same innate sense of rhythm through which the earliest known human communication through music took place.

The historic continuing development of man's musical sophistication upon which Orff based his approach to the study of music required the gradual introduction of melody and harmony into the music and appropriate instruments that were primitive enough to ensure success for amateur performers. He collaborated with the piano maker Karl Maemdler, who understood Orff's thinking and created the first Orff xylophones, which were pitched percussion instruments with removable bars. This construction provided the means through which dance students could learn to freely improvise rhythms, coordinate these with dance movement, and add or combine bars for melody and harmony as their cognitive skills increased. The reverse procedure of beginning with improvised musical composition and adding the dance also became a part of Orff training. The development of Orff rhythm and melody-producing instruments has progressed to include both wooden and metal xylophones called metallophones with removable bars in soprano, alto, and bass timbre and ranges that are easily played by children. Other instruments comprising the Orff instrumentation are a variety of drums, including congo, bass, tom-tom, tympani, and bongo, and other percussion instruments such as claves, cymbals, wooden rattlers, temple blocks, and guiros. Glockenspiels add to the percussion capability and also contribute the ringing sound of the German glockenspiel for melodic effects that were so familiar to Orff. Soprano, alto, tenor, and bass recorder are especially for melody, and guitar, cello, and double bass complete ensembles for advanced players.

In 1948 Carl Orff conducted a series of programs on a Bavarian radio station in which untrained children played his instruments. The success of these programs stimulated his interest in music education for children. Since the Schulwerk was already founded upon a sound philosophical base for children, the only new dimension to be added to the system was singing. Orff believed children's natural responses to rhythmic stimuli to be the base from which the perception of the remaining elements of music emerge. The first of these is melody. Children's speech patterns evolve through chants and rhymes to melody. The song material in the Orff approach begins, therefore, with children's rhythmic speech patterns and continues through childhood chants and rhymes to folk songs. *Musik fur Kinder* is the standard work for teaching music to children through the Orff system. It consists of five volumes of music written by Carl Orff and Gunild Keetman (1955), and has been translated and adapted for use in North America and other world cultures.

In Orff classrooms, rhythmic activities, singing, moving, and speaking are combined and balanced with children's natural propensities such that carefully planned sequential learning appears to be almost incidental. As a result, children learn to respond freely to their feelings through the creation of their own music. In Carl Orff's view, this capacity fosters continuous growth and represents the means through which music education educates the whole person.

The Kodaly Concept

Zoltan Kodaly (1882–1967) was a Hungarian composer, musicologist, and conservatory of music teacher whose enthusiasm for indigenous folk music led to the Kodaly concept of music education. In 1905 he and his friend Bela Bartok initiated the collection and analysis of Hungarian folk songs that is still continued at the Institute of Folk Music Research of the Hungarian Academy of Sciences. The structure of this music, its style, tonal language, and character, so profoundly affected Kodaly that he began to incorporate its melodies into his compositions. As musicologist and nationalist as well, he realized that the strains of this musical heritage heard in his music alone would not preserve it and turned to music education. Through this avenue he sought to make Hungarian youth aware of their own folk music and also to fulfill the long-held dream of a musically literate Hungarian society. In his view, the process of learning to sing, read, and write music was not unlike that of learning to speak, read, and write language. High purpose was assigned to singing:

It is not worth much if we sing for ourselves, it is finer if two sing together. Then more and more, hundreds and thousands until, finally, the great Harmony, in which we can all unite, can be heard. (Williams, 1975)

The philosophical beliefs upon which the Kodaly concept are based belong to Kodaly, but he did not create the implementing techniques. The system gradually developed in Hungary after World War II through the work of his students and musician-teacher colleagues. Kodaly's guiding spirit is clearly present in the classroom teaching strategies, which reveal his thinking concerning such questions as why music, what music, who should study music, and how this study should be approached.

He believed that music literacy was as important as language facility toward the enhancement of life and should belong to ordinary people as well as to the privileged classes. All children, he claimed, babble musical as well as verbal sounds and equally as naturally. The experience of one's own person as a music-producing instrument heightens not only self-esteem but also the enjoyment of life, and is available to everyone; everyone should learn to sing, read, and write music. For Kodaly, indigenous folk music represented a mother tongue that was already available. This body of literature would provide appropriate material for the study of music and also reinforce the sense of national pride that was important to Kodaly. Furthermore, the complex components of more sophisticated music would be embraced without resistance by children whose early training had placed music alongside the "natural" phenomenon, language. Kodaly considered music to be no less valuable than the purely academic subjects toward the intellectual development of children, and to be by far the most valuable resource for emotional and aesthetic growth.

The learning strategies employed to implement Kodaly's philosophical thinking were no more innovative than most of the ideas that he espoused. The strong emphasis upon singing, however, was unique, and herein lies the distinction of the Kodaly approach. All the answers to why, what, who, and how with regard to music learning are found in the singing and study of indigenous folk music. The actual means are a synthesis of Italian, French, English, and Swiss practice. No such amalgamation had been attempted previously. The practice of solfa, or assigning music syllables (do re mi, etc.) to the notes of a melody, came from Italy. The use of syllables to denote rhythm (ti-ti-ta) came from France. Jaques-Dalcroze of Switzerland provided the techniques for employing rhythmic movement to music. The Kodaly approach is probably best known for its utilization of hand signals that interpret the relationships of melodic sounds in space. This practice was invented by John Curven in England in 1870. Finally, the most prominent model for teacher-student interaction can be traced to the influence of the Swiss Johann Pestalozzi, who advocated interest stimulation as precursor to cognitive learning. Kodaly teachers patiently allow children to enjoy singing and gradually implement learning strategies.

In keeping with Kodaly's high regard for authentic music and insistence upon only good music in the classroom, the teaching repertoire begins with childhood chants, singing games, and nursery rhymes. Folk songs are added when appropriate, and the materials evolve through composed music for children to the art music of such composers as Mozart, Beethoven, and Schubert. Treatments for the adaptation of this concept in the United States have been published by several music educators, including Richards (1964), Choksy (1974, 1981), and Szonyi (1973).

Dalcroze Eurythmics

Emile Jaques-Dalcroze (1865–1950) was born in Vienna to Swiss parents. His mother was a music teacher and proponent of the Pestalozzian educational philosophy, which influenced his thinking about life, music, and teaching. Johann Heinrich Pestalozzi (1747–1805) believed music to be a suitable vehicle through which to educate for productivity in life because of its power to evoke feelings. The education of feelings in his philosophy could lead to morality, which he defined as a sense of love for others and the most important of human capacities. The purpose of education was to foster the harmonious development of moral, physical, and mental capability. This basic principle seems to lie at the root of Dalcroze Eurythmics.

The word "eurythmics" from the Greek *eu* and *rhymos*, meaning good movement or flow, describes the study of music through rhythm. Solfege, or singing music notation at sight, and improvisation, or expressing feelings through individual creative music performance, are the two remaining components of Dalcroze Eurythmics. Rhythmic movement is sometimes taught in isolation by Dalcroze teachers. In such cases the full intent of the Jaques-Dalcroze philosophy is unavailable to students. Complete implementation requires the combined effect of physical and intellectual powers for the purpose of getting in touch with, expressing, and controlling the feelings that music evokes. Ultimately this exercise in disciplined freedom is expected to enhance self-knowledge. Participants examine and interpret their feelings in the music environment and become acquainted with themselves in a way that is otherwise unavailable. The transfer of this process into other areas of life experience can be seen to provide a means through which students learn to discriminate intelligently and choose behavior that leads to good consequences. Dalcroze himself maintained that his approach to music education was intended as education of whole persons. Therapists and dancers as well as musician-teachers who relate to this same purpose find a valuable resource in the work of Jaques-Dalcroze.

His accomplishments as composer and writer for the theatre, composer of concert pieces and operas for adults and songs for children, conductor, singer, and pianist led to the 1892 appointment of Jaques-Dalcroze as professor of harmony and solfege at the Conservatory in Geneva. He was dismayed to find student compositions to be mechanical products of the rules of harmony that they themselves could not hear without playing, and also to find an appalling inability among students to sing in tune. Attributing this lack of musicality to the need for training that connects the sounds of music to life itself, he initiated the work that later became Dalcroze Eurythmics. Rhythmic movement in music was for Jaques-Dalcroze the component most closely related to emotive human life. It seemed reasonable that when exposed to practice requiring concentration upon this idea, students could be taught to "become" music and also to create music that expressed themselves. He believed that through the same human facility by which people walk in rhythmic tempo and change pace automatically when appropriate, people learn to compose and improvise musically. Toward this end Dalcroze created thousands of exercises and composed music to stimulate rhythmic movement.

The solfege component of Dalcroze Eurythmics is taught through a system which he labeled "inner hearing." He maintained that humans should be able to hear music by seeing it (hear with the eyes) and write music by hearing it (see with the ears). Solfege, or sight-singing and ear training, in his view awakened the sense of tonal pitch and tonal relationships and allowed the innately possessed consciousness of sound to emerge. In addition to the exercises based upon the principles of movement in relationship to music that he espoused, Dalcroze invented exercises that compelled students to look at musical scores and sing them without the benefit of external music stimuli.

The ability to improvise was, of course, the ultimate aim of Jaques-Dalcroze's philosophy of music education. He described it as "the study of the direct relationship between cerebral commands and muscular interpretations in order to express one's own musical feelings" (Jaques-Dalcroze, 1932). In every Dalcroze lesson, despite the level of student age, experience, and ability, the body's capacity to move and the ears' to hear is coupled with the mental capacity to discern and remember the qualities of combinations of sounds in music. Teachers consistently encourage the employment of individual imaginative powers to transfer these human capabilities into personal (and group) expressions of the feelings that music evokes and music that expresses feelings.

The process begins in nursery school with two different kinds of experiences that Choksy, Abramson, Gillespie, and Woods (1986) referred to as "a relaxed casual type of listening" and "a concentrated musician's listening." Preschool children listen, play singing games, and perform to musical accompaniments of stories. By fifth grade children hear and freely express the complexities of highly sophisticated music through body movements, listen to music and write what is heard, and also sing music at sight with ease.

Comprehensive Musicianship

Among the four major approaches to the study of music education, Comprehensive Musicianship is the only one that originated in the United States and that does not reflect the philosophy and bear the name of a particular person. Implicit in its title is the manner in which it came into being as well as a learning style.

In 1960 Jerome Bruner had advocated the "teaching and learning of structure; rather than the simple mastery of facts" (p. 12), and also proclaimed that "any subject can be taught effectively in some intellectually honest form to any child at any stage of development" (p. 33). The Yale "Seminar on Music Education" convening at Yale University in 1963 under this powerful influence called for the study of music from the inside out. Closely following, the 1965 Northwestern University "Seminar in Comprehensive Musicianship—the Foundation for College Education" studied the problem of fragmentation and the lack of continuity in music curricula, particularly in high schools and colleges. This conference led the way to Comprehensive Musicianship training for children beginning in kindergarten. It appears to be an "intellectually honest form" of music education for youth at "any stage of development."

Comprehensive Musicianship is not represented by a definite set of learning strategies and is not often discussed in philosophical terms. Its creation, however, clearly rests upon the idea that school is a microcosm that should function to prepare youth for personal success and productivity in the world outside. The basic question answered relates to why children go to school as opposed to the "why study music" with which other approaches begin. In the world outside of school people demonstrate abilities, listen to others, are creative, and think logically. Successful people understand the relationships between these functions. Music is performed, listened to, created, and logical; its nature and structure provide opportunities for the development of valuable life skills. Comprehensive Musicianship aspires to teach the nature and structure of music such that students relate to it as performers, listeners, composers, and scholars. Every lesson incorporates activities that provide for development in these areas.

Music is approached on every level of study as a sound source with relationships in time and space to be discovered. Basic concepts of pitch, duration, and texture are explored and seem to combine and produce particular forms in music and forms of music. Children experiment with degrees of high and low through singing and playing instruments; relate to duration through walking and clapping steady beats that become the underlying pulse for rhythmic variety; listen to and create music in relation to the concept of thinness and thickness; and combine the knowledge acquired through experiences such as these to produce new music that achieves a particular purpose in a particular way. In like manner, knowledge of the expressive elements of music, tempo, dynamics, and tone color are acquired experientially. A change of pace, louder or softer or brighter sounds, become important only as a result of student thought, analysis, and discretion.

Performance abilities are seen as means, not ends. Comprehensive Musicianship teachers encourage children to sing, play, and move individually and together and never drill for perfection. A thoughtful presentation that reflects understanding beyond a previous performance achieves its purpose. The child whose galloping horse that previously moved in perfectly even steps now moves unevenly is applauded even though the movement is expressed only by the head. The teacher appeals for evidence of thought and is satisfied to learn that this particular horse is still in the stable and only thinking about galloping.

Comprehensive Musicianship is entirely nondiscriminating and somewhat reminiscent of the open classroom described by Charles Siberman (1973) as "giving" them [children] freedom to explore and supporting them in their exploration." Whatever supports student efforts as performers, listeners, composers, and scholars is acceptable. Along with accepting technically imperfect performances, this approach approves of all music, any form of notation, any sound producer, and any physical expression of music.

In the Comprehensive Musicianship classroom, music representing cultures around the world from childhood chants and songs to high classics may be heard. The musical instruments played are student invented, traditional classroom rhythm band, and popular (such as guitar, ukelele, and piano) as well as electronic and exotic. Physical expression of music incorporates individual and group creations and also the dances of Western and non-Western cultures. Teachers function as facilitators whose leadership skills are highly developed, but almost invisible in the classroom.

Comprehensive Musicianship through Classroom Music (1974) is the best known work for teachers who prefer this approach. It is a product of the Hawaii Music Curriculum Project, which was initiated in Honolulu in 1968 under the sponsorship of the Hawaii Curriculum Center. Like Comprehensive Musicianship itself, this text represents the combined thinking of many musicians and teaching professionals. It is ungraded and divided into zones that are structured to relate to increasing levels of student sophistication in the four areas of interest to Comprehensive Musicianship: composing, listening, performing, and intellectualizing.

Conclusions

The proponents of Orff, Kodaly, Dalcroze, and Comprehensive Musicianship all stress the importance of the philosophical thought that undergirds these approaches to music education. While each clearly extols the value of music in the human experience, each defines this value differently and emerges as a unique learning system. For example, Kodaly began with singing, whereas Orff added it last; Orff emphasized playing instruments, and Kodaly believed instruments to be for the rich; for Kodaly the voice was everyone's instrument, but for Orff the body was everyone's instrument. None of this matters for Comprehensive Musicianship; people should perform and create music by any means.

These differences bring to mind the "note versus rote" controversy, and also explain the current disenchantment among some music educators with the idea of an "eclectic" approach to music learning. Orff, Kodaly, Dalcroze, and Comprehensive Musicianship are the most widely and successfully implemented learning systems in the nations' music classrooms. This success can be attributed to the continuity of why and how within each approach, and also to the differences among them that appeal to the differences among teacher philosophical views.

References

Birge, W. B. (1966). *History of public school music in the United States*, pp. 61–62. Washington, DC: Music Educators National Conference.

Bruner, J. S. (1960). *The process of education*. New York, NY: Random House.

Choate, R. A. (Ed.). (1968). *Documentary report of the Tanglewood symposium*, (p. 39). Washington, DC: Music Educators National Conference.

Chosky, L. (1974). *The Kodaly method*. Englewood Cliffs, NJ: Prentice-Hall.

Chosky, L. (1981). *The Kodaly context*. Englewood Cliffs, NJ: Prentice-Hall.

Chosky, L., Abramson, R. M., Gillespie, A. E., & Woods, D. (1986). *Teaching music in the twentieth century*, (p. 154). Englewood Cliffs, NJ: Prentice-Hall.

Jaques-Dalcroze, E. (1932). Rhythmics and pianoforte improvisation. *Music and Letters*, *13*(4), 371–380.

MENC. (1970). "The GO Project: Where is it Heading?" *Music Educators Journal*, *40*(6), 44–45.

Middleton, J. A. (1980). "The GO Project: Retrospective of a decade." *Music Educators Journal*, *67*(4), 42–47.

Orff, C., & Keetman, G. (1955). *Music for Children* (Vols. 1–5) (A. Walter & D. Hall, Transl. adaptors). Mainz: B. Schott's Sohne.

Richards, M. H. (1964). *Threshold to music*. Belmont, CA: Fearon Publishers.

Silberman, C. E. (Ed.). (1973). *The open classroom reader*, (p. xx). New York, NY: Random House.

Szonyi, E. (1973). *Kodaly's principles in practice*. New York, NY: Boosey & Hawkes.

Thomson, W. (1974). *Comprehensive mmusicianship through classroom music*. Belmont, CA: Addison Wesley.

Williams, M. (1975). Philosophical foundations of the Kodaly approach to education. *Kodaly Envoy*, *2*(2), 4–9.

11
An Analysis of Historical Reasons for Teaching Music to Young Children: Is It the Same Old Song?

THOMAS W. DRAPER and CLAIRE GAYLE

Much of the knowledge base for the discipline of early childhood education comes from logic and tradition rather than from controlled empirical observation. In the area of children's music, in particular, tradition and logic appear to have dominated the written suggestions of early childhood educators. For over 90 years writers of textbooks for teachers of young children have been giving reasons for teaching music to children. The great majority of these reasons, while forming a rather fertile field of hypotheses, have seldom been empirically examined.

The present study seeks to categorize the statements of the textbook writers regarding the value of music in the lives of young children. An examination of these statements could be useful in understanding and improving the discipline of early childhood education. If we value the effects we believe music is having on young children and want to be more efficient in achieving our desired ends, we should systematically study the relationships that are thought to exist. Two of the initial steps in such an examination would be an identification of the variables that are thought to be linked to musical experience and a description of the relationships that are said to exist (Wohlwill, 1973).

Once the relationships have been identified, their magnitude and persistence can be examined. Relationships that are believed to exist by a majority of the textbook authors will perhaps represent the best hypotheses for future study. On the other hand, relationships that are only thought to exist during a particular period may be nothing more than a reflection of the current social Zeitgeist. Shifts in emphasis in the early childhood textbooks may tell as much about how children were regarded and what aspects of their character were valued during different time periods as they will about the development of thought about the teaching of music. In fact, one historian has suggested that those who write books about the care and education of young children are particularly sensitive bellwethers of the social climate, and that social change can be measured and understood by examining the "expert" advice given to those in charge of the young (Graebner, 1980). If this is true, the present study should not only identify some useful hypotheses about the role of music in child development, but also may reveal some interesting information about the relationship between "expert" advice and social trends during the time periods in which different books were written. For example, there may have been a change in thinking in the early to middle 1960s as programs for the disadvantaged proliferated. Other changes have occurred in the early 1970s when the value of programs for young children was severely challenged, and in the late 1970s when the value of early education reasserted itself with a social emphasis (Hodges & Smith, 1979; Lazar & Darlington, 1982).

Early Childhood Education Textbook Survey

In order to determine the ideas and patterns present in textbooks for early childhood educators an attempt was made to survey all such textbooks on the campus of Brigham Young University. The three main sources of textbooks were the two million volume main campus library, the resource library for the early childhood education laboratory, and the elementary music and early childhood education faculty. In all, 114 books were identified. Six of these books were eliminated from consideration because they were either duplicates or they could not be located by the library staff. This left a final population of 108 books. These books are listed in the special bibliography at the end of this paper. All references to music in the table of contents and index of each book were examined and the specific reasons that were given for teaching music to young children were noted. As a reliability check, the complete list of reasons compiled by the first examiner, along with a random sample of six of the textbooks, was examined by a second examiner. There was a correlation of .83 between the categorizations of the two examiners.

The textbooks used in the study were published between 1887 and 1982, with the majority of texts being published more recently. Once the hypothesized relationships between music and the accomplishment of developmental and educational goals had been identified, all volumes (1927 to 1983) of the *Child Development Abstracts and Bibliography* were examined to determine if the specific relationships postulated by the textbook writers had ever received any empirical support.

In order to determine the degree to which the textbooks had been influenced by time, the 96-year span covered by the publication of the textbooks was divided into five time periods and differences in the opinions that were expressed by the textbook authors from each period were noted. The historical paper of Hodges and Smith (1979) was used to divide the evolution of early childhood education into time periods. The categories of Hodges and Smith (1979) were modified somewhat to maintain a sufficient number of books in each time period. The five time periods were:

1. The *early period*, covering from 1887 through 1950 (21 books).
2. *Conception and construction*, 1951 through 1963 (18 books).
3. *Revolution*, 1964 through 1972 (12 books).
4. *Reflection*, 1973 to 1978 (34 books).
5. The *current period*, 1979 to 1982 (23 books).

Each of these periods roughly marks a new type of emphasis in early childhood education. During the early period the thinking about young children was dominated by the writings of the early pioneers such as Froebel (1911) and Montessori (1964). In the 1950s and early 1960s a new conception of early childhood arose. Among the educated there was increased interest in less authoritarian programs for young children. Public reaction to the authoritarian excesses associated with World War II lead to a proliferation of more lenient and less obedience-oriented childrearing philosophies that were reflected in the preschool programs available for the children of socially advantaged parents (Graebner, 1980).

During the 1960s and early 1970s the revolution was beginning. The civil rights movement, the Economic Opportunity Act of 1964, and the beginning of Head Start brought a new awareness of ethnic differences and an increased faith that early intervention could eradicate socioeconomic differences. Professionals from a broad range of disciplines began to see in early childhood education a means of accomplishing social and political goals (Sears, 1975). In addition, theories of cognitive and social development were refined as the study of growth and development became regarded as a more respectable pursuit (Sears, 1975).

In the early 1970s the Westinghouse Study (Cicirelli, 1969) and other studies that sought to evaluate the influence of federal programs for young children shook the nation's faith in the value of early intervention. This caused early childhood specialists to go on the defensive and to reexamine their sometimes lavish promises. In the late 1970s studies like the Lazar and Darlington (1982) consortium report rekindled a redirected faith in the value of early intervention. This time the focus was on social competency rather than on isolated cognitive ability. This successful program defense, based on empirical research, probably increased early childhood educators' appreciation for empirical studies, paving the way for an increased reliance on data to supplement and amend traditional thinking.

If these philosophical shifts occurred, then the reasons given for teaching music from one time period to the next may make some predictable shifts. Textbooks from each of the five periods were examined to determine how the thinking of early childhood educators' about the role of music might have changed over time.

The stated reasons for teaching music to young children fell into the categories shown in Table 11.1. Only those reasons that were mentioned by 5% or more of the writers are listed in the table. An examination of the *Child Development Abstracts and Bibliography* between the years 1927 and 1983 revealed that almost no empirical investigations of the relationships proposed on Table 11.1 had been conducted. The only exceptions were a few studies published in the late 1970s and early 1980s on the role of music in concept formation and conservation (Scott, 1981; Serafine, 1979; Sergeant, 1979; Webster & Zimmerman, 1983).

It is worth noting that, in the 57 years covered by the *Child Development Abstracts and Bibliography*, ideas about research as well as ideas about music were changing. The criteria for inclusion in the *Abstracts* varied at least as much as the thinking about the benefits of music on young children. Many of the works

TABLE 11.1. Percentage of textbook writers ($n = 108$) endorsing each reason for teaching music to young children

Percent	Reason
70	Provides self-expression and creative pleasure
67	Fosters motor and rhythmic development
46	Develops an aesthetic sense
31	Teaches vocal and language development
26	Promotes cultural heritage
25	Promotes cognitive development and abstract thought
20	Teaches social and group skills
11	Helps child feel positive about self
7	Provides a cathartic release of tensions and aggression
6	Develops musicians

abstracted during the early and middle periods were interpretive case studies or reasoned pieces rather than empirical investigations. From these works several new hypotheses about the influence of music on young children could have been garnered—for example, music as a promoter of general health and well-being (Scott, 1931; Van deWall, 1929).

Only in the current period have early childhood educators begun to rely on empirical studies. Traditionally, early childhood educators have not attempted to bolster their ideas and assertions with empirical support. Until recent times the absence of empirical support for the proposed relationships did not seem to bother the textbook writers. Even now, systematically observed relationships do not play a central role in many parts of the early childhood education knowledge base. This indicates that early childhood educational practice is a relatively virgin area where empirical inquiry is needed and where a substantial contribution might be readily made.

In preparing to make such a contribution attention should be first given to the most widely held and enduring beliefs. In the area of music, two hypotheses—"provides self-expression and creative pleasure" and "promotes motor and rhythmic development"—were mentioned by over half of the writers. The majority of textbook writers were confident that music could accomplish these two objectives. Since these two reasons represent the areas of greatest agreement among the writers, they certainly deserve some critical examination.

In terms of hypotheses for future study, it may be somewhat difficult to operationally define, and thereby test, the impact of musical experience on "self-expression" and "creative pleasure." Such variables have always been the nemesis of objective observation. On the other hand, "motor and rhythmic development" might be much more easily operationalized and studied. Studies of this relationship could be conducted using existing measures. Based on a century of assertion, it would seem time for someone to examine the proposed relationship between musical experience and motor development. Likewise, the belief that music can promote language, social, and cognitive development seems widespread enough that investigation is warranted.

Era Comparisons

In order to determine how the thinking of early childhood educators had changed over time, an era analysis was conducted for those seven reasons for teaching music to young children that were mentioned by more than 20% of the textbook writers. As can be seen in Table 11.2, the time period analyses showed that the two most commonly given reasons for teaching music, "provides self-expression and creative pleasure" and "promotes motor and rhythmic development," were not greatly influenced by time. The fact that these beliefs were not only widespread but stable and enduring during the last century is further evidence that they are probably the best hypotheses to be investigated in future work.

All five of the remaining reasons showed time-related changes. The writers from different periods varied in the degree to which they thought music promoted the development of an aesthetic sense, a sense of cultural heritage, group skills, language and vocal ability, and abstract concepts and cognition. In an attempt to isolate the greatest areas of time-related contrast, data for each of

TABLE 11.2. Era-related changes in textbook reasons for teaching music to young children

	Percent of books per time period					
Reasons	< 1951	1951 to 1963	1964 to 1972	1973 to 1978	1979 to 1982	Chi-square[a]
Provides self-expression and creative pleasure	81	61	75	68	70	2.12
Promotes motor and rhythmic develop-ment	81	61	67	68	57	3.26
Develops an aesthetic sense	76	28	50	41	39	10.93**
Promotes vocal and language develop-ment	14	11	50	44	30	10.91**
Promotes cultural heritage	19	11	50	17	43	11.10**
Promotes cognitive development and abstract thought	19	17	17	21	48	8.25*
Teaches social and group skills	24	06	00	26	30	7.87*
Number of books examined in each period	21	18	12	34	23	Total = 108

[a] df = 4 for all chi-squares.
*p < .10.
**p < .05.

these five reasons were partitioned so as to maximize the chi-square with a single degree of freedom. These partitions revealed the following patterns.

The notion that music would develop an aesthetic sense in children was stronger prior to 1951 than it was after that time ($\chi^2 = 7.94$, df $= 1$, $p < .005$). The early writers believed that musical instruction would refine the senses of children and give them an appreciation for beauty more than did the later writers. One possible reason for this change in opinion may be related to the actual content of children's music before and after 1950. The quantity of highly specialized children's music, as we know it today, is a fairly recent innovation. The music children were encouraged to listen to in the latter part of the 19th century and the first part of the 20th century may have been largely light classical rather than specialized children's. That is, there may actually have been an aesthetic difference in the music for children in the two different time periods. This hypothesis requires further study. However, even if the music utilized in teaching children during the early period did have a higher aesthetic quality, the view that young children are capable of perceiving the difference in terms of aesthetics and of being influenced by such music would require further study before it could be accepted. The sheer quantity of children's music also began to change in the 1950s as relatively inexpensive phonographs made possible the mass marketing of specialized children's music designed to appeal to popular tastes.

The view that music promotes vocal and language development has been stronger since 1964 than it was prior to that time ($\chi^2 = 7.79$, df $= 1$, $p < .01$). This shift in emphasis was concurrent with the attempt to erase socioeconomic differences with early intervention. Most likely this addition of emphasis was a logical attempt to use the vocal elements of musical participation to remediate the language deficiencies in some children from the lower socioeconomic levels.

The view that musical experience will promote cultural heritage was stronger between 1964 and 1972 and since 1978 than it was at other times ($\chi^2 = 9.09$, df $= 1$, $p < .005$). This belief appears to be closely tied to the public's regard for the effectiveness of early childhood education programs for the disadvantaged. In Table 11.2 it can be seen that in the middle 1960s there was an upsurge in this belief, followed by a decrease in the belief throughout the middle 1970s, followed by a second upsurge in the late 1970s and early 1980s. Perhaps this up-down-up pattern is an example of the early-childhood-expert-as-social-bellwether phenomenon suggested by Graebner (1980).

The belief that musical training would promote cognitive development and abstract thought has been strongest since 1978 ($\chi^2 = 6.65$, df $= 1$, $p < .01$). The partition point on this relationship was somewhat of a surprise. The view that music could do something for cognitive development and abstract thinking was expected to flourish beginning in the middle 1960s when programs designed to enhance the cognitive development of children were in their heyday. The fact that so many textbook writers resisted the temptation to make a connection between music and a highly desirable child outcome is encouraging. During the middle 1960s cognitive development was much discussed by early childhood educators, yet few of the textbook writers chose to make a connection between musical experience and cognition without additional evidence. Since the bellwether hypothesis does not apply to the relationship between music and cognitive development, it may not be fair to offer a blanket criticism of most of the textbook writers by saying their ideas simply ride rather than guide the social Zeitgeist.

One reason why there may have been more of an emphasis in recent times on the relationship between musical experience and cognitive development is that a number of empirical studies were completed in the late 1970s and early 1980s that supported this relationship (Gardner, 1983; Scott, 1981; Serafine, 1979; Sergeant, 1979; Webster & Zimmerman, 1983). This is one area where the empirical relationship between musical experience and child outcome is receiving some study.

The view that music could promote social interaction and group skills was more prevalent before 1951 and after 1972 than it was during the 22 years between 1951 and 1972 ($\chi^2 = 6.05$, df $= 1, p < .01$). We can think of no reason for this up-down-up pattern. Early childhood education has always claimed to influence socialization. Why the relationship between music and social skill was not considered constant is not apparent.

Conclusion

Having surveyed the ideas of early childhood textbook writers, it appears that there are a number of relationships between musical experience and child outcomes that could be fruitfully studied. As mentioned, the relationship between musical experience and motor and rhythmic development is one prime candidate for inquiry. The relationship between music and cognitive development also appears to be an area that has borne some fruit and is likely to bear more (see Gardner, 1983). There are other possibilities as well, such as the influence of music on language development and social and group skills.

Some of the proposed relationships may be difficult to study because terms like aesthetics, creative pleasure, and self-expression are hard to define. Other relationships that have come and gone in time may represent nothing more than statements on the part of textbook writers caught up in the spirit of their times. Musical experience may promote cultural heritage, provided the children are exposed to the actual music of the culture whose heritage is being promoted. However, we do not find it likely that much of children's music as it exists today will give preschoolers an accurate appreciation of difference among and between people. Singing "Ten Little Indians" does not a cross-cultural experience make.

It is not our intention to suggest that music must provide measurable and demonstrable benefits in order to be included as part of the early childhood education curriculum. A strong argument can be made that music for its own sake certainly has value for human beings (Gardner, 1983). However, we do wish to point out that there is a century of hypotheses suggesting that musical experiences will have definite and specific benefits for young children. It is these relationships we would like to see explored in more detail and it is toward this end that the present paper is directed.

References

Cicirelli, V. G. (1969). *The impact of Head Start: An evaluation of the effects of Head Start on children's cognitive and affective development*. Washington, DC: National Bureau of Standards, Institute for Applied Technology.

Froebel, F. (1911). *Mutter-und kose-lieder*. Leipzig: Witive und Sohns.

Gardner, H. (1983). *Frames of mind: A theory of multiple intelligences*. New York: Basic Books.

Graebner, W. (1980). The unstable world of Benjamin Spock: Social engineering in a democratic culture, 1917-1950. *Journal of American History, 67*, 612-629.

Hodges, W., & Smith, L. (March 1979). *Twenty years of educational intervention with young children: 1958-1978*. Paper presented at the Boyd R. McCandless Symposium on Current Trends in Developmental Psychology, 25th Annual Meeting of the Southeastern Psychological Association, New Orleans, LA.

Lazar, I., & Darlington, R. (1982). Lasting effects of early education: A report from the Consortium for Longitudinal Studies. *Monographs of the Society for Research in Child Development, 47* (2-3, Serial No. 195).

Montessori, M. (1964). *The Montessori method*. New York: Schoken Books.

Scott, C. R. (1981). Progress report on music concept formation in preschoolers. *Bulletin of the Council for Research in Music Education, 66-67*, 74-79.

Scott, G. D. (1931). The psychic value of music and color in infant and child nutrition. *Medical Journal and Record, 133*, 161-165.

Sears, R. R. (1975). Your ancients revisited: A history of child development. In E. M. Hetherington (Ed.), *Review of child development research* (Vol. 5, pp. 1-74). Chicago: The University of Chicago Press.

Serafine, M. L. (1979). Meter conservation in music. *Council for Research in Music Education, 59*, 94-98.

Sergeant, D. (1979). Vocalization as a substructure for discriminatory and cognitive functioning in music: A pilot study. *Council for Research in Music Education, 59*, 98-101.

Van deWall, W. (1929). Music in child rearing. *Review International de l'Enfant, 7*, 3-12.

Webster, P. R., & Zimmerman, M. P. (1983). Conservation of rhythmic and tonal patterns of second through sixth grade children. *Council for Research in Music Education, 73*, 28-49.

Wohlwill, J. (1973). *The study of behavioral development*. New York: Academic Press.

Special Bibliography

Allen, K. E., & Goetz, E. M. (1982). *Early childhood education: Special problems, special solutions*. Rockville, MD: Aspen Systems.

Almy, M. C. (1979). *Ways of studying children: An observational manual for early childhood teachers*. New York: Columbia University, Columbia Teachers College.

Althouse, R. (1981). *The young child: Learning with understanding*. New York: Columbia University, Columbia Teachers College.

Andress, B. (1980). *Music experiences in early childhood*. New York: Holt, Rinehart, & Winston.

Andress, B., Heimann, H. M., Rinehart, C. A., & Talbert, E. G. (1973). *Music in early childhood*. Washington, DC: Music Educators National Congress.

Aronoff, F. W. (1969). *Music and young children*. New York: Holt, Rinehart, & Winston.

Aubin, N., Crook, E., & Walker, D. S. (1981). *Music*. Morristown, NJ: Silver Burdett.

Auleta, M. S. (1969). *Foundation of early childhood education: Readings*. New York: Random House.

Baker, K. R. (1960). *The nursery school: A human relationships laboratory*. Philadelphia: Saunders.

Barnard, H. (1890). *Kindergarten and child culture papers*. Hartford, CT: American Journal of Education.

Barnouw, E., & Swan, A. (1959). *Adventures with children in nursery school and kindergarten*. New York: Crowell.

Batcheller, J. (1975). *Music in early childhood*. New York: Center for Applied Research in Education.

Batterberry, H. L., & Van Dyke, P. (1957). *Wonderland in kindergarten*. New York: Exposition Press.

Bayless, K. M., & Ramsey, M. E. (1978). *Music: A way of life for the young child*. St. Louis: C. V. Mosby.

Beaty, J. J. (1979). *Skills for preschool teachers*. Columbis, OH: Merrill.

Biasini, A., Thomas, R., & Pogonowski, L. (1970). *Manhattanville music curriculum program*. Bardonia, NY: Media Materials.

Blatz, W. E., Millichamp, D., & Fletcher, M. (1935). *Nursery education, theory, and practice*. New York: W. Morrow.

Boardman, E., & Andress, B. (1981). *The music book: kindergarten*. New York: Holt, Rinehart, & Winston.

Bowen, H. C. (1894). *Froebel and education through self-activity*. New York: Charles Scribner's Sons.

Broman, B. L. (1982). *Early childhood education: Creative learning activities*. Boston: Houghton Mifflin.

Burton, L., & Hughes, W. (1979). *Music play: Learning activities for young children*. Menlo Park, CA: Addison-Wesley.

California Bureau of Elementary Education. (1956). *Teachers' guide to education in early childhood*. Sacramento, CA: California State Department of Education.

Christianson, H. M., Rogers, M. M., & Ludlum, B. A. (1961). *The nursery school: Adventure in living and learning*. Boston: Houghton Mifflin.

Clouser, L. W., & Millikan, C. E. (1929). *Kindergarten—Primary activities based on community life*. New York: Macmillan.

Cohen, D. H. (1977). *Kindergarten and early schooling*. Englewood Cliffs, NJ: Prentice-Hall.

Copple, C., Siegel, I. E., & Saunders, R. (1979). *Educating the young thinker: Classroom strategies for cognitive growth*. New York: Van Nostrand.

Crook, E., Reimer, B., & Walker, D. S. (1981). *Music I (teacher's edition)*. Morristown, NJ: Silver Burdett.

Culkin, M. L. (1949). *Teaching the youngest*. New York: Macmillan.

Currie, J. (1887). *The principles and practice of early and infant school education*. New York: E. L. Kellogg.

Debelak, M., Herr, J., & Jacobson, M. (1981). *Creating innovative classroom materials for teaching young children*. New York: Harcourt Brace Jovanovich.

Fontana, D. (Ed.). (1978). *The education of the young child*. London: Open Books.

Forest, I. (1927). *Preschool education: A historical and critical study*. New York: Macmillan.

Forest, I. (1935). *The school for the child from two to eight*. New York: Ginn.

Forest, I. (1949). *Early years at school: A textbook for students of early childhood education*. New York: McGraw-Hill.

Foster, J. C., & Mattson, M. (1929). *Nursery school procedure*. New York: D. Appleton.

Fromberg, D. P. (1977). *Early childhood education: A perceptual models curriculum*. New York: Wiley.

Frost, J. L., & Kissinger, J. B. (1976). *The young child and the educational process*. New York: Holt, Rinehart, & Winston.

Gans, R., Stendler, C. B., & Almy, M. (1952). *Teaching young children in nursery school, kindergarten, and the primary grades*. Yonkers-on-Hudson, NY: World Book.

Garrison, C. G., Sheehy, E. D., & Dalgliesh, A. (1937). *The Horace Mann kindergarten for five-year-old children*. New York: Columbia University: Columbia Teachers College.

Gilbert, A. (1973). *Prime time: Children's early learning years*. New York: Citation Press.

Gilbert, C. B. (1913). *What children study and why*. Boston: Silver Burdett.

Gilley, J. M., & Gilley, B. H. (1980). *Early childhood development and education*. Albany, NY: Delmar.

Gloyn, S., & Frobisher, B. (1975). *Teaching basic skills to infants*. London: Ward Lock.

Gould, J., Lindberg, L., & Spitzer, J. (1957). *Teaching primary children*. Boston: Starr King Press.

Griffin, E. F. (1982). *Island of childhood: Education in the special world of nursery school*. New York: Columbia University, Columbia Teachers College.

Grossman, B. D., & Keyes, C. R. (1978). *Helping children grow: The adult's role*. Wayne, NJ: Averly.

Hammond, S. L. (1963). *Good schools for young children: A guide for working with three-, four-, and five-year-old children*. New York: Macmillan.

Hefferman, H. (1951). *Guiding the young child*. Boston: Heath.

Hendrick, J. (1980). *Total learning for the whole child: Holistic curriculum for children age two to five*. St. Louis: C. V. Mosby.

Hendrick, J. (1980). *The whole child: New trends in early education*. St. Louis: C. V. Mosby.

Hess, R. D., Croft, D. J., & Kirby, A. (1975). *Teachers of young children*. Boston: Houghton Mifflin.

Hildebrand, V. (1971). *Introduction to early childhood education*. New York: Macmillan.

Hipple, M. L. (1975). *Early childhood education: Problems and methods*. Pacific Palisades, CA: Goodyear.

Hodgden, L., Koetter, J., LaFarge, B., McCord, S., & Scharm, D. (1974). *School before six: A diagnostic approach*. St. Louis, MO: Cemrel.

Hurd, H. B. (1955). *Teaching in the kindergarten*. Minneapolis, MN: Burgess.

Hymes, J. L. (1974). *Teaching the children under six*. Columbus, OH: Merrill.

International Kindergarten Union. (1913). *The kindergarten: Reports on the committee of nineteen on the theory and practice of the kindergarten*. Boston: Houghton Mifflin.

Johnson, H. M. (1928). *Children in the nursery school*. New York: John Day.

Johnson, H. M., & Stewart, M. (1924). *A nursery school experiment*. New York: Bureau of Educational Experiments.

Kaplan, S. N. (1975). *A young child's experiences: Activities for teaching and learning*. Pacific Palisades, CA: Goodyear.

Kaplan-Sanoff, M., & Yablans-Magid, R. (Eds.). (1981). *Exploring early childhood: Readings in theory and practice*. New York: Macmillan.

Kellogg, R. (1949). *Nursery school guide: Theory and practice for parents*. Boston: Houghton Mifflin.

Kocher, M. B. (1973). *The Montessori manual of cultural subjects: A guide for teachers*. Minneapolis: T. S. Dennison.

Kost, M. L. (1972). *Success or failure begins in the early school years*. Springfield, IL: Charles C Thomas.

Lambert, H. M. (1958). *Teaching the kindergarten child*. New York: Harcourt Brace Jovanovich.

Lambert, H. M. (1960). *Early childhood education*. Boston: Allyn & Bacon.

Landreth, C., & Read, K. H. (1942). *Education of the young child: A nursery school manual*. New York: John Wiley.

Langdon, G., & Stout, I. W. (1964). *Teaching in the primary grades*. New York: Macmillan.

Lay-Dopyera, M., & Lay-Dopyera, J. E. (1982). *Becoming a teacher of young children*. Lexington, MA: Heath.

Leavitt, J. E. (Ed.). (1958). *Nursery-kindergarten education*. New York: McGraw-Hill.

Logan, M. (1960). *Teaching the young child: Methods of preschool and primary education*. Boston: Houghton Mifflin.

Lundsteen, S. W., & Bernstein-Tarrow, N. (1981). *Guiding young children's learning: A comprehensive approach to early childhood education*. New York: McGraw-Hill.

Malloy, T. (1974). *Montessori and your child: A primer for parents*. New York: Schocken.

Marsh, M. V., Rinehart, C., & Savage, E. (1974). *The spectrum of music: Kindergarten*. New York: Macmillan.

McDonald, D. T. (1979). *Music in our lives: the early years*. Washington, DC: National Association for the Education of Young Children.

Meier, J. H., & Malone, P. J. (1979). *Infant and toddler learning episodes*. Baltimore: University Park Press.

Minor, R. (1937). *Early childhood education: Its principles and practices*. New York: Appleton-Century.

Moore, B., & Richards, P. (1959). *Teaching in the nursery school*. New York: Harper.

Morrison, G. S. (1980). *Early childhood education today*. Columbus, OH: Charles E. Merrill.

Moustakas, C. E., & Berson, M. P. (1956). *The young child in school*. New York: Whiteside.

Newbury, J. (1974). *More kindergarten resources*. Atlanta: John Knox.

Nimmicht, G. P., McAfee, O., & Meier, J. (1969). *The new nursery school*. New York: General Learning Corp.

North Carolina Department of Public Instruction. (1955). *Schools for young children: Nursery schools and kindergartens*. Raleigh, NC.

Nye, V. (1975). *Music for young children*. New York: William C. Brown.

Oxley, M. B. (1976). *Illustrated guide to individualized kindergarten instruction*. West Nyack, NY: Parker.

Parker, S. C., & Temple, A. (1924). *Unified kindergarten and first-grade teaching*. Chicago: University of Chicago, Department of Education.

Petrone, P. (1976). *The developmental kindergarten: Individualized instruction through diagnostic grouping*. Springfield, IL: Charles C Thomas.

Pitcher, E. G. (1974). *Helping young children learn*. Columbus, OH: Charles E. Merrill.

Pratt-Butler, G. K. (1975). *The three-, four-, and five-year-old in a school setting*. Columbus, OH: Charles E. Merrill.

Robinson, G. A. (1973). *A guidance program in nursery school and kindergarten for children one to five*. New York: Heath Cote.

Schwartz, S. L., & Robinson, H. F. (1982). *Designing curriculum for early childhood*. Boston, MA: Allyn & Bacon.

Seefeldt, C. (1973). *A curriculum for child care centers*. Columbus, OH: Charles E. Merrill.

Seefeldt, C. (1976). *Curriculum for the pre-school primary child: A review of the research*. Columbus, OH: Charles E. Merrill.

Sheehy, E. D. (1954). *The fives and sixes go to school*. New York: Holt.

Sheehy, E. D. (1968). *Children discover music and dance*. New York: Columbia University, Columbia Teachers College.

Spodek, B. (1972). *Teachers in the early years*. Englewood Cliffs, NJ: Prentice-Hall.

Spodek, B., & Walberg, H. J. (Eds.). (1977). *Early childhood education: Issues and insights*. Berkeley, CA: McCutchan.

Sweeney, F., & Wharran, M. (1973). *Experience games through music for the very young*. Portola Valley, CA: Richards Institute of Music Education and Research.

Taylor, B. J. (1970). *A child goes forth: A curriculum guide for teachers of preschool children*. Provo, UT: Brigham Young University Press.

Taylor, B. J. (1974). *When I do, I learn: A guide to creative planning for teachers and parents of preschool children*. Provo, UT: Brigham Young University Press.

Thorn, A. G. (1929). *Music for young children*. New York: Charles Scribner's Sons.

Vance, B. (1973). *Teaching the prekindergarten child: Instructional design and curriculum*. Monterey, CA: Brooks-Cole.

Wills, C. D., & Stegeman, W. H. (1950). *Living in the kindergarten: A handbook for kindergarten teachers*. Chicago: Follett.

Winn, M., & Porcher, M. A. (1967). *The playgroup book*. New York: Macmillan.

Wolfgang, C. H. (1977). *Helping aggressive and passive preschoolers through play*. Columbus, OH: Charles E. Merrill.

Woodhead, M. (1976). *Intervening in disadvantage: A challenge for nursery education*. Windsor, Ontario: National Foundation for Educational Research Publishing Co. Ltd.

Yardley, A. (1971). *The teacher of young children*. London: Evans.

Yawkey, T. D. (1976). *Activities for career development in early childhood curriculum*. Columbus, OH: Charles E. Merrill.

12
Children's Musical Behaviors in the Natural Environment

LINDA BRYANT MILLER

When placed within the context of child development, early musical training can provide a foundation for academic instruction. Research has supported the importance of studying the development of early childhood musical behaviors (Greenberg, 1976; Moog, 1976; Petzold, 1981; Zimmerman, 1981) and has recognized the need to provide musical experiences for 3- through 5-year-old children (Gilbert, 1980; Michel, 1973; Rainbow, 1977; Smith, 1963). The purpose of this chapter is to describe the acquisition of spontaneous musical behaviors of young children in a natural environment. The acquisition of conservation, vocal, melodic, rhythm, conceptual, and motor skills during early childhood will be examined.

Literature Review

Conservation Responses

Conservation, the ability to see that certain properties of an object remain the same when the object's appearance is changed, is an essential part of Piaget's theory (Phillips, 1975). Most adults are able to classify music within a conceptual framework of harmony, melody, rhythm, and other formal relationships. Children are increasingly able to separate and analyze these same musical concepts as they grow older and their perceptual responses improve. Believing that conservation is a necessary condition for musical reasoning, Pflederer (1964) tested 18 subjects ages 5 and 8 on tasks of meter, tone, and rhythm. She concluded that 8-year-olds were better than 5-year-olds at conserving meter, tone, and rhythm patterns. The two age groups differed distinctly in their ability to conserve a tonal pattern when the rhythm was changed. Five-year-olds were unable to conserve meter and melody. They also lacked the ability to conserve rhythmic tasks.

Pflederer and Sechrest (1968) tested conservation of instrument, tempo, harmony, mode, rhythm, contour, and interval and found some nonconserving responses in subjects ages 5, 7, 9, and 13. In addition, 5-year-olds lacked the necessary verbal capacity to accurately describe their perceptions.

Two of Pflederer's (1964) findings will have bearing on the present study. First, children obtained more correct solutions to conservation problems when they were actively involved in music. This indicates that opportunities for overt actions involving music can improve some types of problem solving. Second, children can benefit from exposure to a wide range of musical experiences that have been designed to clarify the nature of the problem that is to be solved.

Conservation responses have also been tested in other studies. Schultz (1969) measured the ability of 377 children in grades 2 through 8 to listen to and identify melody, rhythm, tempo, instrumental timbre, mode, and key changes in musical examples. He concluded that these abilities improved with age. Schultz suggested that more developmental research is needed to examine the relationship between musical concepts and cognition.

Schultz's suggestion has been reflected in more recent research. Michel (1973) stated that the musical achievement of young children has been underestimated to a large degree. Michel observed infants as young as 1 month old who reacted to acoustic stimuli and who improved their ability to discriminate pitch, timbre, and intervals with increasing age. Michel concluded that "this steadily improving ability to discriminate acoustic stimuli means that in the second half of the first year of life the child is able to analyze more and more accurately the sound phenomena of the real world" (p. 15). These research results indicate that "active" participation of children in musical activities can be beneficial.

Development of Vocal Responses

The development of vocal ability occurs prior to the preschool years and is dependent upon maturation (Zimmerman, 1971). Music education in preschools and kindergartens should be organized to continue this early vocal development. The following studies review vocal development from birth through the preoperational stage.

Fridman (1973) proposed that the first cry of newborn babies is the generator of musicality and musical rhythm. Observing 2- through 14-month-old children, she found that the child's cry is a pattern of repetitive sounds that develop in potential as the baby grows older. At 4 weeks of age the baby is able to recognize people by their voice timbre, and by 4 months of age his or her voice range is an octave higher than at birth. Fridman stated that a child must be musically nourished from birth and the mother should sing to her baby and echo his or her sounds to build a "sonorous bond" between the two.

In a similar study, Moog (1976) observed a transition from passive to active perception in 4- through 6-month-old infants. Infants responded to music by turning toward the source of sound. When the infant was older he or she began to move in an unorganized manner in response to music. Moog distinguished between babbling as a precursor of speech and babbling that was considered music. Early vocalizations were spontaneous; musical babbling, however, occurred only when the child had been exposed previously to musical sounds.

In contrast to spontaneous music making, other studies have examined the influence of training on vocal abilities of young children. Smith (1963) studied the ability of 3- and 4-year-olds to sing in tune within upper and lower ranges. Findings indicate that large-group vocal training at this age can be successful. In addition, training in the lower range was more effective than in the upper range, suggesting that young children should first learn songs in the range of C' to F' or D' to G' followed by songs in the range of C' to A' and finally C' to E'.

Likewise, Boardman (1964) investigated the effects of preschool vocal training and maturation on the development of vocal accuracy in children. Seven hypotheses were tested with 46 children who had received early training and who were matched to a control group by age, grade level, and socioeconomic background. A recording of 20 tonal patterns was played for each child to repeat. Boardman found that maturation and pretraining were important factors that accelerated rather than improved normal vocal development; and that training did not alter the kind of response or type of errors made. She suggested that the child's failure to reproduce a tonal pattern may be due to perceptual problems.

Ramsey (1983) found that singing ability does not affect preschool children's melodic perception. However, Greenberg (1972) stated that preschool children have difficulty in grasping certain musical concepts. While the relationship of vocal development to maturation and training is plausible during the early years, degree of training was not a consideration in the present study.

Development of Melodic Responses

Extant research seems to imply that melodic skill development begins early in life and that young children's melodic responses should be stimulated by vocal responses. Moog (1976) found that children generally do not copy the rhythm, pitch, or direction of a melody before 1 year of age. However, Gardner (1971) stated that by 1 year and 7 months a child is capable of producing distinct pitches.

Gesell and Ilg (1943) suggested that spontaneous singing of the minor third is characteristic of 2½-year-olds; 4-year-olds create songs during play, using variations of the minor third to tease other children. Such use of songs for particular reasons and in different ways was of interest in the present study.

The ideas of Gesell and Ilg were expanded by Davidson, McKernon, and Gardner (1981) in their developmental study of song acquisition in young children. These authors observed both spontaneous song production and the child's initial ability to produce songs from the culture. They suggested that during the first 3 years of life children engage in constant vocalization, which extends from making noise to acquiring musical competence. Other findings indicated that children begin vocal experimentation with pitch variations, then produce distinct pitches by 19 months of age, later relying on major seconds, major thirds, and minor thirds to sing spontaneous songs.

Updegraff, Heileger, and Learned (1938) found that untrained 3- through 5-year-old children were able to sing back a note and one interval. However, the same children were unable to sing back the model note when it was played on an instrument. Similar research conducted by Williams, Sievers, and Hattwich (1932) tested 2- through 6-year-old children's ability to sing back short musical phrases. These researchers found that 6-year-olds were more accurate than 3- through 5-year-olds. Klanderman (1979) found that 4- and 5-year-old children lacked the ability to sing the correct direction of a melody. He speculated that children would imitate melodies that their peers produced.

Development of Rhythmic Responses

Gaston (1968) defined rhythm as "the organizer and energizer of music.... Whereas music may lack harmony and melody, it always has rhythm" (p. 17). Rainbow (1977) designed a longitudinal study to assess the ability of 3- through 5-year-olds to learn specific rhythmic tasks: maintaining a steady metric beat, rhythmic echoing, rote rhythm patterns, and rhythm patterns presented within a musical context. Results indicated that tasks involving speech rhythms, keeping a steady beat with rhythm sticks, and clapping a steady beat were easiest for the 3-year-olds. All of the tasks could be accomplished by the 4-year-olds, although the order of difficulty was similar to that observed with the 3-year-olds. Tasks involving large muscle movement, such as marching, were difficult for both groups. Children were able to respond most accurately to a spoken rhythm when it was clapped beforehand. Ability to perceive rhythm patterns increased as the children grew older.

In a subsequent report, Rainbow and Owen (1979) found similar results. Speech rhythms were easiest for 3-year-olds to perform. Maintaining and clapping a steady beat was the next easiest task. When 4-year-olds were compared to 3-year-olds, the older children were more successful in completing all tasks. The design of Rainbow's study was replicated by Frega (1979) in Australia. She found that 3-year-olds performed more accurately when they chanted, used speech patterns, and clapped. The 4-year-olds had difficulty clapping, walking, playing a rhythm instrument, and chanting with a drum beat at a moderately fast tempo. Difficult areas for 5-year-olds were walking on beat and singing while clapping. Gardner (1971) found that increasing age influenced the way in which rhythms are acquired and organized.

Development of Motor Responses

Many studies of the relationship between motor responses and body image, psycholinguistic competence, parental attitude, and creativity have been conducted. Music educators would be remiss to attempt the study of music and motor abilities without also considering these other variables. In assessing the motor skill development characteristic of 3- through 6-year-olds, Gilbert (1980) stated:

Music performance is one functional area in which motor skills are integrally involved. Since participation in music activities often requires performance, motor skill is a necessary prerequisite for optimum musical response. Motor skills constitute a central aspect of musical functioning, and professional music educators must acquire as much information as possible concerning the development and manifestation of these skills. (p. 167)

Gilbert's (1979) Motoric Music Skills Test (MMST) was administered to 808 children ages 3 through 6; this test measured motor pattern coordination, eye-hand coordination, range of movement, speed of movement, and compound factors. All children were capable of mastering tasks involving simple motor pattern coordination; tasks of speed, range, eye-hand coordination, and compound factors were easier for the older children. Motor music skills improved with increasing age.

In a follow-up study, Gilbert (1982) "examined the stability of motoric music performance throughout a three-year period, and compared children's motoric music performance to performance on a test of rhythmic and tonal perception" (p. 59). Her MMST and Gordon's (1979) Primary Measures of Music Audiation were administered to children ages 5 through 8. Motor skills improved with increasing age and were strongly related to perceptual and cognitive abilities.

Hulson's (1929) finding that certain tempi were most conducive to rhythmic responses was supported by Zimmerman (1971), who stated that "music with fast tempi should be used first in rhythmic movement experiences. Slower tempi can be gradually inserted as the child becomes more adept in synchronizing movement with music" (p. 26).

Development of Conceptual Responses

Zimmerman (1971) stated that "conceptual development in musical learning is dependent upon aural perception since musical learning begins with the perception of sound" (p. 12). Petzold (1963) recognized that an individual's aural understanding is based upon perceptions of auditory stimuli; that is, children need to make judgments about musical concepts based upon their own aural understanding rather than that of their teachers. Young children may focus on different dimensions of a melody (i.e., pitch level, melodic shape, pitch intervals, and tonality), which will alter perceptual responses (McDonald & Ramsey, 1979; Sergeant & Roche, 1973). This suggests that children process musical information according to their own set of mental structures, and that the way in which music is perceived depends on the way in which it is processed.

The way in which young children process perceptual and conceptual information was investigated by Webster and Schlentrich (1982). The ability of 4- and 5-year-olds to discriminate pitch direction using verbal, gestural, and performance response modes suggested that nonverbal, performance-based modes were used most naturally by children at this age regardless of training. Hair (1977) studied the ability of first-grade children to discriminate tonal direction using verbal and nonverbal tasks; higher scores were indicated on nonverbal tasks.

Scott (1979) investigated the relationship of age (3 through 5) to conceptual development. She found that older children showed more understanding of pitch, register, melodic contour, and interval size than did younger children. Shuter-

Dyson and Gabriel (1981) concluded that "the young child may be able to perceive a difference but has great difficulty in explaining it" (p. 123).

Very few studies have investigated young children's spontaneous musical responses in the natural setting. The present study focuses on active participation of children to create their own music in the unstructured natural environment.

Naturalistic Inquiry Methodology and Procedures

The following sections describe the methods of naturalistic inquiry and how these methods were used to observe young children's musicality in their social interactions with peers. Naturalistic inquiry is a domain of research in which the investigator places few constraints upon antecedent conditions and outputs (Table 12.1).

Selection and Setting

Contrary to quantitative research, where randomization is a concern, naturalists base their inquiry on selection. Ninety-five 3- through 5-year-old children were selected from Montessori, regular day care, church-affiliated, Head Start, and

TABLE 12.1. Derivative postures of the scientific and naturalistic paradigms

Postures about	Paradigm	
	Scientific	Naturalistic
	General Characteristics	
Preferred Techniques	Quantitative	Qualitative
Quality Criterion	Rigor	Relevance
Sources of Theory	A Priori	Grounded
Questions of Causality	Can X Cause Y?	Does X Cause Y in a Natural Setting?
Knowledge Types Used	Propositional	Propositional and Tacit
Stance	Reductionist	Expansionist
Purpose	Verification	Discovery
	Methodological Characteristics	
Instrument	Paper-and Pencil or Physical Device	Inquirer (often)
Timing of the Specification of Data Collection and Analysis Rules	Before Inquiry	During and After Inquiry
Design	Preordinate	Emergent
Style	Intervention	Selection
Setting	Laboratory	Nature
Treatment	Stable	Variable
Analytic Units	Variables	Patterns
Contextual Elements	Controlled	Invited Interference

Reprinted from Guba, E., & Lincoln, Y. (1981). *Effective evaluation*, Jossey-Bass. Used by permission.

public kindergarten schools. Since individual differences are an expected part of naturalistic inquiry, diversity of subjects was desired and achieved. Children from different cultural, religious, and socioeconomic groups were included in the study.

Intact classes were used so as not to disrupt the natural school environment. Classrooms were similar in that each contained a large carpeted area for group activity. The classroom setting was not controlled, contrived, or manipulated in any way. Musical materials were intentionally located in the carpeted area. In addition, each classroom was replete with nonmusical items (e.g., Montessori blocks, toys, games, and dishes). Nonmusical items were not removed because interference was invited rather than controlled. The natural setting was of interest rather than the controlled environment.

Collection of Raw Data

Each classroom teacher was interviewed informally to determine the children's prior exposure to music, the group dynamics of the class, and any salient musical expressions. The interviews also served as a check for naturalistic credibility (internal validity). The teachers' viewpoints were used to determine the biases, perceptions, and ethnocentricities of the children.

Another test of internal validity was a 20-item questionnaire that was completed by the children's parents. The questionnaire assessed subjects' preacademic, social-emotional, motor, and musical skill development outside of class. Items were adapted from standardized assessment scales (e.g., the Denver Developmental Screening Test, Vineland Social Maturity Scale, and Brigance Inventory of Early Development). Raw data collected from the questionnaire enabled the investigator to obtain baseline information useful in planning the observations.

Instrument

In naturalistic inquiry human beings are preferred as data collection instruments because of their multidimensional strengths. The ability of humans to process and ascribe meaning to data simultaneously is particularly useful. Humans are flexible and responsive to the environment and to individuals within the environment, responding to and providing cues during the inquiry. In this study the investigator's body language and facial expressions were important cues that helped to set the mood for observations. For example, a 4-year-old male approached the videotape camera to say that the lens cover had "fallen off" the lens; a nod and smile were accepted by the child, who then continued his music activity.

Another quality of the human-as-instrument is the ability to explore all or part of a context. For example, information was obtained about social interactions, affective behaviors, and musical behaviors of young children during observation. The holistic aspect of young children was observed (a) when subjects used musical materials instead of available nonmusical materials, (b) in their apparent changes in mood with different styles of music, (c) in their verbal responses for preferred music, and (d) with their likes and dislikes of specific instruments. Guba and Lincoln (1983) stated that holistic emphasis gives the inquirer the context and lends itself to mood, climate, tone, pace, texture, and feelings. The ability to collect data on several behaviors simultaneously is an asset in studying the musicality of young children.

The human-as-instrument is able to use both propositional and tacit knowledge, which is appropriate in naturalistic inquiry. As observations progressed, insights and understandings were developed that guided the study and formed an expanded knowledge base. For example, the investigator was able to identify children who were leaders of the group, those who had developed close ties of friendship, and those who explicitly or implicitly needed the teacher's attention or approval.

Finally, the use of humans-as-instruments served to check the credibility of the data, to make certain that information was correct, and to point out key items that may have been missed. In this study, for example, the researcher sought information regarding differences between subjects who were racially mixed, Native American, or Asian.

Source of Theory

A priori theory was replaced by theory that emerged from the data in the process called "grounding." Guba and Lincoln (1981) stated, "it is better to find a theory to explain the facts than to look for facts that accord with a theory" (p. 20).

Musical and social behaviors of young children were grounded during a 30-minute observation phase for each classroom. Criterion behaviors, based on Shelley's (1981) study, and their frequency of occurrence were noted during this phase. The most frequent behaviors that applied to 3-year-olds, 4-year-olds, and 5-year-olds were: (a) observes but does not participate, (b) examines and manipulates instruments, (c) selects and plays records, (d) accompanies record with instrument, (e) sings with accompaniment, (f) sings without accompaniment, and (g) combines music and visual aids. Other criterion behaviors specific to 3-, 4-, and 5-year-olds were based on the work of Andress, Heimann, Rinehart, and Talbert (1973).

Both melodic and nonmelodic instruments, several record albums, and record players were placed in the carpeted area. Children were instructed to play any instrument of their choice; share instruments and materials; make music quietly, alone or in groups, within the carpeted area; and ask the teacher to play records they wanted to hear. Different colored necklaces or bracelets made of yarn or construction paper were used to distinguish 3-, 4-, and 5-year-olds.

Any behavior not listed as a criterion but observed during the grounding phase was included as the inquiry proceeded. In naturalistic inquiry the design varies as the process continues and new information is gathered. Therefore, grounding procedures conclude when behaviors become redundant and no new information is obtained.

Treatment and Design

Because the naturalistic design is emergent, that is, behaviors observed each day depend on observations of the previous day, the treatment in this study was variable. After observing a combined total of 204 behaviors across all eight classrooms, a Musical Behavior Observation Matrix (MBOM) was constructed. This

TABLE 12.2. Musical behavior observation matrix[a]

Children's Musical Behaviors															
Classroom _____ _____ School															
Observation No. _____ Tape No. _____ Date _____															
Frequency[b]															
	Black			White				Native American				Other			
Behavior	In	I3	I4	I5	In	I3	I4	I5	In	I3	I4	I5	In	I3	I4	I5
1. Goes to music area by choice	—	1	2	1	—	7	26	10	—	4	3	—	—	—	—	2
2. Observes but does not participate consistently	—	0	0	0	—	1	0	0	—	0	1	—	—	—	—	0
3. Does not participate	—	0	0	0	—	1	1	0	—	0	0	—	—	—	—	0
4. Examines and manipulates instruments	—	5	10	4	—	21	60	25	—	18	9	—	—	—	—	8
5. Requests record to be played	—	0	1	0	—	0	10	1	—	0	1	—	—	—	—	0
6. Requests certain musical selection	—	0	0	0	—	0	2	2	—	0	0	—	—	—	—	0
7. Listens without playing instruments	—	0	1	1	—	3	6	3	—	1	1	—	—	—	—	0
8. Accompanies records with instruments	—	1	2	1	—	24	64	22	—	16	7	—	—	—	—	6
9. Sings, chants, or moves body parts with recorded music	—	3	8	7	—	5	23	19	—	6	14	—	—	—	—	13

[a] Separate matrices were used for each classroom; however, this example combines the total frequencies of all eight classrooms for males.
[b] In = No interaction, I3 = interaction of 3-year-olds, I4 = interaction of 4-year-olds, I5 = interaction of 5-year-olds; Other = Asian, Spanish-speaking, or mixed racial groups; — denotes not applicable.

TABLE 12.3. Behaviors listed on the MBOM

1.	Goes to music area by choice
2.	Observes but does not participate consistently
3.	Does not participate
4.	Examines and manipulates instruments
5.	Requests record to be played
6.	Requests specific record to be played (demonstrated preference)
7.	Listens without playing instruments
8.	Accompanies records using instruments
9.	Sings, chants, or moves body parts with recorded music
10.	Exhibits musical frustration
11.	Interacts with only females
12.	Interacts with only males
13.	Interacts with both males and females
14.	Makes music alone, does not share
15.	Requests assistance or approval from the teacher
16.	Assists and/or demonstrates to peers
17.	Shares instruments/materials with peers
18.	Uses instruments in a socially appropriate manner
19.	Demonstrates nonmusical use of instruments
20.	Combines music and visual aids
21.	Responds to music vocally and instrumentally
22.	Responds only to recorded music
23.	Imitates spontaneous rhythms
24.	Responds through music to the basic beat
25.	More responsive to music with fast tempos than slower ones
26.	Imitates movement of peers
27.	Plays simple accompaniment ideas while singing
28.	Maintains a steady beat when playing or moving to music
29.	Experiments with sound combinations
30.	Plays drum rhythms resembling primitive patterns

instrument included 30 of the behaviors common to all classrooms (see Tables 12.2 and 12.3). Criterion behaviors were modified or excluded as the study proceeded. For example, those behaviors that were slightly different from the criterion behaviors were changed; if criterion behaviors were not seen during observation they were eliminated. Guba and Lincoln (1981) defined this action as "processual immediacy," the investigator's "ability to process data immediately upon acquisition, reorder it, change the direction of the research based upon it, generate hypotheses on the spot, and test them with the respondent or in the situation as they are created" (p. 136). The matrix was designed to assess musical and social behaviors in terms of age (interaction of 3-, 4-, and 5-year-olds in mixed or same-age dyads or triads), sex (interaction in homogeneous and heterogeneous groups), and race (interaction in similar or dissimilar racial groups).

Phase two observations made use of the MBOM and a videotape. Physical arrangement of the natural classroom environment and instructions given the children remained the same as during the grounding observations. Target behaviors were coded on the MBOM according to the frequency, age, sex, and race of a child or group of children exhibiting the behavior. Event sampling techniques were used to measure the behaviors. For example, the investigator looked for each behavior listed on the MBOM and recorded the number of times it occurred and by whom (age, sex, race).

After the data were collected on site, videotapes were viewed by a second observer. This person was a former preschool teacher who was trained in the method of observation and who had been instructed to look for the target behaviors. While viewing the videotapes she was instructed to use event sampling techniques to record each target behavior by age, race, sex of subject, and frequency of occurrence. Several previews of the videotape by both the investigator and the second observer were made to assure accuracy of data, resulting in interobserver reliability of .92.

Findings and Discussion

Males comprised 56% of the sample. Forty-six percent of the children were between the ages of 4 years 1 month and 4 years 11 months. The racial distribution was 76% white; 14% Native American, Asian, Spanish-speaking, or mixed; and 10% black. The 1982 Census Bureau Report showed the distribution to be representative of the racial makeup in the area where the study was conducted.

Group comparisons by race, age, and sex were determined by calculating the means and by counting the frequency of occurrence for each target behavior. The following descriptions of young children's natural and spontaneous behaviors were a result of data coded on the MBOM and observed from the videotapes.

Throughout the study observations revealed that females were consistently more involved in musical play than were males of the same age. Children who ceased to participate actively observed their peers instead of playing instruments. Data from teacher interviews indicated that children seldom have the opportunity to simultaneously explore several instruments during music time. Andress et al. (1973) stated that instruments become an extension of a child's body. Young children need time to explore how instruments respond and can be controlled. Ramsey (1983) suggested that preschool children's exploratory behaviors rather than their guided manipulations may be more important in their forming perceptions about pitch and melody.

"Instrumental response" was defined as creating rhythms on nonmelodic instruments or creating extemporaneous pitches on melodic instruments. Males used drums frequently and appeared more intent when playing than did females, yet drumming was prevalent among all ages and both sexes. Complex rhythms were sometimes repeated, and accents placed on or off the beat often sounded primitive. Moorhead and Pond's (1941) description of young children's music as embryonic polyphony, linear, and complex in rhythm was affirmed.

Pitch sequences played on melodic instruments were characterized by leaps and steps, yet never repeated. The ability of 3- and 4-year-olds to assimilate pitched and nonpitched sounds, discriminate between pitches, order the direction of sounds, and associate directions on melodic instruments was less developed than that of 5-year-olds. As Scott (1979) indicated, older children had a better understanding of pitch and melodic contour.

For example, 5-year-olds in this study played sequential diatonic and chromatic tones on the xylophone. They were able to press autoharp keys in an orderly sequence and strum simultaneously. Four-year-olds played random diatonic tones on the resonator bells. They pressed keys randomly while continually strumming. Simple rhythm patterns were imitated on pitched instruments; complex patterns were never repeated.

Research suggests that children may learn observable psychomotor skills best through a model of direct imitation (Landers & Landers, 1973). "Imitation" was operationally defined as performing the same behavior as another child. Hand and body movements were performed and imitated largely by older females. Older males and females (ages 4 and 5) imitated rhythms on castanets, blocks, guiro, and bells. Younger children seldom imitated spontaneous rhythms. Imitation among peers yielded increased social interaction in the form of talking, laughing, and more imitation. Vocal rhythms were not imitated often.

"Vocal response" was defined as singing with random pitch sequences. Children of all ages occasionally responded vocally in a group. Four- and 5-year-old white females vocalized independently of their peers. Jersild and Bienstock (1934) found that the number of tones a child could sing increased from age 2 to age 9, and did so rapidly until a child reached age 6.

Children who were familiar with the words sang along with the record. Other children ignored the record and created their own song forms. Chants on a descending minor third were accompanied by fast walking movements in a circle. Contrary to the Pillsbury study (Moorhead & Pond, 1941), chants and speech rhythms were performed alone and never repeated. Vocalizations occurred less among 3-year-old males and females, who were engaged in parallel play and monologue. Rainbow and Owen (1979) found that speech rhythms are easiest for 3-year-olds. Young children begin to imitate songs they have heard. Words are first imitated, followed by rhythm and pitch (Nye, 1983).

Children in this study played simple accompaniment ideas when singing (e.g., a 4-year-old female who played jingle clogs to accompany herself while singing "Jingle Bells"). Twenty-six 4- and 5-year-old females used the xylophone, resonator bells, or autoharp to provide an accompaniment. Younger males and females used rhythm sticks, cymbals, and other nonmelodic instruments to accompany singing. Zwissler (1971) and Hair (1977) suggested that this type of nonverbal performance-based mode is a reliable measure of perception.

Four- and 5-year-old males used drums most often, alternating the left and right hands repeatedly, to accompany improvised songs. Flohr (1984) found that the improvisation of 3-year-olds was rhythmical, 4-year-olds included repetition and similar phrases, and 5-year-olds showed a preference for F' tonality and increased use of rhythmic repetition. Accompaniments to recorded music consisted of strict quarter-note patterns, playing on and off the beat, and imitating rhythmic/melodic patterns of the music.

The majority of males and females who requested records were 4 years old. Musical preferences were expressed mostly by males. Other children sometimes disagreed about records they wanted to hear. Four- and 5-year-old males and females stood next to the record player and listened without playing instruments; no 3-year-olds demonstrated listening in this manner. Those children who did not request records appeared to attend to music that was played (e.g., a 4-year-old female who played triangle or tambourine to every song). It may be that young children of a certain age enjoy or will respond to the same style of music. Research conducted by Greer, Dorow, and Randall (1974) showed that preschoolers through third graders listened to more nonrock music than fifth and sixth graders.

Jazz music played in the present study decreased physical responses, whereas march music (e.g., "Semper Fidelis" and "Washington Post") increased responses. Similar to Zimmerman's (1971) findings, the majority of males and females were more active and responsive to music with fast tempos than with slower ones. For example, dance movements were observed more among 4- and 5-year-old females than any other group, and usually were accompanied by their singing. Gilbert (1980) found motor music skill differences in the performances of boys and girls.

Males of all ages and 3-year-old females were less active unless they were marching. Older children were able to play steady beats when marching, yet females were more adept than were males of the same age. Rainbow's (1977) research concurs that this task would be more manageable by 4-year-olds than by 3-year-olds. All children skipped or alternated feet to "get in time" to the music.

While involved in marching all children stopped playing instruments when the recorded music ended, and did not resume playing until a designated leader began. Some subjects responded to the basic beat of recorded music during the first phase of the observations but demonstrated spontaneity and creativity in the second phase. This may be attributed to reactive effects of the videotape camera or familiarity with the activity and its expectations.

Music listening was combined with the use of visual aids. Album covers and picture books (e.g., Peter Pan and Mary Poppins) were of apparent interest to the children. Norton (1979) found no significant relationship between auditory and visual conservation of kindergarten children. However, Nelson (1984) stated "an important element in the presentation of a conservation task is the need to incorporate visual and physical representation of the concept that might be conserved" (p. 28). The children experimented with sound and pictures and with sound combinations.

Both males and females played two unlike instruments simultaneously and formed ensembles to "see how they sound." Nonmusical use of instruments was observed in each classroom. Symbolic play was observed when some 4-year-olds used wood blocks as microphones for singing and rhythm sticks as batons. Three-year-old males used instruments as cars and made use of onomatopoeia.

While each classroom was replete with other educational materials and toys, no child used these during "free music time." This indicates that the children initially wanted to enjoy the freedom to explore the music area, and they were capable of experimenting with musical sounds appropriately in an unstructured activity. Nye (1983) concurred that "In young children active and spontaneous expression is extremely significant, since sensorimotor behavior is one of the more natural and proven ways they learn" (p. 4).

Many social behaviors were observed during this unstructured activity. Older males and females interacted and demonstrated "how to" play instruments in mixed groups by age, sex, and race. Within group situations children gave and followed directives such as "Let's do this next." Four 5-year-old black females interacted only with each other and one white female. No interaction between males only was observed during phase two. However, 5-year-old males interacted with each other more than with 3- or 4-year-old males or with females of any age. Gesell and Ilg (1949) suggested that children's relationships with each other are influenced by maturation. Only two 3-year-olds were observed to make music alone during observations.

"Musical frustration" implied expressed dissatisfaction with some aspect of the music activity. Two explicit examples were observed. Three 5-year-old females complained of "too much noise" and covered their ears for a brief time. The behavior was initiated by one child and imitated by the others. Zimmerman's (1971) study concluded that young children develop loudness perception first. A 5-year-old male attempted to quiet the class by shouting when he could not hear the music while trying to conduct to the recording. Ramsey and Ramsey (1983) found male and female subjects' loudness discrimination to differ significantly on items of loud dynamics, and found significant differences across age and sex groups in terms of loudness discrimination.

Classroom teachers did not attempt to quiet the class. They were instructed by the investigator to intervene only if social behaviors were inappropriate or if assistance was requested by a child or children. In several classrooms the teacher needed to remind children to share the instruments. Observations showed that the teacher's presence is necessary and desired in an unstructured music activity. Teacher approval was verbally sought by all ages and both sexes. Children asked their teachers to play records, to replace holders on triangles, and to watch their demonstrated musical abilities. While free exploration is a must, Nye (1983) believes that teachers should assist also in guided exploration with both recognition of musical phenomena and the responses to such phenomena through movement.

Summary

Findings of this descriptive study contribute to the knowledge of young children's musicality and provide implications for music education theory and practice. The inquiry revealed that young children are capable of making music freely and spontaneously in their natural environments. They (a) participate consistently within a designated time period, (b) examine and manipulate a wide variety of instruments, (c) demonstrate musical preferences by requesting or playing records, (d) accompany records with instruments or singing, (e) sing, chant, and move body parts with recorded music, (f) demonstrate attentive listening, (g) create songs and rhythms using melodic and nonmelodic instruments, (h) imitate spontaneous rhythms and movements of peers, (i) demonstrate increased physical responses to music with fast tempos, and (j) experiment with instrumental sound combinations. In an unstructured music activity young children can participate without teacher guidance, interact socially appropriately, and increase social interactions via talking, laughing, and imitation. Findings revealed differences among 3-, 4-, and 5-year-olds in terms of some musical skills—which improve with increased chronological age.

Implications for Teaching and Recommendations

The study suggests that 3-, 4-, and 5-year-old children should be allowed to explore the sounds of music to increase their awareness of concepts. Involving children in activities of comparing, classifying, and creating can strengthen their ability to conserve. According to Nye (1983) children should be guided to observe conservation of weight, volume, and size through everyday experiences in their environment. Such concepts are the foundation for subsequent study in mathematics. Activities that focus on body image, body part identification, and gross motor skills should be incorporated into teaching strategies. Young children express their feelings and thoughts through movement. Approaches such as Dalcroze's Eurhythmics assist in developing gross motor skills; playing Orff instruments develops more specific motor skills. Gilbert's (1980) research suggested the need to design specific motor music skills according to the chronological age of children. In view of her findings, music educators should devise motor tasks that incorporate abilities in perceptual and cognitive areas and those upon which later learning can be built.

Weikart, Rogers, Adcock, and McClelland (1977) explained that young children learn by thinking and doing and can gain more knowledge through active manipulation of their environment. The present study allowed children to engage in a nonverbal, performance-based experience to improve their responses to music. The major concern was to determine what a child can do with music and what music does to the child. Petzold (1981) stated that much of what is learned in music is learned through perception and responses to music stimuli.

Results of the study suggest that music activities for 3-year-olds should be structured differently than those for 4- and 5-year-olds. For example, when compared to 4- and 5-year-olds, 3-year-olds lack the ability to march and play steady beats simultaneously. Additional research on the rhythmic skills of young children may provide evidence of rhythmic development at specific ages.

In terms of creativity, Flohr's (1984) finding that older children spent more time in free exploration with pitched instruments than did younger children concurred with observations in the present study. Thus, 4- and 5-year-olds may need longer time periods for exploratory (discovery) learning whereas 3-year-olds may need guided instruction. Conservation tasks reveal that 3-year-olds deal with the present, 4-year-olds begin to add concepts of past events, and 5-year-olds begin to add to their concepts of past and present those related to the future. In singing, 3-year-olds may lag behind or sing other words, 4-year-olds can match some pitches and sing alone, and 5-year-olds can recognize songs and sing five-note ranges (Nye, 1983).

The research cited in this study recognizes the effect of age on the musical abilities of young children. Greenberg (1976) stated that instructional methodology and evaluation techniques using music with young children have often been simplified versions of elementary methodologies and techniques. Based on this study and others, a set of musical skills and concomitant developmental activities should be identified that relate specifically to 3-, 4-, and 5-year-olds. The skills can be used by classroom teachers to facilitate musical development. Skills and activities may then be incorporated into music education methods courses to broaden preservice teachers' awareness of musical capabilities of young children, later providing a foundation for devising curricula during the elementary years. The study agrees with Aronoff's (1969) statement that:

It is not enough to know that young children can be taught to move, sing and play instruments and that they thrive on these activities and accomplishments; we must identify the conditions for transfer of pre-verbal understandings, provide for the acquisition of needed skills and musical repertoire, and devise teaching strategies to help children develop heuristic techniques for further cognitive and affective growth in music. (p. 6)

In addition, the pioneering efforts of teaching and learning developed by the Pillsbury School (Moorhead & Pond, 1941) need to be extended for use in today's classroom. It can be argued that traditional methodology may have exhausted its efforts to reach children of all ages, resulting in a lack of musical training during the preschool years. Brand (1985) stated, "two constituencies that have been traditionally ignored by music educators—preschool children and their parents —may be the populations that can benefit most from music education" (p. 29). The development of musicality is most effectively examined via the young child's exploration of music in the natural environment, and is therefore recommended by the investigator.

Naturalistic inquiry, concerned with human behaviors, assumes that no single reality exists in relation to the research; multiple truths combine to form one's understanding. This inquiry has systematically examined the holistic musical development of young children and is merely a starting point. Both the Musical Behavior Observation Matrix and on-site observations could be extended over a longer period of time. Further studies should examine both qualitative and quantitative methods simultaneously, to compare results and to expand the body of knowledge in early childhood music.

References

Andress, B. L., Heimann, H. M., Rinehart, C. A., & Talbert, E. G. (1973). *Music in early childhood*. Reston, VA: Music Educators National Conference.

Aronoff, F. W. (1969). *Music and young children*. New York: Holt, Rinehart, and Winston.

Boardman, E. (1964). *An investigation of the effect of preschool training on the development of vocal accuracy in young children*. Unpublished doctoral dissertation, University of Illinois, Champaign.

Brand, M. (1985). Lullabies that awaken musicality in infants. *Music Educators Journal, 71*, 28–31.

Davidson, L., McKernon, P., & Gardner, H. (1981). The acquisition of song: A developmental approach. In *Documentary report of the Ann Arbor symposium*. Reston, VA: Music Educators National Conference.

Flohr, J. W. (1984). *Young children's improvisations: A longitudinal study*. Paper presented at the Music Educators National Conference, Chicago.

Frega, A. L. (1979). Rhythmic tasks with three-, four-, and five-year-old children. *Bulletin of the Council for Research in Music Education, 59*, 32–34.

Fridman, R. (1973). The first cry of the newborn: Basis for the child's future musical development. *Journal of Research in Music Education, 21*, 264–269.

Gardner, H. (1971). Children's duplication of rhythmic patterns. *Journal of Research in Music Education, 19*, 355–360.

Gaston, E. T. (Ed.). (1968). *Music in therapy*. New York: Macmillan.

Gesell, A., & Ilg, F. (1943). *The infant and child in the culture of today*. London: Hamilton.

Gesell, A., & Ilg, F. (1949). *Child development*. New York: Harper & Row.

Gilbert, J. P. (1979). *The development of motoric music skills in children ages three through six*. Unpublished doctoral dissertation, The University of Kansas, Lawrence.

Gilbert, J. P. (1980). An assessment of motor skill development in young children. *Journal of Research in Music Education, 28*, 167–175.

Gilbert, J. P. (1982). Motoric music skills: A longitudinal investigation and comparison with children's rhythmic and tonal perceptions. In P. E. Sink (Ed.), *Proceedings of the research Symposium on the Psychology and Acoustics of Music 1981*. Lawrence, KS: The University of Kansas Printing.

Gordon, E. (1979). *Primary measures of music audiation*. Chicago: G.I.A. Publications.

Greenberg, M. (1972). A preliminary report of the effectiveness of a preschool music curriculum with preschool Head Start children. *Bulletin of the Council For Research in Music Education, 29*, 13–16.

Greenberg, M. (1976). Research in music in early childhood education: A survey with recommendations. *Bulletin of the Council for Research in Music Education, 45*, 1–20.

Greer, R. D., Dorow, L., & Randall, A. (1974). Music listening preferences of elementary school children. *Journal of Research in Music Education, 22*, 284–291.

Guba, E., & Lincoln, Y. (1981). *Effective evaluation*. San Francisco: Jossey-Bass.

Guba, E., & Lincoln, Y. (1983). Epistemological and methodological bases of naturalistic inquiry. *Educational Communications and Technology Journal, 30*, 233–252.

Hair, H. I. (1977). Discrimination of tonal direction on verbal and nonverbal tasks by first grade children. *Journal of Research in Music Education, 24*, 197–210.

Hulson, E. L. (1929). Tempo in rhythm for young children. *Childhood Education, 6*, 78–80.

Jersild, A. T., & Bienstock, S. F. (1934). A study of the development of children's ability to sing. *Journal of Educational Psychology, 25*, 481–503.

Klanderman, N. (1979). *The development of auditory discrimination and performance of pitch, rhythm, and melody in preschool children*. Unpublished doctoral dissertation, Northwestern University, Evanston, IL.

Landers, D. M., & Landers, D. M. (1973). Teacher versus peer models: Effects of model's presence and performance level on motor behavior. *Journal of Motor Behavior, 5*, 129–239.

McDonald, D., & Ramsey, J. H. (1979). A study of musical auditory information processing of preschool children. *Contributions to Music Education, 2*, 2–11.

Michel, P. (1973). The optimum development of musical abilities in the first six years of life. *Psychology of Music, 1*, 14–20.

Moog, H. (1976). The development of musical experience in children of preschool age. *Psychology of Music, 4*, 38–45.

Moorhead, G., & Pond, D. (1941). *Music of young children*. Santa Barbara: Pillsbury Foundation for the Advancement of Music.

Nelson, D. J. (1984). The conservation of rhythm in Suzuki violin students: A task validation study. *Journal of Research in Music Education, 32*, 25–34.

Norton, D. (1979). Relationship of music ability and intelligence to auditory and visual conservation of the kindergarten child. *Journal of Research in Music Education, 27*, 3–13.

Nye, V. T. (1983). *Music for young children* (3rd ed.). Dubuque, IA: William C. Brown.

Petzold, R. G. (1963). The development of auditory perception of musical sounds by children in the first six grades. *Journal of Research in Music Education, 11*, 21–43.

Petzold, R. G. (1981). Child development. In *Documentary report of the Ann Arbor symposium*. Reston, VA: Music Educators National Conference.

Pflederer, M. (1964). The responses of children to musical tasks embodying Piaget's principles of conservation. *Journal of Research in Music Education, 12*, 251–268.

Pflederer, M., & Sechrest, L. (1968). Conservation-type responses of children to musical stimuli. *Bulletin of the Council for Research in Music Education, 13*, 19–36.

Phillips, J. L. (1975). *The origins of intellect: Piaget's theory*. San Francisco: W. H. Freeman.

Rainbow, E. L. (1977). A longitudinal investigation of the rhythmic ability of preschool age children. *Bulletin of the Council for Research in Music Education, 50*, 55–61.

Rainbow, E. L., & Owen, D. (1979). A progress report on a three-year investigation of the rhythmic ability of preschool age children. *Bulletin of the Council for Research in Music Education, 59*, 84–86.

Ramsey, J. (1983). The effects of age, singing ability, and instrumental experiences on preschool children's melodic perception. *Journal of Research in Music Education, 31*, 133–145.

Ramsey, D., & Ramsey, J. (1983). *A study of musical loudness discrimination of three- to five-year-old children*. Paper presented at the Early Childhood Music Research Session, Chicago.

Schultz, S. W. (1969). *A study of children's ability to respond to elements of music*. Unpublished doctoral dissertation, Northwestern University, Evanston, IL.

Scott, C. R. (1979). Pitch concept formation in preschool children. *Bulletin of the Council for Research in Music Education, 59*, 87–93.

Sergeant, D. C., & Roche, S. (1973). Perceptual shifts in the auditory information processing of young children. *Psychology of Music, 1*, 39–48.

Shelley, S. J. (1981). Investigating the musical capabilities of young children. *Bulletin of the Council for Research in Music Education*, *68*, 26–34.

Shuter-Dyson, R., & Gabriel, C. (1981). *The psychology of musical ability* (2nd ed.). London: Methuen.

Smith, R. B. (1963). The effect of group vocal training on the singing ability of nursery school children. *Journal of Research in Music Education*, *11*, 137–141.

Updegraff, R., Heileger, L., & Learned, J. (1938). The effect of training on musical abilities and interest. In *University of Iowa Studies in Child Welfare* (No. 14). Iowa City: University of Iowa Press.

Webster, P. R., & Schlentrich, K. (1982). Discrimination of pitch direction by preschool children with verbal and non-verbal tasks. *Journal of Research in Music Education*, *30*, 151–161.

Weikart, D., Rogers, L., Adcock, C., & McClelland, D. (1977). *The cognitively-oriented curriculum*. Urbana, IL: University of Illinois Press.

Williams, H. M., Sievers, C., & Hattwich, M. (1932). The measurement of musical development. In G. Stoddard (Ed.), *University of Iowa Studies in Child Welfare* (No. 7). Iowa City: University of Iowa Press.

Zimmerman, M. P. (1971). *Musical characteristics of children*. Washington, DC: Music Educators National Conference.

Zimmerman, M. P. (1981). Child development and music education. In *Documentary report of the Ann Arbor symposium*. Reston, VA: Music Educators National Conference.

Zwissler, R. N. (1971). *An investigation of the pitch discrimination skills of first grade children identified as accurate singers and those identified as inaccurate singers*. Unpublished doctoral dissertation, University of California, Berkeley.

13
The Virtue and Vice of Musical Performance Competitions for Children

IRENE WEISS PEERY, DALE NYBOER, and J. CRAIG PEERY

For more than two decades the authors have been involved in music performance competitions. We have collective experience as organizers, participants, judges, parents of participants, and teacher of participants in competitions ranging from the local to the international level. We have been impressed at the powerful events competitions are, and have become increasingly aware of their potential outcomes, most positive and some negative. These events have been largely bypassed by experts in child development and education in their study of children. We believe performance competitions have much to offer young people and their families, and are worthy of consideration when the topics of music and child development merge.

An Introduction to Competitions—What They Are

From the earliest times games and competitions have captured the interest of mankind. We seem innately endowed with a desire to improve our skills, and then to test them against others. From the Egyptian game of senat, which represented the perils of the journey through life and the afterlife, to the first Olympic games in Greece, to the Super Bowl, everyone loves a winner and enjoys the process of selecting a small group of "the best" from the pack of participants. Watching a Mary Lou Retton amazes and entertains as we thrill to observe levels of performance that are seemingly impossible. Additionally, participating in such competitions can inspire both the participants and the audience; one frequently comes away with a renewed sense of determination, and increased faith in developing one's own potential through practice and perseverance.

In this spirit of selecting the "best," music competitions have long been a part of the serious music scene as an opportunity for conscientious young performers to launch a career by "winning" one of the top prizes in an international event. The Van Cliburn piano competition and the Tchaikovsky competition in Moscow are examples of these large and famous encounters. State and county fairs, state and local orchestras, music teacher organizations, and occasionally music businesses also sponsor performance competitions.

Competitions are becoming increasingly popular for musicians of all ages. These contests are remarkable events that can have both positive and negative outcomes on the lives of children, their families, and their teachers.

As the number of competitions proliferates, and as competitions seek to incorporate younger contestants, another—and we think potentially more important—motivation for competition participation is emerging. Increasingly there is a healthy shift away from perceiving competitions *only* as a mechanism for identifying "winners," and toward the notion of using competitions as an integral part of music education. Increasingly competitions are seen as an opportunity for students, parents, and teachers to get together, share skills, test abilities, compare notes, and learn from each other and from the experience. It is our belief that instead of fringe benefits these opportunities and experiences can be a major source of value to competition participants. Competitions can provide valuable insights into music, society, and individual development. Our purpose here is to help explicate the idea of music competitions for young people as an educational experience, and to discourage the tendency to emphasize the "winners and losers" as the exclusive value of competitions with the attending potential pitfalls of such an outlook.

Typical Competition Format

There are two indispensible groups in competitions: judges and competitors. An individual judge, or more frequently a panel of judges, sits in a room and listens as competitors play. Usually an audience is allowed. Typically the competitors enter the room individually, play, and leave, although they frequently return as part of the audience.

Attending at least one music competition is a "must" on the agenda of anyone who is interested in children and/or child development. There are several categories of contest: local, state, and national/international. To the uninitiated first-time attender, the quality of performance of the young people at a typical "local" contest, like a county fair, can be truly surprising. The first-time listener at a "state" level competition will be amazed at the skill of the youthful performers from across the state. Inevitably in the "national" and "international" competitions the level of performance skill displayed by even the very young (4–6-year-olds) is truly astounding both to the novice listener and to the experienced competition-goer. Anyone who believes that the age of prodigious playing by 6-, 8-, or 12-year-olds ended with Mozart simply has not attended an international music competition for young people. Rather than being uncommon, it is the order of the day at such competitions to hear 6-year-olds execute Bach fugues with nonchalance, 8-year-olds rip through Chopin Polonaises with gusto, and 12-year-olds play the Mozart K.467 C major Concerto, which Mozart's father declared was too difficult even to play at all, with astonishing technical fluency, grace, and maturity.

Judges make notes about the playing, and sometimes fill out a judging form. After all the competitors have performed the judges usually retire and deliberate.

Their task is to select a first-, second-, and third-place winner; frequently honorable mentions are also chosen.

In competitions with large numbers of competitors, and always in national and international competitions, there are preliminary (sometimes more than one level) and final rounds. Preliminary screening can be accomplished by having would-be competitors send tapes, or go to on-site auditions. The Young Keyboard Artists Association piano competition holds auditions in dozens of states by flying judges to major cities in every geographic area. Final rounds for competitions are accomplished in one location with a panel of knowledgeable judges.

Competitions for young children sometimes have as much action outside the performance hall as inside. Everyone is wanting to use a "warm-up" room or piano. There are always fewer warm-up facilities than there are students who want to use them, so creative (and sometimes devious) techniques can be invented to gain practice time before the performance. Competitors listen attentively in the audience, or outside the doors. Parents pace up and down corridors. Teachers provide support and encouragement. Grandparents take pictures.

At the end of the competition, and as a final celebration, there is usually some kind of convocation, dinner, or awards ceremony where winners are announced and prizes given. Wide-eyed facial anticipation followed by squeals of excitement and stiff-upper-lip behavior are prevalent. Congratulations and condolences are exchanged and the competition ends.

Potential Pitfalls of Music Performance Competitions

Having introduced the competition format, we will now turn attention to avoiding potential pitfalls for competition participants. First, there ar some myths to dispel.

Myth #1: Those Who Win Prizes Are the Only Ones Who Really Benefit from a Competition

As a general rule those who win the prizes combine musical talent with diligence, patience, hard work, good training, and not a little luck. The greater each of these attributes is the more likely an individual is to win a prize. However, each competitor has developed these musical and personal characteristics to a substantial degree or they would not be attending the competition in the first place. Consequently, all of the participants are "winners." They are winners in the sense that through their efforts they have set themselves apart from their larger group of peers by developing proficiency that would have otherwise remained dormant. And they are winners because they are willing to put this expertise up for public and professional scrutiny. They are putting their light on the candlestick.

It is true that at any given point in time a competition will select three or four from the ranks to give special recognition as "winners," but this can be a mixed blessing even to them. Trophies can be put on a shelf, but they bring no persisting benefit. Indeed they can lure one into a false sense of confidence. The procedures and competencies that one develops that stimulate entering a musical competition are the enduring prizes. The evaluation in the competition gives some measure of skill at a given moment in time, among a group who have developed like abilities, but it is the existence of the abilities themselves that is paramount. The expression often heard before prizes are awarded, "all these children are winners," needs to be integrated into every competitor's consciousness.

Myth #2: Competition Winners Are the Best Musicians. If I Don't Win, I Must Not Be Good, or Perhaps I'm Wasting My Time Studying Music

Competition results are a function of a given panel of judges, on a given day, with a particular group of competitors in a given sequence. Changing any one of these elements can change the outcome. Consequently, the list of "winners" can change with the circumstances. We have already discussed the error of the view that prize winners are the only winners. The same holds true with the ideas relating to musicianship, and the purpose of music study. For most children it would be a grave mistake to undertake the study of music and music performance with the initial purpose of becoming a prize winner in performance competitions. Involving children with music can be justified by a large number of considerations related to the inherent value of music itself, and to the adjunct capabilities that music study can nurture (see Peery & Peery, Chapter 1, this volume). The student, the parents, and the teacher are always going to be better able to judge whether satisfactory progress is being made toward broader goals. Performance at competitions is one kind of information, but certainly not definitive, and not the most important for determining success.

Myth #3: Judge's Views Are Always Consistent, Accurate, and Completely Objective

Competition organizers usually try to be objective in selecting judges, and judges try to be objective in their evaluation, but complete objectivity is never possible. Political prejudices can and do influence competitions at every level, from determining physical location, to which piano to use, to judge selection, to choosing prize winners. Judges have biases about pieces, styles, and people. They share these frailties with the rest of mankind. A given panel of judges will have its own chemistry. It is not uncommon to see a winner in one competition fail to make the preliminary screening in the next. Performers, parents, and teachers are well advised to consider all of the circumstances, including the individual judge's background, training, and experience, when putting competition outcomes into perspective.

Coping with Stress

There are healthy kinds of stress, and some kinds that may not be so healthy, in competitive situations. David Elkind's book, *The Hurried Child* (1981), is highly recommended to parents whose children enter performance competitions because he identifies the kinds of stress we sometimes subject children to that are not helpful. Elkind is justifiably concerned that we as a society are pushing children to grow up too soon, and requiring them to cope with their world in ways they, as children, are not capable of. We do not believe that competitions, per se, necessarily lead to the kinds of stress Elkind describes for hurried children. However, we have seen instances where children have been pushed by parents or teachers into experiences that went beyond the child's ability to cope and produced undue stress.

Children in music competitions are children first, and must be allowed to integrate the experience into their world. They cannot be expected to "give up" a part of being a child in order to excel in music performance. That is not to say that children do not give up *time* to study music, because they do. However, the needs to play, to develop socially, and to enjoy family relationships, for example, should not be compromised by involvement with music.

Potential problems that can turn competitions into unnecessarily stressful, hurried experiences develop when parents use the child to fill *parental* needs. Two kinds of parental "hurrying" Elkind identifies are precisely potential traps for parents of music competitors:

1. "The child as self surrogate" —in this case parental dissatisfaction pushes the parent into using the child to bolster his or her own self-esteem.
2. "The child as status symbol" —Elkind feels mothers, especially, who are staying home with children are vulnerable to using child accomplishments to overcome a perceived stigma for being "just" homemakers and mothers.

Compelling the child to act in a way that requires him or her to compensate for a parental problem (low self-esteem, feelings of inadequacy) is likely to put stress on the child beyond his or her ability to deal with it effectively. Parental expectations can influence children's expectations (Entwisle & Baker, 1983). Parents can be justifiably proud, but should not expect children to compensate for their own weaknesses.

There are benefits accrued from experience. Once parents and teachers decide to enter a competition, they should commit themselves to competing in more than one. Experience in competing itself increases the likelihood of winning (Scanlan, Lewthwaite, & Jackson, 1984). Beyond that, experience with more than one competition is necessary to bring the process into perspective. Conclusions based on only one competition exposure are likely to be incorrect.

Coping with Evaluations and Criticism

Most of the time involved in studying a musical instrument is spent alone in individual practice. After many lessons and hours of practicing the student (sooner or later) steps onto the stage and performs for an audience. The performance represents all the lessons and those many long, lonely hours of practice. The performance puts everything on the line. It is customary for the audience to be appreciative, to applaud, and to support the individual and the musical efforts. When the audience includes a judge, who is there to be critical and to make discriminating judgments, those judgments can be seen as attacks on the performer's innermost self.

Standing up and performing is very ego exposing in itself. Being criticized on the weaknesses of the performance can be devastating. Both younger and older students alike must be cautioned and forewarned by parents and teachers. Some of the following concepts may aid in preparing students for the feedback from judges, and in evaluating judge's remarks: What the judge has to say about your playing is his own opinion. Judges are trying to be helpful. Just because judges may criticize parts of your playing does *not* mean they are criticizing you as a person. In fact just the opposite is true. Judges have the greatest admiration for performers, they are usually musicians themselves, and they know how hard performing is. They are only doing their best to make evaluations. Their comments should be considered as possible suggestions, not as absolute truth. A different judge would have had different views.

The challenge for many students and teachers is maintaining self-esteem while expanding one's perspective, hearing another person's views, and gaining performance experience under exacting conditions. Both winning and losing can be learning experiences, but both must be kept in perspective.

Why Competitions Are Needed

Two Views of What Competitions Accomplish

The major public rationale for competitions is identifying and recognizing the "best" among competitors. Resembling tests of skill in other domains, major international competitions are frequently used for launching professional careers. Competitions can also achieve meaningful results in the amateur realm. At state and county fairs, for example, the skills of young musicians can be judged and compared along with other skills, hobbies, and other activities of regional interest. At such state and local levels, competitions exist not so much with the hope of launching a professional career as with the intent of giving an audience and recognition to young people for developing talents and abilities of which the community is justly proud.

Beyond the view of competitions as "an opportunity for recognition of the best," we are proposing an additional view that competitions can supplement traditional music "lessons" and should be integrated as a part of music education. We are persuaded that a major, possibly even the most significant, contribution competitions can make is as part of the process of music education by filling several needs usually not completely met in private lessons. Because music performance education involves developing specific motor skills, teaching one-on-one is usually required. The child then practices those skills alone. By its very nature, then, music performance training is both personally demanding and socially isolated. Competitions can be an integral part of performance training aimed at opening the natural isolation of the training, and at providing expanded opportunities to meet the needs of students and teachers that individual study alone cannot supply.

The Need for Support

It has been said that no one is as lonely as the child practicing a musical instrument. Emotional and social support can be the difference between success and failure at such a solitary task. We believe parents and, if possible, other family members should be involved in the weekly process of music study. Beyond the daily family environment, which both Freeman (1976) and Shuter-Dyson (1979) found to be a crucial ingredient in developing musical talent, preparing for and participating in competitions can bring both parents and peers into the child's social support network.

One of the most striking aspects of piano competitions we have observed over the years is the support children receive from parents. During the competition parent and child practice together, walk and talk together, and sometimes jump for joy or cry together. Parents coach, encourage, and support children as performance time nears; then they listen with pride and intense concentration as children play. They are the first—and possibly most important—judges of the performance; they provide comfort and reassurance while waiting for results and then they help interpret the results and put outcomes into perspective. From this standpoint competitions can be powerful family-oriented experiences.

Parents need to be sensitive to take advantage of the opportunities that present themselves. If an atmosphere of healthy social process is fostered, choice opportunities can develop. Of course, sometimes competitions can serve to amplify difficulties between parent and child. Parents who are overprotective, overcontrolling, or overly critical can find competitions are a strain. Occasionally a child will be brought to tears by a parent who insists on asking, "Why did you make that mistake?" The overall aftermath of competition participation should be satisfaction and enjoyment for both parent and child. If competitions engender harshness or long-lasting discomfort this can point toward potential difficulties in parent or child expectations of each other or of the competition. Such feelings are worth thinking about and discussing, and may provide helpful insight into ways to improve family functioning.

Such negative outcomes occur much less often than one might expect given the intense efforts competitions foster. It has been our experience that families usually display behavior that is supportive and nurturing. In these times of increased family breakdown and parent-child alienation, we have often reflected that the opportunities for parent-child involvement in performance competitions seem to draw families together in powerful, lasting ways. The influence performance competitions have on strengthening families by fostering support, communication, and joint labor on a difficult task may be one of competitions' most significant ancillary benefits.

Fellow students can also provide significant support. Performance competitions differ from competitive sports because there is no direct conflict between contestants. Instead of trying literally to "beat" the other person, with the parents standing on the sidelines yelling, "Kill him, Kill him," as is sometimes the case in Little League sports, each individual has a solitary opportunity to take the spotlight and do his or her individual best. Contestants may acknowledge an occasional secret wish that another person will have a memory lapse, but by and large the relationships between contestants and parents of contestants are very congenial. Contestants frequently make new acquaintances and sometimes lasting friendships. Students frequently band together to listen, hearten, and brace each other up. Being able to be with others who are under the pressure of preparation and performance can provide an atmosphere of true empathy. Friends' opinions and views can be extremely meaningful in evaluating the entire experience and the specific judging outcomes.

The Need for Evaluation

Sometimes reinforcement beyond the parent and the teacher can be a vital ingredient in successful music study. Particularly as adolescence approaches, familiarity with parents and teachers can lead to a saucy, "what do you know" attitude. Evaluation by someone completely detached can add credibility to comments from teachers and parents. Testing reality outside the child's more narrow background can be an important skill that has significance that generalizes beyond music.

Comparison with peers can be one of the most forceful and convincing influences on children of any age. Typically a child who has developed the ability to perform musically up to the competition level is the only one of his or her playmates absorbed in such daily discipline. In response to parental encouragement for practicing one may frequently hear something like, "None of the other kids in the neighborhood have to practice an hour-and-a-half every day." Children can feel singled out, and fail to understand the broader motivations for music study, seeing only the demands on time and energy. Attendance at a competition quickly makes it abundantly clear, "You aren't the only one who has to practice." Suddenly one is surrounded with peers who all are very involved. Levels of performance ability frequently correlate with years of study and hours of practice time. The discussion shifts from "Do you have to practice?" to "How long do you practice every day?"

Beyond facilitating the realization that there are many peers involved in music, comparing one's playing with others' can have very beneficial consequences. Parents, grandparents, and siblings make very enthusiastic audiences. However, they usually cannot provide accurate views on how one is progressing vis-à-vis other students from other teachers or other areas. A student may come to feel unrealistically proud or critical or his or her progress if there is not a reasonably broad representative group of peers with which to compare. Competitions can be invaluable in bringing some perspective and comparison of the student's progress. If one learns what level of pieces the typical 8-year-old was playing at the competition, one has a much better idea about how one's own level compares.

Given our philosophies of education that try to insulate children from criticism or failure, it is perhaps surprising to discover that, if a child finds he or she is playing considerably below the level of his or her cohort, the child is rarely discouraged in the long run. At the end of the competition day such a child may feel like giving up, but usually by the next lesson he or she comes with new resolve. Teachers are frequently pleased to find an attitude of "If he (or she) can do it, I can do it" manifest after exposure to being outperformed by peers. "Winning at the competition" may not be as effective a motivation as understanding how one compares in the normative scheme of things (Coady & Brown, 1978). Consequently, competitions can provide motivation for continued progress and achievement in music study.

Competitions provide opportunities for the serious student to improve skills as a listener. Performers need to become intelligent evaluators of their own and others' playing, a kind of self-critic. This sharpening of listening skills can lead to or integrate with a more intelligent analytical study of one's practicing. Learning from competitions is based upon comparison and contrast of hearing others perform. One can also learn to compare and contrast one's own performance from practice session to practice session. A maturing ear can measure progress according to a specific standard of excellence or set of standards encouraged by the teacher, but increasingly comprehended by the student because he or she has "heard" it before at the competition.

Competitions can provide development and professional stimulation for the teacher as well as the student. Competitions augment other professional training and enrichment. They provide a view of student progress where "the rubber hits the road" in actual public performance. Teachers experience professional enrichment by hearing others' students, and by observing others' performing styles. They can evaluate their work, and the progress of their students, with respect to that of other teachers. The one-on-one teaching required in music performance can isolate teachers as well as students. Competitions are analogous to professional workshops for teachers where ideas, repertoire, and fellowship can enhance the teacher's range of experience.

The Need for Recognition

We have noted that practicing is a lonely business. Encouraging recalcitrant children to practice can also be a seemingly thankless task. Both parents and children find themselves asking, "Why am I making this sacrifice?" When the answers are phrased in vague, very long-term goals, immediate nagging doubts can remain. Competitions provide short-range, exciting, and visible occasions for both parents and children to gain recognition and reward for their efforts.

School attendance is mandated by law because society generally recognizes the value of education. Parents are involved in back-to-school nights, parent-teacher conferences, PTA, and a variety of school-related activities. "What did you do in school today?" is a universal foundation for parent-child conversation.

When parents embark on extraschool learning like music lessons they leave the well-worn, and legally mandated, social requirements for education. Such privately motivated education requires investing large sums of money and considerable amounts of time and energy. Examining the results from outside the family system over the long range, one sees progress and the development of many positive attributes that result from such parental investment. However, on a day-to-day basis music lessons can seem to parents like a maneuver in masochism where one pays a monthly fee for the opportunity to prompt surly offspring to perform a disagreeable task.

Competitions provide an opportunity for parents of music students to see some tangible results from their efforts. Parents can be fortified by seeing other parents who are also working with their children. The broader experience of hearing many children play at a competitive level is very reinforcing and reassuring that music lessons are making the world a better place. Parents receive congratulations on their children's performances; smiles, pats on the back, even a chance to brag a little are all part of a parent's experience at the competition. Realizations that music lessons are worthwhile and that progress is being made bolster parents and give them renewed conviction about the reasons for pursuing music lessons.

From the child's viewpoint there is no activity in his or her life that requires so much effort, time, and hassle yet seemingly results in so little reward. Children enjoy having goals, and they need something tangible like a competition to prepare for. It is only natural to want recognition when one works on a difficult task and brings it to successful completion. Opportunities to perform, listen, discuss, and celebrate must be part of a musical education. Otherwise the only reward for perfecting one piece is to put it away and begin another.

Of course, winning a prize is a great thrill. Being able to be selected as one of the best in the group can be reinforcing and gratifying. There can be difficulties and complications associated with winning prizes, which parents and teachers can help to avoid. Children can be lured into a false sense of superiority, which can come crashing down at the next competition if they do not win. They can also have anxiety because they feel they will not be able to measure up and win again. In both cases the same kind of dialogue about putting prizes into perspective as one set of judges' opinions at one given time and place can be very helpful. Trophies are wonderful, and look great on the shelf. They only document achievements in the past, however; they are part of the journey, not the destination. They are neither a guarantee nor a threat for the future.

Competitions are made to order as grand celebrations of completion and developing art. However, because the actual process of the competition is so intense and absorbing, the "grand celebration" aspect may not emerge spontaneously. Parents and teachers need to be sure these positive aspects are created and emphasized.

Plenty of hugs and smiles are always in order. Every competitor should hear "You worked hard to prepare, you did your very best, and we are so proud of you." Prize or no prize, the pride in working on a hard task and finishing masterfully with the flourish of a public performance is something every young competitor should be encouraged to feel. If such a fundamental lesson about life can result from music lessons the cost seems justified indeed. Picnics, parties, a favorite activity, and/or possibly cash (if you don't believe us, ask the young musician) all contribute to making the competition a milestone for recognition, if parents capitalize on the opportunity. In addition to prizes and trophies, frequently all competitors receive a certificate recognizing their participation; they hang such accolades up, put them in personal journals, show them to grandparents, frame them. Such mementos provide well-deserved recognition for membership in what is really quite an exclusive club.

Those who organize and run the competition should be sensitive to these needs of recognition that *all* the competitors experience. A certificate of achievement speaks volumes and costs pennies. Anything that can be done to organize, foster, and assemble community, regional, and even national recognition should be encouraged. Media coverage for the competition is usually easy to obtain and builds pride both in the community and in the competitors and their families.

In our electronic, prerecorded age the performing arts need visibility and encouragement. Even more important, young performers are a local and national treasure. Few competitors will become professional musicians, but all will remember the lessons from life learned during competitions. One young man, just after completing his first high school debate tournament, was heard to remark, "After competing in an international piano competition this debating is a piece of cake." When parents are willing to give support and children are willing to put forth the effort to discipline themselves to learn to play an instrument well enough to enter a competition at any level, something remarkable has happened. If the positive elements of musical training and competition could be generalized to our other efforts at promoting child development and education it would cause a transformation in many aspects of family life and society that would be truly inspirational.

Conclusion

Although largely ignored by professionals in education and/or child development, music performance competitions enjoy a lively and growing viability that involves thousands of children each year. In addition to awarding prizes these competitions can foster emotional and social support from family and peers, provide evaluation and sharpen self-assessment, and give personal and public recognition for what can otherwise be a lonely task.

Children of all ages achieve such remarkable skill at performance, we wonder if aspects from these competitions might not serve as models for other facets of our educational system. We believe competitions promote musical performance, enhance child development, and build family strengths to such a degree that they deserve national recognition alongside (possibly before) sports competitions as objects of national recognition and pride.

References

Coady, H., & Brown, M. (1978). Need for approval and the effects of normative and competitive incentives on children's performance. *Journal of Genetic Psychology, 132*, 291–298.

Elkind, D. (1981). *The Hurried Child*. Reading MA: Addison-Wesley Publishing.

Entwisle, D. R., & Baker, D. P. (1983). Gender and young children's expectations for performance in arithmetic. *Developmental Psychology, 19*, 200–209.

Freeman, J. (1976). Developmental influences on children's perception. *Educational Research, 19*(1), 69–75.

Scanlan, T. K., Lewthwaite, R., & Jackson, B. L. (1984). Social psychological aspects of competition for male youth sport participants: II. Predictors of performance outcomes. *Journal of Sport Psychology, 6*, 422–429.

Shuter-Dyson, R. (1979). Music in the environment: Effects on the musical development of the child. *International Review of Applied Psychology, 28*(2), 127–133.

14
Influences of Home and Family on Musical Opportunities of Educationally Advantaged Second-Grade Children

JEAN M. LARSEN

The development of young children's musical awareness, preference, and abilities has become an area of interest for many developmental psychologists as well as for music educators and early childhood educators. Yet, surprisingly little research has been conducted with young children on these aspects of development. Past studies addressing music preferences of older children and adolescents have provided two general insights. First, there is a preference for the type of music one is repeatedly exposed to (Bradley, 1971; Getz, 1966; Peery, Peery, Gaynard, & Crane, 1979), a phenomenon more commonly referred to as the "What you hear is what you like" hypothesis. Second, there is a steady age-related increase in children's preference for popular (or rock) music (Greer, Dorow, & Randall, 1974; Rogers, 1957); this latter hypothesis might be described as "You like what your peers or significant others like." Applying these hypotheses to younger ages, it may be speculated that young children would develop an affinity for nonrock or classical music if it were the type of music most frequently listened to at home.

It is generally accepted that the increased preference for popular music with age is linked to environmental experiences. As reported by Greer et al. (1974), nursery school children and children in the first grade showed an equal preference for both rock and nonrock music. However, Rogers (1957) noted that as children grew older there was a decrease in their preference for classical music. Rogers also found socioeconomic status to be related to children's musical taste. When children of upper and lower socioeconomic status were compared, a consistently larger number of choices for classical music were made by the higher status group. This difference between groups was present through the 12th grade. No data were collected beyond the 12th grade.

For the most part, recent research exploring the development of musical preferences and abilities has focused on the relationship between musical characteristics as well as categories of music style, and media, peers, teacher approval, and school experience (Dorow, 1977; Greer, Dorow, Wachhaus, & White, 1983; LeBlanc, 1979, 1981; LeBlanc & Cote, 1983; LeBlanc & McCrary, 1983). All of these studies have examined samples of older school-age children. Few studies have used samples of young children or the home setting to investigate the beginning influences of musical preference. Therefore, it seemed important to conduct a study that would contribute to a better understanding of young children's early musical experiences in the context of home and the family.

The present chapter is concerned with a number of experience factors peculiar to educationally advantaged children in the home setting that ultimately may influence the development of musical preferences. It is an examination of the relationships between family demographic variables that include activities in the home setting and musical opportunities for educationally advantaged children. Specifically, the present study was concerned with exploring the impact of family size, employment, income, education, and time spent on different tasks by children on the frequency and type of music most often listened to as a background to other home activities, the taking of piano and violin lessons, and participation in music performance and dance groups.

Method

Subjects

The study sample was comprised of the parents of 132 second-grade children, 74 females and 58 males. These subjects represent two of the five waves of parents and children currently under study in the longitudinal research project. Longitudinal study subjects were randomly selected from a large pool of applicants to the Brigham Young University (BYU) preschool. Each of the study waves is composed of an experimental group with children who attend preschool and a control group with children who did not attend preschool.

The subjects in the study were determined to be parents of low-risk/educationally advantaged children since in the majority of families both parents were present, and the parents' education level, as well as the levels of father's occupation and family income, were above average for the Mountain States region of the country (United States Department of Commerce, 1983). Approximately 97% of the fathers and 93% of the mothers had attended some college. Fifty-five percent of the families reported income of more than $30,000, with under 3% indicating an income of less than $15,000 (1983 dollars).

In addition to these socioeconomic factors, almost all of the families applying to the BYU preschool maintain a very active religious affiliation (Mormon) that emphasizes child-centered family activities. As an institutionalized part of their religious activity, both mothers and fathers are encouraged to spend time teaching and building positive relationships with their children. It may be further noted that Mormon parents have been shown to have very high achievement expectations for their children, which are likely to influence the opportunities they provide (Dewey & McKinney, 1976). Church members are also encouraged by their leaders to seek uplifting experiences from the cultural arts—music, art, dance, and the like (Packer, 1980). While the home and family experiences of the children in the sample may not be typical of many preschool children in America, they are probably similar to those of children of other achievement-oriented and well-educated parents.

Questionnaire

In connection with the longitudinal study, parents were asked to complete questionnaires when their children were in second grade. These questionnaires provided an update of demographic information about families. For the present study, items were added to the family information questionnaire in order to obtain data on the musical listening practices in the home and music and other lesson-taking opportunities for the children.

Specific items that were added to the parent questionnaire asked parents to estimate the percentage of time during an average day that music would be played in their home as a background to other activities. Then parents were asked to classify this music as being more often classical, easy listening, rock or popular, Western, or "other" (respondents were asked to define or describe "other"). Since this classification was not presented as a forced choice, more than one type of music was often indicated. All choices were recorded, resulting in some families having more than one preferred type of background music. Questionnaires also asked parents to indicate if their children were taking lessons, to specify what type of lessons were being taken, and to indicate the length of time their children had been taking lessons. In addition, information concerning children's out-of-school time spent in routine and leisure activities (e.g., doing homework, watching TV, practicing or taking music lessons), was obtained from the questionnaires.

Descriptive Data

Summary information from the questionnaire is presented in Tables 14.1, 14.2, and 14.3. Some of the family characteristics were briefly discussed earlier in describing the sample. Included with the demographic variables in Table 14.1 is the perceived time per weekday mother and father spend with their child in a one-on-one situation. Fathers spent considerably less time with their children than did mothers. Less than 15% of fathers reported spending more than a half-hour per day with the child, while more than 50% of the mothers reported spending more than 30 minutes per day.

Concerning the reported time spent in out-of-school activities, the educationally advantaged children comprising the study sample seem to be directing larger portions of time toward cognitive activities (including homework) and outdoor play than to watching TV or practicing and taking lessons. The majority of children in this sample spent less than 1 hour per day watching TV. Children in the present sample were less involved in doing household chores such as cleaning their room, washing dishes, feeding pets, and the like than any other category of activity.

TABLE 14.1. Family demographic characteristics and time spent in out-of-school activities of educationally advantaged second-grade children ($N=132$)

Demographic characteristics	Percent
Preschool	
Attended	66.2
Did not attend	33.8
Sex	
Male	44.4
Female	55.6
Household type	
One parent	3.0
Two parent	97.0
Number of older siblings	
0	17.3
1	17.3
2	17.3
3	17.3
4	18.0
4+	12.9
Number of younger siblings	
0	13.5
1	30.8
2	30.1
3	21.8
3+	3.8
Father's occupation level	
Low	6.2
High	93.8
Father's highest education level	
High school graduate	3.0
Some college	17.3
College graduate	21.8
Some graduate school	9.8
Master's degree awarded	17.3
Working on doctorate	4.5
Doctoral degree awarded	26.3
Mother's highest education level	
High school graduate	6.8
Some college	33.1
College graduate	38.3
Some graduate school	11.3
Master's degree awarded	9.8
Working on doctorate	.8
Doctoral degree awarded	.0
Mother's employment	
Full	6.8
Part	18.2
No employment	75.0
Family income	
Less than $15,000	2.3
$15,000–30,000	42.2

TABLE 14.1. *Continued*

Demographic characteristics	Percent
$30,000–45,000	42.2
$45,000+	13.3
Time father spends with child per weekday	
Less than 15 minutes	49.2
15–30 minutes	35.7
31–60 minutes	3.2
More than 60 minutes	11.9
Time mother spends with child per weekday	
Less than 15 minutes	7.8
15–30 minutes	38.0
31–60 minutes	17.1
More than 60 minutes	37.3
Average minutes per day spent in out-of-school activities	
Cognitive and/or small muscle activities	
0–15 minutes	2.3
16–30 minutes	7.6
31–60 minutes	35.6
61–90 minutes	32.6
More than 90 minutes	22.0
Watching TV	
0–15 minutes	15.4
16–30 minutes	22.3
31–60 minutes	41.5
61–90 minutes	14.6
More than 90 minutes	6.1
Outdoor and/or large muscle play	
0–15 minutes	5.3
16–30 minutes	13.0
31–60 minutes	39.7
61–90 minutes	21.4
More than 90 minutes	20.7
Practice and in lesson time	
0–15 minutes	41.4
16–30 minutes	38.7
31–60 minutes	10.8
More than 60 minutes	9.0
Household chores	
0–15 minutes	30.8
16–30 minutes	61.5
More than 30 minutes	7.7

Table 14.2 presents the number and type of music and music-related lessons in which study children were involved. Sixty-one percent of the sample took music lessons. However, more than twice as many females took lessons as males. This difference can be attributed to the number of girls who took dance lessons. While the percentages of males and females who took chorus, piano, and violin were comparable, over 50% of the females and less than 4% of the males were taking dance lessons.

TABLE 14.2. Participation in music lessons and music-related activities by educationally advantaged second-grade children ($N=132$)

	Total[a]		Male[b]		Female[c]	
	Frequency	%	Frequency	%	Frequency	%
Taking lessons	80	61.0	22	37.9	58	78.4
Chorus	10	7.6	2	3.4	8	11.0
Dance	40	30.3	2	3.4	38	52.1
Piano	50	38.0	20	34.5	30	41.1
Violin	8	6.1	3	5.1	5	6.8
Not taking lessons:	52	39.0	36	62.1	16	21.6

[a] Approximately one third of children involved take more than one type of lesson.
[b] Five males take more than one type of lesson.
[c] Twenty-one females take more than one type of lesson, with one female involved in three types of lessons.

The estimated percentage of time and the type of music played as a background to other activities in the home is presented in Table 14.3. The majority of families reported playing music less than half of the time. The most frequent type of music being played was "easy listening," with classical being the next most frequently reported. Rock and "other" (described by most of those listing this type to be music especially for children) were a distant third and fourth. Western music was played infrequently.

Data Analysis and Discussion

The data analysis took place in two steps. First, the Pearson product-moment coefficients were computed between all of the family characteristics (exogenous variables) and outcome measures (endogenous variables). Second, all of the

TABLE 14.3. Reported percent of time music is played as a background to other activities and type of music most often played in the homes of educationally advantaged second-grade children ($N=132$)

	Response frequency	Percent of total sample
Percent of time during average day music played		
Less than 20	48	36.4
20–50	56	42.4
More than 50	23	17.4
No response	5	3.8
Type of music most often played[a]		
Classical	53	40.2
Easy listening	93	70.5
Rock	39	29.5
Western	8	6.1
Other[b]	34	25.8

[a] Over 95% of the sample reported more than one type of music played.
[b] Described by the majority of respondents as "children's" music.

exogenous variables that were significantly ($p < .05$) related to each of the endogenous variables were entered into a series of stepwise multiple regression analyses. The intercorrelations between the exogenous and endogenous variables are presented in Table 14.4. It is recognized that some of the exogenous variables (e.g., mother/father time with child as well as child's out-of-school activities) could easily be considered outcome rather than predictor variables. It was determined more appropriate to enter them as independent rather than dependent variables in the analysis in order to focus on the musical opportunities as the outcome variables.

The SPSS stepwise regression technique, developed by SPSS Inc. (1983), was the method selected for the regression analysis. This technique allows for the specification of multivariate models yielding the predictive equation for each endogenous variable with the highest R^2 using the fewest numbers of variables. For the purpose of selecting the best regression equations the following basic criteria were used as limiting factors: (a) the final model had to have an F ratio significant at the .05 level or lower; (b) no new equation would be considered unless it demonstrated an increase of at least .01 in the coefficient of determination (R^2) over the previous equation; and (c) any variable added to the model must be significant at the .10 level or lower. Any equation established under the SPSS stepwise technique that failed to meet any of these basic criteria was not considered for the final model.

Separate regression models were constructed for seven of the endogenous variables. Predictor variables emerged from six of the models. The variables in each of the regression models are presented in Table 14.5. The beta weights from the SPSS Inc. (1983) program are as shown in Table 14.5, so that the relative impact of each variable might be compared.

The influences on children's musical opportunities as identified in this study were varied. No particular family factor seemed to dominate or be generally consistent as an influence. However, preschool attendance was shown to be associated with taking dance and piano lessons and with the type of music most often played as a background to other activities in the home. Preschool attendance positively correlated with "easy listening" as the type of music played most often at home. A negative correlation was shown between preschool attendance and the playing of "other" music.

Time watching TV emerged as the single predictor of involvement in children's chorus. Being female was the strongest of three predictors remaining in the final regression model for taking dance lessons. The other predictor variables for taking dance lessons were having attended preschool and number of older siblings (the negative relationship indicates the fewer the number of older siblings the more likely the subject is to be in dance). This equation seems to indicate that in this middle-socioeconomic status/educationally advantaged sample, girls, especially those who are firstborn rather than later born and who have attended preschool, are more likely to have the opportunity to be taking dance lessons. It may be further speculated from the number of girls taking dance lessons that such an opportunity was highly valued in the sample studied.

TABLE 14.4. Correlations between family demographic and out-of-school activity variables presented in Table 14.1 and music opportunity variables displayed in Tables 14.2 and 14.3 ($N = 132$)

	Taking lessons				Time music played	Type of music most often played				
	Chorus	Dance	Piano	Violin		Classical	Easy	Rock	Western	Other
Preschool attendance	-0.09	.23**	.17*	.05	.02	-0.08	.14*	.07	-0.02	-0.25**
Sex, female	.14*	.52***	.07	.04	.07	-0.11	.03	.04	.03	.07
One-parent household	-0.05	-0.17*	.05	-0.05	.02	.04	.02	-0.02	-0.04	.10
Number older sibling	-0.12	-0.27**	-0.08	.08	.02	.30***	-0.03	.13	.04	-0.04
Number younger sibling	.06	.02	.05	-0.02	.07	-0.12	-0.12	-0.19*	-0.10	.06
Father's occupation	-0.05	.03	.13	.07	-0.02	.01	.11	-0.05	-0.20*	.01
Mother's employment	.05	-0.08	-0.02	-0.03	.02	-0.05	-0.04	-0.04	-0.02	.05
Father's education	-0.15*	-0.13	.06	.14*	.08	.24**	-0.06	.12	-0.12	-0.02
Mother's education	-0.12	.07	.09	.15*	.15*	.10	-0.08	-0.10	-0.11	.03
Family income	-0.10	-0.07	.12	.06	.12	.07	-0.06	.04	-0.10	-0.03
Father's time with child	-0.11	-0.08	-0.15*	-0.05	-0.04	-0.06	.02	.10	.28**	-0.03
Mother's time with child	-0.02	-0.01	-0.09	-0.01	-0.03	-0.01	.03	.10	.25**	.16*
Time spent in										
Cgntv/small muscle act	.04	.05	-0.08	-0.03	-0.11	-0.12	.05	.21*	-0.00	.09
Watching TV	.24**	.09	-0.06	-0.06	.04	-0.01	-0.04	.02	.05	-0.04
Outdoor/large muscle play	.12	-0.17*	-0.25**	-0.09	-0.10	.02	.05	.09	.13	-0.03
Practice and in lesson time	.12	.07	.39***	.36***	-0.11	.03	-0.15*	.05	.02	-0.23*
Household chores	.07	.01	-0.07	.02	-0.11	.00	-0.12	.12	.10	-0.06

$*p < .05.$ $**p < .01.$ $***p < .001.$

TABLE 14.5. Influences of family factors and out-of-school activities on children's musical opportunities ($N=132$)

	beta
Participating in children's chorus	
Time watching TV	.24
Mult $R = 0.24$, $R^2 = 0.06$	
Taking dance lessons	beta
Sex (female)	.53
Number of older siblings	$-.21$
Attended preschool	.21
Mult $R = 0.61$, $R^2 = 0.37$	
Taking piano lessons	beta
Time spent in outdoor/large muscle activities	$-.22$
Mult $R = 0.22$, $R^2 = 0.04$	
Classical music most often played	beta
Number of older siblings	.29
Mult $R = 0.29$, $R^2 = 0.09$	
Rock (popular) music most often played	beta
Time spent in cognitive/small muscle activities	.21
Mult $R = 0.21$, $R^2 = 0.04$	
Other music most often played	beta
Attended preschool	$-.26$
Practice and in lesson time	$-.23$
Mult $R = 0.35$, $R^2 = 0.12$	

It was surprising that the amount of television watching was positively correlated with children taking chorus. It was expected that television watching would be negatively associated with all types of lesson taking. It may be that children who take chorus have an interest in the performance aspects of television. However, there are no data on the types of television programs viewed by the children to confirm this guess.

Nearly as many boys as girls were taking piano lessons. This was the only lesson area where boys had more than a token representation. In reviewing the influence variables that were associated with taking piano lessons (see Table 14.4), it would seem that children were more likely to be taking piano if they had attended preschool, had less time alone with their fathers, did not spend out-of-school time in outdoor or large muscle play, and spent out-of-school time practicing and taking lessons. Time practicing was not included in the regression model because it was felt that the high correlation between this variable and lesson taking would mask other influences. Of the three variables that were entered in the regression analysis, only time spent in outdoor or large muscle play emerged as a predictor of piano lessons.

Although comparatively few children in the study had the opportunity to take violin lessons, both boys and girls were represented among those who did (see Table 14.2). The influence variables entered in the regression analysis for taking violin lessons were the education levels of both the mother and the father. As was the case with piano lessons, practice time was not entered in the regression model because of an expected masking effect. In the regression analysis neither the mother's nor the father's education met the specified criteria to be considered a predictor of taking violin lessons.

The education level of the mother was the only significant correlate associated with the percent of time music was played as a background to other activities in the home. The higher the education level of the mother, the more likely music was played in the home.

It was assumed that the musical preference findings in the present study would be consistent with the findings of earlier studies. For example, Rogers (1957) had found that socioeconomic status was an important factor in musical preference. Preference for classical music was stronger in children from higher status families than it was in children from lower status families. It was expected that the middle-class/educationally advantaged subjects in the present study would also show a strong preference for classical music. However, families in this study indicated "easy listening" music was preferred, with classical music in second place.

As expected, the level of father's education was associated with the playing of classical music in the home. However, it was not expected that the number of older siblings in the home would be a stronger predictor of the playing of classical music. The reason for this relationship is not apparent.

The relationship between the playing of rock music and time spent in cognitive and small muscle activities was also unexpected. One could speculate that large muscle activity, rather than cognitive and small muscle activity, would be associated with rock music. Again, we do not have data for more than speculation.

Although the playing of Western music was included in the correlation table, no regression analysis was conducted because of the small number of families that reported listening to this type of music. Nevertheless, it would seem that if fathers have a lower level occupation and both parents spend a greater amount of time with the child, it is more likely Western music will be played in the home. There is a temptation to stereotype the association of fathers in a lower level occupation with playing Western music, but the same cannot necessarily be said for parents spending a greater amount of time with their child and playing Western music. Other than perhaps the fact that children and families are mentioned more in the lyrics of Western music than other music, there does not seem to be a logical explanation for this association.

When parents were asked to identify the type of music most often played as a background to other activities, the selection of "other" required a definition. The majority described "other" to mean special music tapes and/or records for young children. Such audio programs are designed to teach concepts and feelings through music as well as to provide musical entertainment for children. Two predictors for playing this type of music emerged from the final regression model: preschool attendance and out-of-school practice and lesson time. Both were negatively related to the playing of "other" music. It may be that specialized children's music is played as a compensatory measure for those children who have not attended preschool or are not involved in music lessons.

In summary, no clear pattern of family influence seems to be associated with musical opportunities for this low-risk/educationally advantaged population of second-grade children. A higher percentage of girls than boys had the opportunity to take music and dance lessons. The sex of the child did not have an effect on time nor type of music played as a background to other home activities. In addition, previous attendance in preschool, parents' education, number of siblings, time with parent, father's occupation, and various out-of-school activities all were shown to have an influence on one or more aspects of the musical opportunities provided the children in this study sample.

The relationships presented in this report cannot be considered definitive. They represent only a beginning of an ongoing process that will be necessary to identify specific influences on musical opportunities afforded young children. While these findings do give some indication of musical exposure provided low-risk children in educationally advantaged families during the important formative years, many questions remain to be answered. For example, it was not always possible to determine from the parents' responses if one type of music was consistently played more often than another. Also, it was not possible to determine which family members usually selected the type of music played in the home. This information, along with the source of the music (e.g., radio or record player), would have allowed for a more complete interpretation of the musical opportunities generated by the families of educationally advantaged children. It will be necessary to continue research with young children in the home environment in order to fully understand the factors that influence musical abilities and preferences in young children.

References

Bradley, I. L. (1971). Repetition as a factor in the development of musical preference. *Journal of Research in Music Education, 19,* 295–298.

Dewey, T., & McKinney, D. (1976). *Independence training as an index of achievement motivation: A study of LDS families.* Unpublished paper, Harvard University.

Dorow, L. G. (1977). The effect of teacher approval/disapproval ratios on student music selection and concert attentiveness. *Journal of Research in Music Education, 25,* 32–40.

Getz, R. P. (1966). The influence of familiarity through repetition in determining music preference. *Journal of Research in Music Education, 14,* 178–182.

Greer, R. D., Dorow, L. G., & Randall, A. (1974). Music listening preferences of elementary school children. *Journal of Research in Music Education, 22,* 284–291.

Greer, R. D., Dorow, L. G., Wachhaus, G., & White, E. R. (1973). Adult approval and students' music selection behavior. *Journal of Research in Music Education, 21,* 345–354.

LeBlanc, A. (1979). Generic style music preferences of fifth-grade students. *Journal of Research in Music Education*, *27*, 255–270.

LeBlanc, A. (1981). Effects of style, tempo, and performing medium on children's music preference. *Journal of Research in Music Education*, *29*(2), 143–156.

LeBlanc, A., & Cote, R. (1983). Effects of tempo and performing medium on children's music preference. *Journal of Research in Music Education*, *31*(1), 57–66.

LeBlanc, A., & McCrary, J. (1983). Effect of tempo on children's music preference. *Journal of Research in Music Education*, *31*(4), 283–294.

Packer, K., (1980). The arts and the spirit of the Lord. In S. P. Sondrup (Ed.), *Arts and Inspiration, Mormon Perspectives*. Provo, UT: Brigham Young University Press.

Peery, J. C., Peery, I. W., Gaynard, L., & Crane, P. (1979, September). *Effects of exposure to classical music on the musical preferences of preschool children*. Paper presented at the Annual Convention of the American Psychological Association, New York City.

Rogers, V. R. (1957). Children's musical preferences as related to grade level and other factors. *Elementary School Journal*, *57*(8), 433–435.

SPSS Inc. (1983). *SPSS user's guide: A complete guide to SPSS language and operations*. Chicago, IL.

United States Department of Commerce, Bureau of the Census. (1983). *1980 census of population, general social and economic characteristics, Utah*. PC80-1-C-46. Washington, DC: U.S. Government Printing Office.

Author Index

Subject Index